Metaphor and Intercultural Communication

Also available from Bloomsbury

Fire Metaphors, *Jonathan Charteris-Black*

Intercultural Contact, Language Learning and Migration, *edited by Barbara Geraghty and Jean Conacher*

Metaphor in Educational Discourse, *Lynne Cameron*

Metaphor and Intercultural Communication

Edited by

Andreas Musolff, Fiona MacArthur and Giulio Pagani

Bloomsbury Academic India
An imprint of Bloomsbury Publishing Plc

BLOOMSBURY

NEW DELHI • LONDON • OXFORD • NEW YORK • SYDNEY

BLOOMSBURY INDIA
Bloomsbury Publishing India Pvt. Ltd
Second Floor, Building No. 4
DDA Complex LSC, Pocket C – 6 & 7
Vasant Kunj, New Delhi 110070
www.bloomsbury.com

BLOOMSBURY, Bloomsbury Academic India and the Diana
logo are trademarks of Bloomsbury Publishing Plc

First published in India 2020
First published 2014
Paperback edition first published 2015

British Library Cataloguing-in-Publication Data
A catalogue record for this book is available from the British Library.

Library of Congress Cataloging-in-Publication Data
A catalog record for this book is available from the Library of Congress

ISBN: 978-93-89351-78-1

For Sale in the Indian subcontinent only

Typeset by Newgen Knowledge Works (P) Ltd., Chennai, India
Digitally Printed and bound in India by Replika Press Pvt. Ltd. In 2019.

Contents

Notes on Contributors

Sadia Belkhir is 'Maître-assistante' in the Department of English at Mouloud Mammeri University of Tizi-Ouzou, Algeria. She is particularly interested in animal-related proverbs and metaphor in cognition and culture. Among her recent publications is 'Variation in source and target domain mappings in English and Kabyle dog proverbs', in Kleinke, S., Kövecses, Z., Musolff, A. and Szelid, V. (eds), *Cognition and Culture – The Role of Metaphor and Metonymy* (Eötvös University Press, Tàlentum 6, 2012).

Gabriela Iuliana Colipcă-Ciobanu is associate professor at the 'Dunărea de Jos' University of Galaţi, Romania. She is a member of the Galaţi University research team in the FP7 project 'Gender, Migration and Intercultural Interactions in the Mediterranean and South-East Europe' (GeMIC). Among other works, she is the author of *Literary Journeys and Cross-Cultural Encounters* (Galaţi University Press, forthcoming). Her research interests include literary theory and criticism, film studies, translation studies, imagology, critical discourse analysis and cognitive metaphor theory.

Tatjana Đurović is an associate professor at the Faculty of Economics, University of Belgrade. She received her PhD degree in linguistics in 2006. Her fields of interest include cognitive linguistics, applied linguistics and ESP. She is the author of a monograph on neurolinguistic aspects of foreign language learning and co-author of a monograph on metaphors in Serbian public discourse.

Claudia Förster Hegrenæs is a PhD student in the Department of Professional and Intercultural Communication, Norwegian School of Economics. Her research interests include translation studies, cognitive linguistics and terminology management.

Patrick Goethals is a senior lecturer in Spanish linguistics and multilingual communication at the Department of Translation, Interpreting and Communication, Faculty of Arts and Philosophy, Ghent University. His research interests include contrastive linguistics, translation theory, intercultural and multilingual communication, discourse analysis and tourism communication. Among his major recent publications are 'Demonstratives on the Move: What Translational Shifts Tell Us about Demonstrative Determiners and Definite Articles in Spanish and Dutch', *Linguistics*, 51 (2013): 517–53; and 'A Multi-layered Approach to Speech Events. The Case of Spanish Justificational Conjunctions', *Journal of Pragmatics*, 42 (2010): 2204–18.

Geert Jacobs is professor in the Department of Linguistics of Ghent University, Belgium. He received a PhD in Linguistics in 1997 from the University of Antwerp, where he wrote a dissertation on the metapragmatics of press releases. His research focuses on the study of professional and institutional discourse in a pragmatic perspective. He is the head and co-founder of the international NewsTalk&Text research group and has published widely in international peer-reviewed journals.

Zoltán Kövecses is professor in the Department of American Studies, Eötvös Loránd University, Budapest. Among his major publications are *Metaphor and Emotion* (Cambridge University Press, 2000); *Metaphor in Culture* (Cambridge University Press, 2005); and *Metaphor: A Practical Introduction*, 2nd edn (Oxford University Press, 2010). His research interests lie in the theory of metaphor and metonymy, metaphor and culture, metaphor and context and American English.

Fiona MacArthur is a senior lecturer in the Department of English at the University of Extremadura. She is co-editor of *Metaphor in Use: Context, Culture, and Communication* (John Benjamins, 2012) and is the author of numerous research articles published in international peer-reviewed journals on the topic of metaphor and the learner of English as a second language. Her current research focuses on the use of metaphor in office hours' consultations involving Spanish Erasmus students spending a period of time at European universities where teaching is carried out in English.

Celia Martín de León is a lecturer in the Department of Modern Philology at the Universidad de Las Palmas de Gran Canaria, Spain. Her research focuses on cognitive translatology, translation processes, implicit theories and metaphor. She is the author of *Contenedores, recorridos y metas. Metáforas en la traductología funcionalista* (Frankfurt: Peter Lang, 2005) and has published a number of articles on translation in international, peer-reviewed journals such as *Target*.

Andreas Musolff is professor of Intercultural Communication at the University of East Anglia, Norwich. His monographs include *Metaphor, Nation and the Holocaust* (2010), *Metaphor and Political Discourse* (2004) and *War against the Public: The Language of Terrorism* (1996, in German). He has co-edited further volumes on political discourse in Europe and is the author of articles and book chapters on metaphor theory.

Mariana Neagu is an associate professor at the 'Dunărea de Jos' University of Galaţi, Romania. She is the author of *Categories in Natural Languages: The Study of Nominal Polysemy in English and Romanian* (Buzău: Alpha, 1999); and editor of *Understanding and Translating Metaphor* (Bucureşti: Editura Didactică şi Pedagogică, 2005), among other works. Her research interests include cognitive linguistics, semantics, critical discourse analysis, cognitive metaphor theory and cross-cultural communication.

Anna Ogarkova is a senior researcher at the Swiss Center for Affective Sciences, University of Geneva. She is the author of numerous publications on emotion concepts in cross-cultural comparison. Her major research interests are corpus-driven cognitive linguistics (primarily with regard to metaphoric representation of emotion concepts) and cross-cultural emotion semantics. She is also interested in emotion conceptualization and expression in bilinguals.

José L. Oncins-Martínez is a senior lecturer in the Department of English at the University of Extremadura, Spain. He has published numerous book chapters and articles in peer-reviewed journals on the language of Shakespeare and Anglicisms. His research interests include cognitive stylistics, corpus stylistics, the influence of English on Spanish and translation.

Giulio Pagani is lecturer in Discourse and European Politics at the University of East Anglia, United Kingdom, where he teaches linguistics, discourse analysis, intercultural communication and their applications in political studies. His main fields of research include systemic-functional linguistics, social semiotics, multimodality and political discourse analysis, particularly in relation to public sector discourse in the United Kingdom and France. He has published a number of articles in international peer-reviewed journals on the representation of the relationship between the citizen and the state.

Dafni Papadoudi is translation project manager at Kleos SA (a consulting company). Her research interests include the translation of metaphor, conceptual metaphor and technology, and metaphor use in second-language learning.

Marisa Presas is head of the Department of Translating and Interpreting at the Universitat Autònoma de Barcelona, Spain. She has published numerous articles on translating and the training of translators in national and international peer-reviewed journals. Her research focuses on cognitive translatology, implicit theories, research methods and translation didactics.

Farzad Sharifian is a professor and director of the Language and Society Centre at Monash University, Australia. He is the author of several works, including *Cultural Conceptualisations and Language: Theoretical Frameworks and Applications* (John Benjamins, 2011). His main research interests lie in the fields of cultural linguistics, cognitive linguistics, intercultural communication, and language and politics.

Nadežda Silaški is an associate professor at the Faculty of Economics, University of Belgrade. She received her PhD degree in Linguistics in 2005. Her fields of interest include discourse analysis, cognitive linguistics and ESP. She is the author of a monograph on Anglicisms in Serbian economic register and co-author of a monograph on metaphors in Serbian public discourse.

Cristina Soriano is a senior researcher at the Swiss Center for Affective Sciences, University of Geneva. She conducts interdisciplinary (linguistic and psycholinguistic) research on emotion semantics, the metaphorical representation of concepts and the affective meaning of colour. She is also the executive officer of the GRID Project, a large international study of the meaning of emotion words across languages and cultures. She has published numerous book chapters and articles in international peer-reviewed journals on the topic of metaphor and emotions.

Jasper Vandenberghe is a research assistant and a PhD candidate at the Department of Translation, Interpreting and Communication (Faculty of Arts and Philosophy – Ghent University). His research focuses on the discursive representation of Spanish foreign direct investment in media discourse (newspaper articles) and business discourse (press releases). His research interests include discourse analysis, media studies and business communication. Among his most recent publications is '"Repsol Meets YPF": Displaying Competence in Cross-Border M&A Press Releases', *Journal of Business Communication*, 48(4) (2011): 373–92.

Xia Xiang obtained her MA in Interpreting and Translating from Bath University. She is a lecturer in translation and interpretation at the College of Science and Technology, Ningbo University, and has served as a freelance conference interpreter and translator for ten years. Her research focuses on theories of translation and interpretation, and the teaching of interpreting. She has published papers in *Babel* and *Foreign Language Teaching & Research* (bimonthly), among other journals.

Binghan Zheng is a lecturer in Translation Studies in the School of Modern Languages & Cultures, Durham University. His research focuses on contemporary translation theories, in particular empirical studies on the process of translation and interpretation. He is the author of *Choice-Making in the Process of English-to-Chinese Translation: An Empirical Study*, which is regarded as a breakthrough in process-oriented translation research in China, and is one of the major contributors to *A Dictionary of Translation Studies in China*, published by Shanghai Foreign Language Education Press in 2011. He has also published papers in *Babel, Perspectives: Studies in Translatology, Foreign Language Teaching & Research* (bimonthly), and *Chinese Science & Technology Translators Journal* (quarterly), among other journals.

List of Figures

List of Tables

Foreword

Zoltán Kövecses

We now live in an era of interculturality more than ever before. Whether we like it or not, we constantly interact, and are confronted, with language, signs, objects, people, ideas, forms of behaviour and so on that come from cultures other than what we may be most likely to call our own. However, in many cases we are not aware that the language, signs, objects, people, ideas, forms of behaviour and so on that we interact with come from another culture. We live in a world of increasing hybridization that blurs the distinction between our culture and that of the other, or, in short, the distinction between the self and the other.

In my view, the main topic of intercultural communication as a discipline should be, and, perhaps, is the phenomenon of hybridization mentioned in the previous paragraph. The chapters in this volume all represent efforts to deal with the challenge of handling such a diverse and complex set of phenomena and the human issues that arise from them. As such, the volume stands out as a major new effort to provide a basis for the scientific study of a fledgling field. The editors of the volume made several wise decisions in this enterprise. First, they limited the topic to be studied to the phenomenon of metaphor, which is a relatively well-defined area in human communication. Second, they limited the range of chapters to some of the best-known cases of intercultural communication: the issues of translation, of universality and specificity, and of globalization. All three are undeniably paradigmatic examples of intercultural communication with a long and well-studied history, thus making it possible to do some restructuring in the foundational ideas of the new discipline.

One of these new foundational ideas is 'conceptual metaphor'. Conceptual metaphors play a significant role in how we think about the world. As a result, they are prime carriers of our feelings, lay and expert theories, values and ideologies, and they are highly susceptible to variation in different contexts. Thus, any theory of intercultural communication should incorporate the study of conceptual metaphor. It is also clear that the theory of conceptual metaphor should be modified and adjusted according to the requirements of the new discipline to make it a more flexible and reliable tool for the study of the diverse phenomena interculturality involves. Several of the chapters in the volume point to a need for such changes. Authors rely, explicitly or implicitly, on some new theoretical concepts in more recent versions of conceptual metaphor theory, such as 'scene', 'meaning focus', 'metaphor identification procedure', 'context sensitivity' and so on. The new topics also require new methodologies. Some chapters make use of corpus linguistics, which enables us to see the subtleties and finer details of intercultural hybridization that were not available previously. Others employ empirical-experimental methods in an effort to lend substance to our claims in capturing what actually happens in cognitive terms in the process of hybridization.

The framework the various authors work within can and should be expanded. In addition to the conceptual process of metaphor, a number of other cognitive operations will have to be carefully studied in a larger project. These should include metonymy, blending, perspective-taking, figure and ground phenomena, force dynamics and others. In other words, all the cognitive processes that are studied by cognitive linguists should become a part of the enterprise. This makes cognitive linguistics a major conceptual tool of intercultural communication. And obviously, the range of topics would also have to be broadened to include all the many and incredibly diverse forms of linguistic and pictorial hybrids that pervade our lives.

But the significance of the volume goes beyond providing some foundational work for a potential new scientific discipline. This is seen in the new insights and perspectives that such foundational work can open up. The issues that can be discussed given the new framework challenge us to reconsider our time-honoured and cherished positions on who we are, who other people are, what kind of world we live in, what kind of world we would like to live in, how and why we think about the world in the way we do, how our views have emerged, what keeps them alive or what makes them disappear, whether we should accept or change all this, and several others.

In summary, the volume confronts us with new questions and challenges that are not only relevant to scientific inquiry but also essential to the way we live in human societies.

Introduction: Metaphor in Intercultural Communication

Andreas Musolff, Fiona MacArthur and Giulio Pagani

Why is it important to study metaphors across cultures and in intercultural communication? The question may almost seem self-evident given the ever-growing traffic among different cultures, which produces all kinds of linguistic and conceptual phenomena that strike their users as 'foreign', or difficult to understand on account of their different cultural backgrounds. However, with regard to metaphor, the difficulties of interlingual and -cultural communication may seem to be smaller than for other language structures. Unless we wish to adopt a radical version of linguistic relativism, surely all metaphors are 'translatable' in the sense that they can at least be paraphrased across all languages (perhaps with explanatory notes that provide information on a particular cultural background where the respective text genre and communicative context allow for such a luxury). Furthermore, from a cognitive perspective one could argue that – since human conceptualization is largely body-based or 'embodied'[1] – metaphors in all languages can in principle be derived from fundamental bodily experiences that are shared by all humans on account of our common physique. From this viewpoint, we might still allow for some variation across languages but once all metaphors have been broken down into their components and the latter into something like Anna Wierzbicka and Cliff Goddard's universal 'semantic primes', we should be able to account in principle for all essential meaning aspects of metaphors.[2]

Let us consider these propositions in the light of a few examples from a metaphor-interpretation task that was given to two groups of British and international MA students at the University of East Anglia in 2010–12,[3] that is, with a brief to describe the concept of the nation state in terms of a (human) body. Here are six exemplary responses:

(1) Student A: 'If one organ or part of the national body suffers, the whole body would suffer from fever. In other words, having a healthy body requires healthy parts. As a nation, a problem in one area of a country should attract the attention of the whole people in that country.'

(2) Student B: 'The head of the body represents the Queen of England, as she is in charge of the whole country and she is royalty. The features of the head (eyes, nose, mouth and ears) represent the different official people, such as politicians, the Prime Minister, the Government.'

(3) Student C: 'This is Britain, a vast body of forty-eight million people, sucking in resources, processing them, and spewing out fumes and ideas.'
(4) Student D: '*Beijing*: Heart and Brain, *Shanghai*: Face, economic centre; *Hong Kong and Taiwan*: Feet; *Tianjin*: Hands (= army close to Beijing); *Shenzhen*: Eyes (= the first place open to the world).'
(5) Student E: '*Beijing*: brain (government); *Shanghai*: hug/arm (welcome to foreign people); *Guangzhen*: feet (keep China going); *Hong Kong*: face (familiar to everyone, representative); Taiwan: hair (we can live without hair but it is necessary for beauty).'
(6) Student F: '*Beijing*: the heart of the country, dominates the whole country and symbolizes life; *Chengdu and Shanghai city*: right and left hands of China: create food and money for the body; *Hainan island and Taiwan*: right and left feet, help China to stand up in the world.'

Examples (1)–(3) were produced by one American (A) and two British students (B and C), whereas students D, E and F are Chinese. While all answers are 'correct' in the sense that they fulfil the task, the responses fall into two clearly distinguishable classes: the first three responses describe a 'Western' political system in terms of a body's health, anatomy and metabolism; answers (4)–(6), on the other hand, identify geographical places in China (both the mainland and islands, including the de facto separate state of Taiwan) and link them to parts of the human anatomy on the basis of functional correspondences between activities performed by the respective body parts and politically significant characterizations of the locations (see, for instance, the categorization of Taiwan as beautiful but non-essential *hair* or of China as one of the *feet*).[4] They are at the same time more geographically specific/concrete than the British/American answers and more 'personalized' in the sense that they use the bodily source domain as an inventory for characterizing China as an agent/subject.[5]

Despite such differences, the metaphor of the state as a body is fully understood and successfully interpreted in all these examples, and we may interpret this as evidence of the cross-cultural accessibility of the 'state-as-body' mapping. Insofar as the physical source domain categories, *health, brain, head, heart, hands, feet, face, eyes* and *hair*, are basic level terms (Taylor, 1995, pp. 46–8), which require no specialized anatomical or medical knowledge, we may assume that they do indeed reflect a universal or near-universal concept derived from phenomenological human physique. Such an interpretation would seem to support the universalist view that a globally shared basic knowledge of the body serves as the source for conceptualizing abstract objects such as the 'state'. On the other hand, however, we have found a consistent, possibly systematic, difference between two main methods of interpreting the metaphor, which calls for further explanation. In this context it seems significant that the British/US students' answers can be related to a prominent metaphor tradition in British and American political culture, which is embodied in the phrase *body politic* in English to this day and can also be found across other European languages and public discourse communities (de Baecque, 1997; Hale, 1971; Harvey, 2007; Musolff, 2010a,b; Sontag, 1978). Apart from the topical reference to the institution of a 'prime minister' in response (2), the first group of responses is compatible with famous formulations of *body politic* theories by medieval or Renaissance political thinkers, such as John of Salisbury, Sir John Fortescue or Thomas Hobbes (Musolff, 2010a, pp. 81–120). Of course, the existence of such a tradition – as a construct of learned research – does not mean that British/US students in the twenty-first century are consciously aware of it. Nevertheless, *body politic* terminology still permeates British and American public discourses, for example, in lexicalized expressions such as *head of state/head of government, long arm of the law, organ (of a party), heart of Britain/Europe* and in creative new coinings, such as the repeated self-description of a British politician as 'the toenail of the body politic' (Deignan, 1995, p. 2; Musolff, 2004, pp. 83–114; 2010b, pp. 23–5; Obama, 2007, p. 10). It is therefore not unreasonable to conclude that the students' answers reproduce parts of that tradition into which they have become enculturated, for example, through educational exposure to the works of Shakespeare and other famous authors in the cultural history of English-speaking countries, which include *body politic* references.[6] This tradition is part of a wider long-term impact of the theory-complexes of the 'four humours' and the 'Great Chain of Being' that Western culture has inherited from ancient Greek and Roman thought: while known in detail only to historians of thought today, they are still present in popularized and simplified versions in present-day idioms and discourse, long after they have been discarded in modern science.[7]

The Chinese students' responses, on the other hand, show a different perspective of metaphor interpretation. They are perfectly acceptable solutions to the given task because they provide as plausible interpretations of the 'state-as-body' metaphor as the British and American students' responses. However, quite apart from the China specific geographical frame of reference, their interpretative approach differs from that of the US/British students by not echoing the Western *body politic* theory tradition. Instead, the Chinese responses include different combinations of metaphor and metonymy. It would seem that in the first place, a basic mapping – 'shape of body > shape of nation (China)' – is applied; on this foundation, salient parts of China's geo-political 'body' are identified on the basis of metonymic geographical-political relationships (e.g. 'Beijing – seat of government'). These metonymies are in turn associated with specific functional interpretations, some of which are politically loaded and biased, for example, the (non-)allocation of political functions to Taiwan and the assertive characterization of special economic zones such as Shenzen and Hongkong.[8]

The reasons for this contrast between the Chinese and British/US responses obviously need to be investigated on a broader data basis but, if confirmed, they link to important findings of cross-cultural studies of acquisition, usage and understanding of metaphor and metonymy. Empirical studies have already shown that in interpretation tasks for metaphors, Chinese children and adults tend to give more psychological interpretations than English speakers (Wang and Dowker, 2010), which might link to the 'personalized' interpretations in the *body politic* responses; other further culture-specific interpretation patterns have also been observed in second-language metaphor acquisition (Golden, 2010; Philip, 2010; Piquer-Piriz, 2010). Cross-cultural differences have also been found in metaphor construction. Ning Yu (1998, 2001, 2008a,b, 2009) has demonstrated that the *face*-metaphor of folk-psychology (as in English *to save/maintain/lose face*), while based on primary body-based metonymies linking face and emotion, is differentially composed in Chinese and English and leads to subtly differing versions of complex conceptual metaphors DIGNITY IS FACE AS A VALUABLE POSSESSION and PRESTIGE IS FACE AS A VALUABLE POSITION. Both these conceptual metaphors exist in the two languages but their conceptual architectures are different, and so is the respective distribution of idioms and proverbs based on them: 'Face saving is more reciprocal in Chinese. Apparently, Chinese is richer than English with conventional expressions involving the body part of the face' (Yu, 2008a, p. 257). In conclusion, it would seem that the link to primary experiences shared by Chinese and English for 'face'-related psychological metaphors and 'body'-related political metaphors does not automatically entail a one-to-one correspondence of the complex metaphors that are built on them.

Such findings of culturally mediated differences in the construction, acquisition and usage of body-based metaphors and metonymies can hardly be regarded as surprising because Chinese culture has, of course, as complex and distinctive philosophical traditions of body-conceptualization, which have become 'sunken', popularized folk-theories, as has the West. In the case of Chinese, for instance, Yu has pointed to the 'theories of *yin-yang* and five elements of Chinese philosophy and medicine' that have shaped 'the way Chinese culture sees the world' (2008b, p. 401) as background for present-day idioms. For Japanese, Shogimen (2008a,b) has shown that ancient taboos concerning body-dissection influenced the development of anatomical and surgical metaphors for many centuries and led to different perspectives in the application of body-based metaphors to the state compared with the classical Western tradition: 'The European notion of medical treatment as the eradication of the causes of diseases highlighted coercive and punitive aspects of government as the final solution to political conflicts while the Japanese notion of medical treatment as controlling physical conditions seems to create the image of government as an art of daily healthcare and preventative medicine' (2008a, p. 103). In a series of studies on body-based metaphors of emotions, Kövecses (1986, 1990, 1995, 2000, 2005, 2006) has convincingly argued that, despite the physiologically observable (and thus, by definition, universal) link between body temperature and the experience of anger emotions, metaphors of 'anger-as-heated-and-pressurized substance in a container' are by no means identical across languages. They show historical variation even within English, which leads Kövecses to the conclusion that 'universal physiology provides only a potential basis for metaphorical conceptualization – without mechanically constraining what the specific metaphors for anger will be' (2006, p. 171). In this perspective, the aforementioned common-sense assumptions of universal translatability and the cognitive theories about the 'embodied' nature of metaphorical conceptualization are both vindicated and at the same time relativized: cultural specificity is not a contradiction but a complementary characteristic in the acquisition, online production and understanding of metaphors, and therefore has to be taken into account at every level of their linguistic and conceptual analysis.

The consequences of such differences in conceptualization for actual communication between speakers with different cultural and linguistic backgrounds are only slowly beginning to be explored, largely because research into the relationship between metaphorical conceptualization and culture has tended to focus more on describing and comparing the motivation of metaphorical expressions used by different cultural groups, rather than what actually happens when speakers with differing cultural conceptualizations come together and interact with each others' linguistic productions. Of course, this comparative/contrastive perspective is a necessary first step in understanding the ease or difficulty with which speakers from different backgrounds will be able to communicate with each other and, to a certain extent, predict some of the difficulties which may arise. However, it is becoming increasingly clear that this is not the whole story.

Our growing understanding of the complex role played by metaphor in intercultural communication comes in large part – though by no means exclusively – as a result of research in one particular setting: the university. The ever more prevalent use of English as academic lingua franca – not only in written scientific communication but also as a medium of instruction in universities worldwide – has made academic discourse in English an important area of applied linguistics research generally, and of metaphor research in particular.[9] When compared with fiction, newspapers or conversation in English, academic discourse has been shown to display the highest density of metaphorical language use (Steen et al., 2010), for metaphor plays an important role in both constituting and communicating concepts in all academic disciplines. It has long been acknowledged that metaphors pervade scientific thinking and communication (e.g. Boyd, 1993; Kuhn, 1993; Montuschi, 2000), and the close description of metaphors and models used in different disciplines has shed light on this aspect of academic reasoning (e.g. Aitchison, 2003; Alejo, 2009; Caballero, 2006; Carroll et al., 1991, Goschler, 2007; or Mio, 1996). A direct consequence of the pervasiveness of metaphor is that disciplinary enculturation into fields such as economics, architecture, technology, politics or psychology will involve becoming familiar with the metaphors used conventionally in those fields and – to a greater or lesser extent – with its conceptual underpinning (see, e.g., Martín de León and Presas, Chapter 1 in this volume, for a discussion of students' metaphors for translation). This poses a challenge for communication in educational contexts generally, regardless of the novice's linguistic or cultural background (see, e.g., Cameron, 2003; Halliday, 2004).

However, when we look at communication in academic settings where interlocutors do not share the same mother tongue, the problems are magnified, as is only to be expected. Studies of the comprehension of lectures in university settings where English is lingua franca have shown that the possibilities for misunderstanding when metaphor is used are quite astounding – but these potential misunderstandings are very often not perceived either by lecturers or by the students themselves. Lecturers do not seem to feel the need to explain the metaphors they use or to flag metaphorical words or phrases lexically, by using tuning devices such as 'sort of', 'like' and 'as it were' (see Cameron and Deignan, 2003; Goatly, 1997, pp. 168–94). For example, in the seven UK lectures examined in Low (2010) and Low et al. (2008), no more than half a dozen similes were found. That is, no overt markers of comparison were used to aid comprehension of the vast majority of the metaphors used (Low et al., 2008; Low, 2011). And while it is true that lecturers may use metaphors deliberately[10] as a way of explaining a concept,[11] most of the metaphors used in lectures seem to be highly conventional and hence unmarked as being figurative. In particular, many of the verb phrases and phrasal verbs used to flag agenda or discourse management are conventional linguistic metaphors in English, for example, 'wrap something up', or 'go through something (quickly)' (see Low, 2011). As Littlemore (2001, 2003) and her colleagues (Littlemore et al., 2011) have shown, students are very likely to misunderstand such metaphors. That is, if feedback is not available, they will think they have understood them. For example, Littlemore (2001, 2003) found that Bangladeshi students studying International Development at a university in the United Kingdom were 'repeatedly misled by metaphoric evaluations and metaphor-based cultural references' (Low et al., 2008, pp. 428–9), something that went unnoticed by the lecturers (who presumably thought the metaphors they used were quite transparent) and the students (who had come up with a meaning that made sense to them, even though it did not match the intended meaning). Unfortunately, feedback on this kind of misunderstanding often only becomes available in university settings when examination scripts are read. For example, in Spanish universities, lecturers who appeal to the concept of 'face' or 'facework' in courses taught in English on sociolinguistics, pragmatics or other related subjects may discover that this metaphor needs special explanation, particularly when they discuss Face-Threatening Acts (FTAs).[12] Unless the motivation for this metaphor is fully explicated, students will tend to interpret metaphorical uses of 'face' on the basis of familiarity with uses of the equivalent word in their mother tongue (*cara*). In many Spanish idioms, *cara* is used in phrases that describe situations of conflict or challenge, where FACE is not the 'locus of dignity or prestige' (Yu, 2001), as in English or Chinese, but rather the visible manifestation of audacity (even 'nerve' or 'cheek'). As the following examples show, Spanish is rich in phrases instantiating this mapping:

(7) *tener cara* (lit: have face, 'to have a cheek')
(8) *caradura* (lit: a hardface, 'bold/insolent person')
(9) *dar la cara* (lit: give the face, 'own up to something'/'accept the consequences for [another's] actions')
(10) *verse las caras* (lit: to see each other's face, 'to have it out')
(11) *echar en cara* (lit: throw in (someone's) face, 'to reproach')
(12) *tener cara para algo* (lit: to have face to do something, 'have the nerve to do something') or its variant forms, such as *tener más cara que espalda* (lit: to have more face than back)
(13) *encararse con algo/alguien*, (lit: to face oneself with something/someone, 'confront something/someone')

It is thus not altogether surprising that entrenched linguistic and conceptual routines in the first language (L1) should lead students to interpret an *FTA* as having to do with the self's projection of hostility or defence, rather than understanding that it is another's self-image that may be offended and need protection. The conceptual mapping that underlies such expressions in Spanish is quite unlike that described by Yu for English 'face' or Chinese *lian/mian*, and it may lead to deep misunderstandings in university classrooms.[13]

The explorations of university students' misunderstanding of metaphors carried out to date highlight one important fact about metaphor use that can easily be overlooked if our focus is solely on the conceptual aspect of metaphorical reasoning: if metaphorical conceptualizations are to be communicated, they must be realized in words, gestures or other modes. Metaphor in intercultural communication implies the deployment of specific modes of communication and the conventional forms associated with them by members of the same cultural group. That is to say, there may be nothing intrinsically difficult about understanding a metaphor or analogy per se, as long as speakers realize that this is what they are being invited to do (but see Azuma, 2012). Metaphors are produced and understood by ordinary adult language users everywhere, and their power to induce new ways of understanding situations and events are well known. Why then should their use in communication be especially problematic?

One reason is that metaphorical expressions in most discourse contexts are not signalled explicitly as figurative, and listeners or readers are thus not alerted to the fact that they are being asked to 'see' something in terms of something else. Rather, as Steen (2008) and Cameron (2003, 2008) have pointed out, linguistic metaphors in English are mostly 'invisible' or 'non-deliberate' in discourse, and most often realized not in an 'A is B' form but rather by everyday verbs, verb phrases, noun phrases with 'of', prepositions and particles. Most metaphorical expressions – in English, at least – are realized by high-frequency words, whose polysemous senses are so familiar to native speakers that they are fluent in recognizing and understanding their intended sense in the discourse context in which they are used. A further cue that the use of particular words in context is metaphorical seems to be provided by the fact that many figurative uses are associated with fixed phraseological patterns (Deignan, 2005). However, a speaker communicating in his/her second language may lack the conceptual and linguistic fluency necessary to recognize and understand a conventional metaphor in the target language when this is used in a specific communicative situation, particularly in the rapid give and take of face-to-face conversation. For example, MacArthur and Littlemore (2011) found that even after forty years living in the United Kingdom, a highly educated university professor (L1 Polish) misinterpreted a student's figurative use of the verb 'push' to signify 'too strongly encourage someone to do something', understanding the use literally, although the discourse context showed that this interpretation was not fully coherent with the topic being discussed. A further example of miscommunication arising as a result of otherwise unremarkable (figurative) language uses in a conversation between a Spanish Erasmus student and a lecturer at a university in the United Kingdom is discussed fully in MacArthur (2011) and Littlemore et al. (2012). In this conversation, the lecturer and student were talking about the problems associated with written assignments. Throughout their conversation, the lecturer (Jim) was attempting to explain to the student (Carmen) that when answering an exam question or doing any other type of written assignment, it is important that she think critically and not simply repeat what her lecturer or textbooks explained. The lecturer was seeking to understand the kind of difficulties this student was experiencing and the way she approached the tasks set her, specifically asking how she 'would <u>go about</u>'[14] doing a particular written assignment. In the extract reproduced here, we can see how the conversation takes a very strange turn: the two participants begin by discussing an academic topic ('features of speech') and end up talking about the television programmes Carmen watches.

The words in the extract reproduced here are highlighted in different ways depending on how they are being used: when the use is evidently figurative (e.g. SEEING IS UNDERSTANDING in 'I see' [T16]) it is underlined; when a word from the same source domain is used literally (e.g. '**look** in the dictionary' [T2]) it is signalled by bold type. When a use could be taken either literally or figuratively, this is signalled by a dotted underline (e.g. 'a lot of people in linguistics have talked about these things'):

(14)	T1:	Carmen:	So I will look for this words on Internet, and I use them
	T2:	Jim:	Ok, you'll look at, yeah, will you look at any – because one of the strange things about you studying applied linguistics is that you are – you're studying what you're doing in a way, so a lot of people in linguistics have talked about these things. They sometimes call them discourse markers, yeah? They call them linking words, they call them discourse markers so they – there've been a lot of studies on these. Would you consider that kind of thing, looking at the things that linguists say about these things or would you just **look** in the dictionary or internet, urm, because, so, in the, in the urm, in the last, the last lecture, you looked at some of the features of speech
	T3:	Carmen:	Yes
	T4:	Jim:	So things like when people reformulate what they say, start again and say it in a different way, and I think academic essays they have their own features and well like you're not
	T5:	Carmen:	For example have we do – have we got to do any essay in [*name of course*]?
	T6:	Jim:	Not for the moment, not for months
	T7:	Carmen:	It will be okay
	T8:	Jim:	So you're not worried about it?
	T9:	Carmen:	I could practise.
	T10:	Jim:	Yes, you can practise, and it **sounds** like it will be ok, yeah.
	T11:	Carmen:	Also I can do it by myself because I study at home English, I **watch** TV every day, I'm reading books
	T12:	Jim:	Do you **watch** the television, do you?
	T13:	Carmen:	Yes
	T14:	Jim:	English telly, what do you **watch**?
	T15:	Carmen:	I **watch** some series like Friends and Desperate Housewives, the Vampires Diaries,
	T16:	Jim:	I see, yeah
	T17:	Carmen:	All many programmes I **watch** TV

Carmen declares that she isn't worried about this written assignment because she can 'practise', but this practice turns out to involve watching popular television series such as 'Friends' or 'Desperate Housewives', an activity that could hardly be seen as particularly useful when writing an academic essay. However, the fact that Carmen regards watching TV as relevant practice can plausibly be seen as a consequence of the foregoing use in the discourse by both interlocutors of words related to the domains of SEEING and TALKING/HEARING (both of which are involved in watching television). The highlighting reveals the density of words referring to sight (look, see) and speech (talk, say) that Jim uses in T2 in ways that can be taken literally or figuratively. Academics often communicate by means of the spoken word, so when Jim says that 'a lot of people in linguistics have talked about these things' he could be referring to actual speech. But he could equally well be using 'talk' here to signify 'consider' or 'write about'. In the same way, Carmen may well have literally seen ('looked at') features of speech in the lecture hall or seminar room, if a lecturer has used visuals like a PowerPoint presentation to illustrate a talk (and, of course, 'features' and 'things' can literally be 'seen'). But Jim may again be using the verb with the abstract sense of 'think about'. If Carmen – consciously or unconsciously – used 'look for' in T1 to refer literally to using her eyes to find information on a computer screen (she would have a memory of the specific event which involved the use of her eyes), and expected Jim's contribution to the conversation to be relevant to her own, it seems likely that she would lean towards a literal interpretation of her conversational partner's repetition of the same word in his reply ('you'll look at'). This would explain why she is able to relate watching television with academic assignments, since both involve sight and speech – television only literally but academic work both literally and metaphorically.

The interpretation offered of this extract from a particular conversation rests on the recognition that it is often difficult to decide whether words and phrases are being used literally or figuratively in particular contexts, even when a trained analyst uses a method for identifying metaphorically – used words such as MIP (Pragglejaz Group, 2007). And if it is difficult for an analyst to make such distinctions, it is even harder for the non-native speaker of a language when engaged in face-to-face conversation. In these and other circumstances the strategy adopted may be to take the most familiar literal meaning of a word as the default intended sense in unclear contexts of use.

The misunderstandings of metaphors used in academic communication described here are not simply local problems associated with particular contexts of use (e.g. the office hours' consultation or the lecture), but problems that are potentially capable of having an impact on students' overall academic achievement at university and on their future professional lives. If international students who have been sent to acquire specific training at universities in the United Kingdom, America or Australia (such as the Bangladeshi students considered in Littlemore's 2001 and 2003 studies) return home having ill understood their lecturers, this may well have practical consequences for their own countries' developing economies. In the political sphere, international relations may be strained by failure to understand what is being implied by the metaphorical use of words and phrases. Likewise, the failure to render what is being implied through the metaphorical uses of language in translated texts may seriously compromise the fidelity of those texts and their full comprehension by the target language audience (see Papadoudi, Chapter 2 in this volume). Our increasingly globalized world, with increased opportunities and need for contact between different cultural groups, implies a hitherto unknown inter-dependence of nations and communities. In this world, intercultural dialogue is of vital importance. For these reasons, scholarly interest in the role of metaphor in impeding or facilitating intercultural communication is necessary in order to be able to provide the kind of feedback that will serve to make this dialogue possible.

The chapters in this volume contribute to this discussion by providing empirical, often corpus-based analyses of three key areas of metaphor in intercultural communication. The first of these is the challenge of metaphor translation, specifically issues of choosing between alternative translation strategies and translators' own reflection and awareness of cultural background knowledge. The second area concerns the fundamental problem of establishing metaphors cross-culturally: what counts as metaphorical in the context of one language/culture is not necessarily considered to be equally metaphorical (or not at all metaphorical) in another. Even in cases where comparability appears to be guaranteed, as in proverbs, the respective weight of cultural traditions and of the culture-specific experiential basis may differ to such an extent that the degree of figurativeness is affected. The third dimension of intercultural metaphor use highlighted in this volume is its role in the multifaceted process that is commonly referred to as 'globalization'. Metaphors that deal with the internationalization of businesses and national economies, the restructuring of national sovereignty or multinational cooperation migrate from one culture to another and both generate and become part of perceptions of hybridized cultures. These three key areas and their associated issues are reflected in the grouping of the following chapters into three parts.

In Part I, we begin with an empirical study by Celia Martín de León and Marisa Presas into novice translators' own perceptions and practices of translation. This hinges on an interrogation of how the development of the translators' work, and their understanding of it, seems to be influenced by the development of their metaphorical conceptualization of the discipline. This is followed by Dafni Papadoudi's investigation into the (in)compatibility of metaphors used by the (English) authors and (Greek) translators of popular computing magazines. Identification of similarities and differences in the way that technology is conceptualized plays a key role here, along with consideration of how these impact on communication between the respective cultures. Chapter 3 shifts the focus towards sight translation and interpreting; Xia Xiang and Binghan Zheng describe how their experiment on the effect of providing English-Chinese interpreters with background information (or depriving them of it) reveals that effective (swift and/or 'correct') sight translation of metaphorical expressions is significantly correlated with such provision. The final contribution to Part I is Claudia Förster Hegrenæs's study of the quantitative distribution of expressions of the TIME IS MOTION metaphor in corpora of 'original' and translated English texts. Overrepresentation of the metaphor in the latter is detected, which raises implications for future research into translation strategies and culture-specific conceptual mappings.

In Part II, Anna Ogarkova and Cristina Soriano examine the universality, or otherwise, of metaphoric concepts by mounting an extensive quantitative investigation of the representation of ANGER concepts in three languages and cultures. Their assessment of the shared versus culture-specific aspects of this representation highlights the existence of common categories of ANGER in tandem with cross-cultural divergences in its positive/negative appraisal, expression and regulation, and physiological saliency. In Chapter 6, Farzad Sharifian analyses miscommunication between speakers of Aboriginal and non-Aboriginal varieties of English in Australia. Such miscommunication, he argues, can be accounted for in terms of an underlying cross-cultural mismatch in conceptual systems. Implications of this finding are twofold: first, societal indifference to this mismatch works to compound the social disadvantages faced by speakers of Aboriginal English; and second, theorizing in conceptual metaphor needs to take full account of cross-cultural mapping as a vital component of cross-domain mapping in the broader sense. Part II ends with Sadia Belkhir's chapter which mounts a comparison of proverbs in English and Kabyle that map human behaviour onto the behaviour of dogs. Both cultures are rich in such proverbs, and both tend to negatively characterize the latter behaviour, a propensity that is examined in the light of the potential influence of the *Great Chain of Being* idea across cultures.

The final part of the volume begins with a chapter by José Oncins-Martínez that focuses on the evolution of a metaphorical expression in Spanish and its use in idiomatic language in the fields of politics and business. Oncins-Martínez uses data from corpora to trace the cross-cultural 'marriage' of a Spanish ball-sport metaphor with a similar one borrowed from English. The offspring of this merger is an entirely new hybrid that, albeit not entirely conceptually coherent in the cognitive sense, provides an example of metaphorical creativity which illustrates the power of cultural coherence in influencing speakers' behaviour. The remaining three chapters work with data gleaned from newspapers or related media. Chapter 9, by Jasper Vandenberghe, Patrick Goethals and Geert Jacobs, investigates the use of discourse metaphors and scenarios in English-language headlines reporting on the international business activities of Spanish companies in the 1990s and 2000s. The authors find that the media discourse repeatedly falls back on stereotypical, historically based representations of the Spanish as aggressive colonialists which could have important negative consequences for the intercultural understanding of Spain in the Anglophone world. In Chapter 10, Nadežda Silaški and Tatjana Đurović examine discourse emanating from Belgrade and Brussels on the subject of Serbia's ongoing application to join the EU, concentrating on journey-related metaphors based on *steps* and *traffic lights*. While there may be cross-cultural consistency in understanding these metaphors at face value, there is, contrary to expectations, no such consistency in their actual use by the political elites of the respective capitals. The strategic choices of these political elites attempt to realign the metaphors' meanings to suit their own ends but in so doing they arguably only serve to cause conceptual, and political, confusion and alienation on the part of citizens. The closing chapter, by Mariana Neagu and Gabriela Iuliana Colipcă-Ciobanu, focuses on representations of citizens of a state that has reached the 'destination' of EU membership – Romania. The phenomenon of migration by Romanians to other EU states, especially to the United Kingdom, and the use of metaphors in media reporting of it is examined and interpreted by means of a critical analysis of five metaphor groups which seem to point to the prevailing (ideological) conceptualizations of this process. As the authors point out, such an analysis is of importance in understanding how the world is subject to the discursive construction and consolidation of an 'us' and 'them' dichotomy and thus demonstrating the potential of metaphor use in determining the course of intercultural communication and understanding in its widest sense.

Notes

1 See Gibbs (2005); Johnson (1987); Lakoff and Johnson (1980, 1999).
2 See Goddard and Wierzbicka (2002) and Wierzbicka (1972, 1997); for a polemic about the 'universality' of metaphors in this sense, see Goddard (1996) and Mühlhäusler (1995, 1996).
3 The task was given to students of a master's degree module on 'Metaphors across Cultures' that ran in consecutive academic years (2012–13). The low number of available student responses collected so far makes a statistical analysis pointless. The task will be given to larger groups in future and form the basis for further empirical research. The examples quoted here have been corrected for a few grammatical and spelling errors but otherwise have been left as they were given.
4 The category of 'hair' as part of the 'body politic' appears only in responses given by Chinese students, with different interpretations: 'The hair represents the law, as it is situated at the very top of the body and it has great power and control over the body'; 'The head of the government: hair (if one goes down, always some other one will grow up)'.
5 As regards this personalization or agentivization, response (3), given by a British student, slightly resembles the Chinese answers but it still lacks their geographical grounding.
6 In Shakespeare's oeuvre alone, the tragedies *Coriolanus*, *Macbeth*, *Hamlet* and the historical plays are full of *body politic* imagery; see Armitage et al. (2009); Clemen (1977); Harris (1998); Leggatt (1988); Patterson (1991); Tillyard (1982).
7 See Geeraerts and Grondelaers (1995); Lakoff and Turner (1989); Lovejoy (1936); Niemeier (2000); Tillyard (1982).
8 This description is based on post-test discussions with the students and does not claim to reflect a 'psychological reality' as regards the 'online' metaphor construction process. Any hypothesis on the latter would require detailed psycholinguistic corroboration by observation and experiment.
9 This is a particularly pressing issue for universities in the English-speaking world, because they are receiving ever higher numbers of international students in search of specific training and expertise. For more information on the spread of English as the medium of instruction in higher education across Europe, see Coleman (2006).
10 For discussion of the much debated notion of what a 'deliberate' metaphor is, see Charteris-Black (2012); Deignan (2011); Gibbs (2011); Steen (2011a,b).
11 See Beger's (2011) examples from three psychology lectures, for example, or Brick (2010) for the use of similes in a three-phase explanatory sequence in history lectures in Australia.
12 The second author had this experience when teaching a course in sociolinguistics for the first time.
13 Similar types of expressions are also found in Chinese (see Yu, 2001) but they do not appear to be as numerous as they are in Spanish.
14 In line with standard practice, words that are used metaphorically are underlined.

References

Aitchison, J. (2003), 'Metaphors, Models and Language Change', in R. Hickey (ed.), *Motives for Language Change*, Cambridge: Cambridge University Press, pp. 39–53.

Alejo, R. (2009), 'Where Does the Money Go? An Analysis of the Container Metaphor in Economics: The Market and the Economy', *Journal of Pragmatics*, 42: 1137–50.

Armitage, D., Condren, C. and Fitzmaurice, A. (eds) (2009), *Shakespeare and Early Modern Political Thought*, Cambridge: Cambridge University Press.

Azuma, M. (2012), 'English Native Speakers' Interpretation of Culture-Bound Japanese Figurative Expressions', in F. MacArthur, J. L. Oncins-Martínez, M. Sánchez-García and A. M. Piquer-Píriz (eds), *Metaphor in Use: Context, Culture, and Communication*, Amsterdam and Philadelphia: John Benjamins, pp. 195–216.

Beger, A. (2011), 'Deliberate Metaphors? An Exploration of the Choice and Functions of Metaphors in US-American College Lectures', *metaphorik.de*, 20: 39–60.

Boyd, R. (1993), 'Metaphor and Theory Change: What is "Metaphor" a Metaphor For?', in A. Ortony (ed.), *Metaphor and Thought* (2nd edn), New York: Cambridge University Press, pp. 481–532.

Brick, J. (2010), 'The Use of Metaphor in History Lectures', Paper presented at the RaAM-8 Conference, VU University, Amsterdam, 30 June–3 July.

Caballero, R. (2006), *Re-Viewing Space. Figurative Language in Architects' Assessment of Built Space*, Berlin and New York: Mouton de Gruyter.

Cameron, L. (2003), *Metaphor in Educational Discourse*, London: Continuum Press.

—(2008), 'Metaphor and Talk', in R. W. Gibbs (ed.), *Metaphor and Thought*, New York: Cambridge University Press, pp. 197–211.

Cameron, L. and Deignan, A. (2003), 'Using Large and Small Corpora to Investigate Tuning Devices around Metaphor in Spoken Discourse', *Metaphor and Symbol*, 18(3): 149–60.

Carroll, J. M., Mack, R. and Kellogg, W. (1991), 'Interface Metaphors and User Interface Design', in M. Helander (ed.), *Handbook of Human-Computer Interaction*, Amsterdam: Elsevier, pp. 67–85.

Charteris-Black, J. (2012), 'Forensic Deliberations on "Purposeful Metaphor"', *Metaphor and the Social World*, 2(1): 1–21.

Clemen, W. (1977), *The Development of Shakespeare's Imagery* (2nd edn), London: Methuen and Co.

Coleman, J. A. (2006), 'English-Medium Teaching in European Higher Education', *Language Teaching*, 39(1): 1–14.

de Baecque, A. (1997), *The Body Politic: Corporeal Metaphor in Revolutionary France 1770–1800*, Stanford, CA: Stanford University Press.

Deignan, A. (1995), *COBUILD English Guides. Vol. 7: Metaphor Dictionary*, London: HarperCollins.

—(2005), *Metaphor and Corpus Linguistics*, Amsterdam and Philadelphia: John Benjamins.

—(2011), 'Deliberateness Is Not Unique to Metaphor: A Response to Gibbs', *Metaphor and the Social World*, 1(1): 57–60.

Geeraerts, D. and Grondelaers, S. (1995), 'Looking Back at Anger: Cultural Traditions and Metaphorical Patterns', in J. R. Taylor and R. E. MacLaury (eds), *Language and the Cognitive Construal of the World*, Berlin and New York: de Gruyter, pp. 153–79.

Gibbs, R. W. (2005), *Embodiment and Cognitive Science*, Cambridge: Cambridge University Press.
—(2011), 'Are "Deliberate" Metaphors Really Deliberate? A Question of Human Consciousness and Action', *Metaphor and the Social World*, 1(1): 26–52.
Goatly, A. (1997), *The Language of Metaphors*, London and New York: Routledge.
Goddard, C. (1996), 'Cross-Linguistic Research on Metaphor', *Language and Communication*, 16(2): 145–51.
Goddard, C. and Wierzbicka, A. (2002), 'Semantic Primes and Universal Grammar', in C. Goddard and A. Wierzbicka (eds), *Meaning and Universal Grammar – Theory and Empirical Findings Vol. 1*, Amsterdam and Philadelphia: John Benjamins, pp. 41–85.
Golden, A. (2010), 'Grasping the Point: A Study of 15-Year-Old Students' Comprehension of Metaphorical Expressions in Schoolbooks', in G. Low, Z. Todd, A. Deignan and L. Cameron (eds), *Researching and Applying Metaphor in the Real World*, Amsterdam and Philadelphia: John Benjamins, pp. 35–59.
Goschler, J. (2007), 'Metaphors in Cognitive and Neurosciences: Which Impact Have Metaphors on Scientific Theories and Models?', *metaphorik.de*, 12: 7–20.
Hale, D. G. (1971), *The Body Politic: A Political Metaphor in Renaissance English Literature*, The Hague and Paris: Mouton.
Halliday, M. A. K. (2004), *The Language of Science* (ed. J. J. Webster), London: Continuum.
Harris, J. G. (1998), *Foreign Bodies and the Body Politic*, Cambridge: Cambridge University Press.
Harvey, A. D. (2007), *Body Politic: Political Metaphor and Political Violence*, Newcastle-upon-Tyne: Cambridge Scholars Publishing.
Johnson, M. (1987), *The Body in the Mind: The Bodily Basis of Meaning, Imagination, and Reason*, Chicago: University of Chicago Press.
Kövecses, Z. (1986), *Metaphors of Anger, Pride, and Love: A Lexical Approach to the Structure of Concepts*, Amsterdam and Philadelphia: John Benjamins.
—(1990), *Emotion Concepts*, New York: Springer.
—(1995), 'Anger: Its language, Conceptualization, and Physiology in the Light of Cross-Cultural Evidence', in J. R. Taylor and R. E. MacLaury (eds), *Language and the Cognitive Construal of the World*, Berlin and New York: de Gruyter, pp. 181–96.
—(2000), *Metaphor and Emotion: Language, Culture, and Body in Human Feeling*, Cambridge and New York: Cambridge University Press.
—(2005), *Metaphor in Culture: Universality and Variation*, Cambridge and New York: Cambridge University Press.
—(2006), *Language, Mind and Culture: A Practical Introduction*, Oxford and New York: Oxford University Press.
Kuhn, T. S. (1993), 'Metaphor in Science', in A. Ortony (ed.), *Metaphor and Thought* (2nd edn), New York: Cambridge University Press, pp. 533–42.
Lakoff, G. and Johnson, M. (1980), *Metaphors We Live By*, Chicago: University of Chicago Press.
—(1999), *Philosophy in the Flesh: The Embodied Mind and its Challenge to Western Thought*, New York: Basic Books.
Lakoff, G. and Turner, M. (1989), *More than Cool Reason: A Field Guide to Poetic Metaphor*, Chicago and London: University of Chicago Press.
Leggatt, A. (1988), *Shakespeare's Political Drama: The History Plays and the Roman Plays*, London and New York: Routledge.
Littlemore, J. (2001), 'The Use of Metaphor in University Lectures and the Problems That it Causes for Overseas Students', *Teaching in Higher Education*, 6: 331–51.

—(2003), 'The Effect of Cultural Background on Metaphor Interpretation', *Metaphor and Symbol*, 18: 273–88.

Littlemore, J., Chen, P., Koester, A. and Barnden, J. (2011), 'Difficulties in Metaphor Comprehension Faced by International Students whose First Language Is Not English', *Applied Linguistics*, 32(4): 408–29.

Littlemore, J., MacArthur, F., Cienki, A. and Holloway, J. (2012), 'How to Make Yourself Understood by International Students: The Role of Metaphor in Academic Tutorials', *ELT Research Papers: British Council Publications*, 12-06: 1–27.

Lovejoy, A. O. (1936), *The Great Chain of Being. A Study of the History of an Idea*, Cambridge, MA: Harvard University Press.

Low, G. (2010), 'Wot No Similes: The Curious Absence of Simile in University Lectures', in G. Low, Z. Todd, A. Deignan and L. Cameron (eds), *Researching and Applying Metaphor in the Real World*, Amsterdam and Philadelphia: John Benjamins, pp. 291–308.

—(2011), 'Pin Me Down a Bit More. Researching Metaphor in University Lectures', *International Journal of Innovation and Leadership in the Teaching of Humanities*, 1(1): 6–22.

Low, G., Littlemore, J. and Koester, A. (2008), 'Metaphor Use in Three UK University Lectures', *Applied Linguistics*, 29(3): 428–55.

MacArthur, F. (2011), 'On the Use of Metaphor in Office Hours' Consultations Carried Out in English between Lecturers and Students with Different First Languages', *International Journal of Innovation and Leadership in the Teaching of Humanities*, 1(1): 23–44.

MacArthur, F. and Littlemore, J. (2011), 'On the Repetition of Words with the Potential for Metaphoric Extension in Conversations between Native and Non-native Speakers of English', *Metaphor and the Social World*, 1(2): 202–39.

Mio, J. S. (1996), 'Metaphor, Politics and Persuasion', in J. S. Mio and A. N. Katz (eds), *Metaphor: Implications and Applications*, New Jersey: Lawrence Erlbaum, pp. 127–46.

Montuschi, E. (2000), 'Metaphor in Science', in W. Newton-Smith (ed.), *A Companion to the Philosophy of Science*, Oxford: Blackwell, pp. 277–82.

Mühlhäusler, P. (1995), 'Metaphors Others Live By', *Language and Communication*, 15(3): 281–8.

—(1996), 'Rejoinder to Goddard on Cross-Linguistic Research on Metaphor', *Language and Communication*, 16(4): 401–2.

Musolff, A. (2004), 'The *Heart* of the European *Body Politic*. British and German Perspectives on Europe's Central *Organ*', *Journal of Multilingual and Multicultural Development*, 25(5/6): 437–52.

—(2010a), *Metaphor, Nation and the Holocaust: The Concept of the Body Politic*, London and New York: Routledge.

—(2010b), 'Political Metaphor and *Bodies Politic*', in U. Okulska and P. Cap (eds), *Perspectives in Politics and Discourse*, Amsterdam and Philadelphia: John Benjamins, pp. 23–41.

Niemeier, S. (2000), 'Straight from the Heart – Metonymic and Metaphorical Explorations', in A. Barcelona (ed.), *Metaphor and Metonymy at the Crossroads: A Cognitive Perspective*, Berlin and New York: De Gruyter, pp. 195–213.

Obama, B. (2007), *The Audacity of Hope: Thoughts on Reclaiming the American Dream*, Edinburgh: Canongate.

Patterson, A. M. (1991), *Fables of Power: Aesopian Writing and Political History*, Durham, NC: Duke University Press.

Philip, G. (2010), 'Drugs, Traffic, and Many Other Dirty Interests: Metaphor and the Language Learner', in G. Low, Z. Todd, A. Deignan and L. Cameron (eds), *Researching and Applying Metaphor in the Real World*, Amsterdam and Philadelphia: John Benjamins, pp. 63–80.

Piquer-Piriz, A. M. (2010), 'Can People Be Cold and Warm? Developing Understanding of Figurative Meanings of Temperature Terms in Early EFL', in G. Low, Z. Todd, A. Deignan and L. Cameron (eds), *Researching and Applying Metaphor in the Real World*, Amsterdam and Philadelphia: John Benjamins, pp. 21–34.

Pragglejaz Group (2007), 'MIP: A Method for Identifying Metaphorically Used Words in Discourse', *Metaphor and Symbol*, 22(1): 1–39.

Shogimen, T. (2008a), 'Treating the Body Politic: The Medical Metaphor of Political Rule in Late Medieval Europe and Tokugawa Japan', *The Review of Politics*, 70: 77–104.

—(2008b), 'Imagining the Body Politic: Metaphor and Political Language in Late Medieval Europe and Tokugawa Japan', in T. Shogimen and C. J. Nederman (eds), *Western Political Thought in Dialogue with Asia*, Lanham, MD: Lexington Books/Rowman and Littlefield, pp. 279–300.

Sontag, S. (1978), *Illness as Metaphor*, New York: Vintage Books.

Steen, G. J. (2008), 'The Paradox of Metaphor: Why We Need a Three Dimensional Model of Metaphor', *Metaphor and Symbol*, 23(4): 213–41.

—(2011a), 'What Does "Really Deliberate" Really Mean? More Thoughts on Metaphor and Consciousness', *Metaphor and the Social World*, 1(1): 53–6.

—(2011b), 'From Three Dimensions to Five Steps: The Value of Deliberate Metaphor', *metaphorik.de*, 21: 83–110.

Steen, G. J., Dorst, A. G., Herrmann, B., Kaal, A., Krennmayr, T. and Pasma, T. (2010), *A Method for Linguistic Metaphor Identification: From MIP to MIPVU*, Amsterdam and Philadelphia: John Benjamins.

Taylor, J. R. (1995), *Linguistic Categorization* (2nd edn), Oxford: Oxford University Press.

Tillyard, E. M. W. (1982), *The Elizabethan World Picture*, Harmondsworth: Penguin.

Wang, C. and Dowker, A. (2010), 'A Cross-Cultural Study of Metaphoric Understanding', in G. Low, Z. Todd, A. Deignan and L. Cameron (eds), *Researching and Applying Metaphor in the Real World*, Amsterdam and Philadelphia: John Benjamins, pp. 105–22.

Wierzbicka, A. (1972), *Semantic Primitives*, Frankfurt am Main: Athenäum.

—(1997), *Understanding Cultures through Their Key-Words. English, Russian, Polish, German, and Japanese*, Oxford and New York: Oxford University Press.

Yu, N. (1998), *The Contemporary Theory of Metaphor: A Perspective from Chinese*, Amsterdam and Philadelphia: John Benjamins.

—(2001), 'What Does Our Face Mean to Us?', *Pragmatics and Cognition*, 9(1): 1–36.

—(2008a), 'Metaphor from Body and Culture', in R. W. Gibbs (ed.), *The Cambridge Handbook of Metaphor and Thought*, Cambridge: Cambridge University Press, pp. 247–61.

—(2008b), 'The Relationship between Metaphor, Body and Culture', in R. M. Frank, R. Dirven, T. Ziemke and E. Bernárdez (eds), *Body, Language and Mind. Vol. 2: Sociocultural Situatedness*, Berlin and New York: Mouton de Gruyter, pp. 387–407.

—(2009), *From Body to Meaning in Culture: Papers on Cognitive Semantic Studies of Chinese*, Amsterdam and Philadelphia: John Benjamins.

Part One

Metaphor in Translation

1

The Evolution of Translation Trainees' Subjective Theories: An Empirical Study of Metaphors about Translation

Celia Martín de León and Marisa Presas[1]

Introduction

Traditionally, when reflecting on the translation process, metaphors such as TRANSFER, CHANGE or IMITATION are used. Several studies have shown that these metaphors are something more than just 'a way of saying'. On the one hand, they shape the concept of translation of a specific social group or translation theory (Chesterman, 1997; D'hulst, 1992; Martín de León, 2008); on the other, they serve to structure and express individual translators' knowledge (Martín de León, 2010).

In the fields of sociology, psychology and pedagogy the concept of implicit or subjective theories is linked to that of everyday knowledge, that is, non-scientific or lay knowledge. It is assumed that subjective theories are unconscious but may become conscious and explicit if the corresponding stimulus is provided. Their main function is to explain the way in which the world functions, as well as one's own behaviour and that of others (Mandl and Huber, 1983; Scheele and Groeben, 1998).

Translators' knowledge about translation has been studied from sociological and cognitive perspectives. Both approaches hold that the knowledge translators possess – not only procedural knowledge but also declarative knowledge – determines the characteristics of the final product, the translated text. Sociologists work with an abstract, 'ideal' translator in an attempt to discover theoretically based criteria or 'norms' (Toury, 1995) that are generalizable and that may be induced from the study of translated texts. Cognitive studies have sought to develop problem-solving models and have focused on, among other aspects, the identification and classification of strategies used by expert and novice translators to solve translation problems. Many of the studies investigating the translation process of novice translators have used Thinking Aloud Protocols which have enabled informants to spontaneously manifest their theoretical concepts of translation. Researchers have paid little or no attention to this form of lay knowledge – which was not the aim of their research – because they consider it to be idiosyncratic, erroneous or incoherent (Hönig, 1997; Krings, 1986).

Within the framework of a research project being carried out by the PETRA[2] group, we have begun a study of the subjective theories of translation of novice translators. We are particularly interested in determining the structure and content of their theories; how they evolve as a result of the effects of translation practice and the study of scientific theories; and to what extent students apply these theories to solving translation problems. The general principles of the conceptual theory of metaphor (Lakoff, 1993; Lakoff and Johnson, 1980) serve as the basis for our analysis. Our first findings showed that novice translators do in fact have initial subjective theories about translation; that these theories may be structured and articulated through metaphor; and both experience in translating and the study of scientific theories can modify their initial theoretical positions. In an earlier publication we focused our attention on modelling the role of subjective theories in the translation process and analysing the basic tenets of these theories (Martín de León and Presas, 2011). In this chapter we discuss our analysis of the metaphoric expressions used by students to describe the translation process, giving some examples, and present our conclusions concerning conceptual changes in students' subjective theories of translation as a result of formal learning.

Subjective theory, formal learning and conceptual change

Educational research has found that students in general have difficulty in understanding scientific concepts not only in "abstract" domains like philosophy and mathematics, but also in more "concrete" fields like history or biology (see Vosniadou et al., 2008 for a review). To a large extent, this difficulty may be attributed to the fact that insufficient attention has been paid to the problem of conceptual change (Vosniadou et al., 2008, p. 1). Vygotsky (1962) had already differentiated between 'spontaneous concepts' and 'scientific concepts' and pointed to the fact that changes and restructuring of spontaneous concepts were brought about as a result of formal education. Over the past twenty years, research into conceptual change has attempted to identify the mechanisms regulating these changes and their implications for curriculum design. Although most of the studies have focused on children and adolescents, their conclusions are applicable to adults as well (Pozo, 2003).

Studies on conceptual change are based on the assumption that students' initial knowledge is organized into a relatively coherent structure of domain specific knowledge, which has an ontology and a causality ('framework theory'). Conceptual change is the gradual substitution of the beliefs and presuppositions of subjective theories when they come into conflict with new knowledge that is acquired. The difficulty lies in the fact that a framework theory is a coherent explanatory system which is constructed on the basis of experience that is, moreover, repeatedly confirmed within the context of lay culture. More important still is the fact that students are not aware that others may have different beliefs, or that their beliefs are not true facts about the world but hypotheses that may be tested and falsified. That is why they do not test hypotheses to evaluate their relevance to reality and, if necessary, begin a conscious process of conceptual change (Vosniadou, 2008, p. xviii). Research into the process of acquisition of scientific theories shows that students, unconsciously and over time, use mainly additive enrichment types of learning mechanisms to revise their initial theories. Often these learning mechanisms give rise to so-called synthetic models, which evidence students' attempts to synthesize two incompatible concepts or pieces of information, one coming from their prior knowledge and the other from knowledge acquired through formal instruction (Vosniadou et al., 2008, p. 9).

Following Posner et al. (1982), the traditional approach to promoting conceptual change within an academic context involves creating 'cognitive conflict' in order to provoke students' dissatisfaction with their preconceptions. The method generally used is to encourage students to verbalize their initial theories. It has been noted, however, that cognitive conflict as a pedagogical strategy, and verbalization of students' theories in particular, may be counterproductive because it focuses on inappropriate or erroneous prior knowledge that cannot be used constructively in the learning process (diSessa, 1993). More recent research (Potvin et al., 2012) shows that encouraging students to make their initial theories explicit is not counterproductive as long as this is carried out in combination with other strategies used to create cognitive conflict (Clement, 2008), or in association with the development of metacognitive or conscious strategic learning skills, such as the testing of hypotheses (Clement, 2008; Wiser and Smith, 2008).

Research findings in the field of conceptual change are consistent with those of studies carried out in the use of metaphors to explain spontaneous as opposed to scientific concepts. Studies in the use of metaphors in advanced knowledge acquisition (Spiro et al., 1989) and in school educational discourse (Cameron, 2003) conclude that metaphors can play an important role in the process of cognitive restructuring as a result of acquiring scientific concepts, although they may become an obstacle to learning, in particular when great store is set by a metaphor that was useful at one point in time but which is now unable to reflect the complexity of the corresponding domain.

Theoretical and methodological framework used in the analysis of metaphor

The general framework of the conceptual theory of metaphor was used for our study, although theoretical and methodological contributions were incorporated from studies on metaphors in discourse carried out over the past decade. Cognitive linguists (Lakoff, 1987, p. 386; Núñez, 2000, p. 135) have described 'conceptual metaphors' as mental operations that enable us to understand the world by establishing systematic mappings of inferential structures between domains of experience that are best known or accessible to bodily experience and others that are more difficult to structure conceptually. Cognitive linguistics holds that these structures orientate experience and action and can be fairly stable, that is, they can function as cultural models shared by a social group and are reflected in their language (e.g. Kövecses, 1986, 2005;

Lakoff and Kövecses, 1987). The notion of the cognitive nature of metaphor and its function in orienting experience and action is the keystone of our research since one of our hypotheses is derived from it: that ideas about communication, language and translation implicit in the metaphors used by students influence the way they translate. Also of interest to our study is the extent to which the implicit theories reflected in the metaphors used by students are socially shared, and to which they are unique to individual students and the result of work carried out in the classroom.

That said, we believe that the conceptual theory of metaphor, because it focuses exclusively on cognitive aspects, has tended to overlook linguistic aspects of metaphor on the one hand, and aspects of the communicative situation in which metaphors are produced and interpreted on the other. As regards the linguistic aspects of metaphor, Lakoff and Johnson (1980) consider language to be a secondary element which gives expression to cognitive processes but is not an integral part of those processes: 'Metaphor is primarily a matter of thought and action and only derivatively a matter of language' (p. 153). Nevertheless, if we focus our study of metaphor on spoken discourse, linguistic aspects of metaphor can provide important clues for cognitive analysis. For example, Cameron (2003) found systematic differences between how nominal metaphors and verb metaphors were processed in English. It should be noted that there is a conflict between cognitive linguists' desire to make language secondary and their use of language as their main source of evidence for describing conceptual metaphors (p. 19).

As regards the communicative situation, cognitive linguists' initial research did not involve the empirical study of spoken discourse but rather phrases obtained as a result of introspection and studied out of context. However, as shown by Cameron (2003), one and the same expression can be interpreted as literal or as metaphorical depending on the context and the communicative situation. The analysis of metaphors must take into consideration all those contextual aspects that have a bearing on the interpretation of an expression as metaphoric, that is, those aspects that determine whether or not a metaphor may be interpreted as such.

Analysis of metaphors

The theoretical and methodological framework of the conceptual theory of metaphor has been expanded in our work to include contributions from the study of metaphors in spoken discourse (e.g. Cameron, 2003, 2007; Cameron and Deignan, 2006; Cameron and Stelma, 2004; Kövecses, 2009; Musolff, 2004; Musolff and Zinken, 2009). Following these authors, the analysis of the linguistic aspects of metaphors is essential if we are to understand how we use metaphors to organize our experiences and how we interpret them (Cameron, 2003, p. 2). Moreover, when analysing metaphors in spoken discourse, the specific context within which they are used must be taken into consideration. The term 'context' is used here in the broadest sense and includes physical, social, interactional and linguistic factors, among others (p. 4). Applied linguistics focuses on 'language in use', and always takes into consideration the situatedness of the discourse. By taking into account the communicative situations in which metaphors are used, we have assumed a dynamic approach in our study, recording the evolution in the use of specific metaphors or the substitution of one metaphor for another. We have not, therefore, studied metaphoric expressions in isolation but rather the relationship between such expressions within discourse, and their evolution over the period in which data were collected.

Identification of linguistic metaphors

The basic criteria proposed by Cameron (2003, pp. 59–61) and the method proposed by the Pragglejaz Group (2007), with some modifications, were used to identify the metaphoric expressions in students' discourse.

First, expressions were identified that could give rise, at a superficial level, to semantic or pragmatic incongruity between a 'Focus' or 'Vehicle' (Black, 1962; Cameron, 2003) and the discourse ('Topic') in which they were embedded. To do this, we compared the contextual meaning of these expressions and their primary meaning as in, for example, a dictionary (Pragglejaz Group, 2007). Thus, when a student referred to 'the phrases they've put into your head'[3] (subject JKL, semi-structured interview held in November 2008) potential incongruity was detected between the physical action of putting one object into another, and the subject of the dialogue: education. The basic meaning of the verb 'put' (physical action of introducing an object into a place) is incongruent within the immediate context ('phrases', 'in your head').

Second, an attempt was made to determine whether the potential incongruity could be resolved by establishing a link between the two domains of experience (Cameron, 2003, p. 60, refers here to interaction or conceptual blending between the Vehicle and the Topic of the metaphor). In the example given earlier, the incongruity detected can be resolved by linking knowledge of the domain of the manipulation of physical objects to the domain of education. An analogy can be established between the action of teaching or modelling behaviour and the action of introducing objects into a container: ideas or 'phrases' are 'put' into the head of subjects who receive education. The objects put into the head represent cognitive and behavioural changes that are the result of the education process.

It should be noted that it is often difficult to establish the boundaries of metaphoric expressions which may extend to the length of a word, a clause, a sentence or even a paragraph. In our study, units of greater length than those proposed by the Pragglejaz Group (2007) have been analysed in those cases in which there are systematic and coherent relationships between the elements of the unit. For example, the phrase 'transport some ideas from one language to another' (subject B, interview) was, as a whole, considered to be a metaphoric expression. The Vehicle of the metaphor, 'transport', extends its metaphoricity to 'ideas' and 'languages', which tend to be understood as transported objects and as places between which transport takes place.

Analysis of linguistic metaphors

Our analysis of metaphoric expressions focused, on the one hand, on the domains of experience between which links were established and, on the other, on the context within which the metaphors were used. We perceive the category of metaphor as radial, open and defined by *family resemblance*, not by a list of sufficient and necessary conditions for membership (Cameron, 2003; Lakoff, 1987; Wittgenstein, 1953). Not all expressions identified as metaphoric, therefore, enjoy the same degree of metaphoricity (belong to the category to the same degree), that is, in each case there may be greater or lesser probability of metaphoric expressions being mentally processed as metaphors.

> Metaphoricity does not inhere in the word or even necessarily in the Topic-Vehicle contrast, but can increase and decrease through the nearby use of other words related to the Vehicle domain and also through non-linguistic or non-verbalized phenomena. (Cameron, 2003, p. 69)

When analysing metaphoric expressions, there is always the danger of overgeneralizing data, filling in the gaps in linguistic metaphors in order to reconstruct a conceptual metaphor described earlier. The move from metaphoric expressions to conceptual metaphors requires using large doses of inferencing, but this must be done with great caution (Cameron, 2003, pp. 240–1). This is why the systematicity and coherence of metaphoric expressions in discourse must be studied. By analysing the domains of experience involved in the example given earlier ('the phrases they've put into your head'), we may infer a metaphoric projection by which to teach or communicate ideas to another person involves putting those ideas into his or her head. This metaphor forms part of a model of communication and, by extension, of teaching as the transmission of ideas through language (Reddy, 1993). However, the isolated use of the metaphoric expression cannot lead us to suppose that the speaker is using a conceptual metaphor to refer to the domain of education since the expression is a very common one in Spanish and is often used without thinking. This metaphoric expression occurs when the student claims that every translation is different because everybody is different: 'Always . . . because it depends too on your environment, with your parents, how you were brought up, *the phrases they've put into your head* . . .' (subject JKL, interview). If, however, we analyse the wider context, we will find a little earlier on in the same interview other metaphoric expressions the student uses to refer to her difficulties in expressing herself: '*I've got it in my head* but I don't know how to explain it to other people'; 'I could never *get it out*'. These linguistic metaphors would appear to coincide with the aforementioned metaphoric model in which the head is conceived as a container of ideas and to express these ideas is akin to 'getting them out of the container'. The emergence of these metaphoric expressions close together in context increases the probability that the domain of manipulation and transfer of physical objects was activated when referring to communication and education. We cannot be sure that this is what happened but in general our analysis of the context has enabled us to determine the degree of systematicity with which the linguistic metaphors have been used and, as a result, the greater or lesser probability that they function as cognitive metaphors.

Context of the study

The study was carried out with a group of ten students (nine females and one male) in the first semester of the Degree in Translation and Interpreting at the Universidad de Las Palmas de Gran Canaria, 2008–9. Data were collected during the course of the subject 'Theory and Practice of Translation B German-Spanish'. The subject was designed to introduce students to theoretical reflection and hands-on experience of translation from German to Spanish. Data were collected throughout the semester by the researcher, who was also the teacher responsible for the subject. How much the integration of research into the learning process influenced the results obtained is difficult to say since once the students had completed the first questionnaires they began to participate in the formal learning process that would increasingly influence their metaphoric models of translation. The main objectives of this course were to encourage students to: (1) become aware of the metaphors they used to refer to translation; (2) think critically about the view of translation and communication that those metaphors reflected; and (3) develop new theories based on their experience and study of different scientific theories of translation.

To a large extent the methodology consisted in providing students with tools, cognitive support and opportunities to restructure their views on translation by making them aware of the theories implicit in the metaphors they used, as a first step to developing new theories based on their experience and on scientific models. Following Vygotsky (1962), we could say that the aim was to ease the changeover from 'spontaneous concepts' to 'scientific concepts' by using new metaphors (Spiro et al., 1989).

Data collection

Data were collected using four questionnaires, a semi-structured interview, four theoretical essays, two commentaries on students' own translations and the Translog[4] transcript of students' activity while translating four different texts. At the beginning of the semester (September 2008) students were required to complete a questionnaire providing sociolinguistic data, followed by another on translation. Several weeks later (October 2008), in a third questionnaire, they were asked to sketch what they understood to be the translation process and to explain, using an image or a metaphor, what happens when a text is translated. In the fourth questionnaire, they had to answer questions about the metaphors they had used. During the months of November and December 2008, interviews were conducted in which informants were required to carry out a metalinguistic reflection on the metaphors they had used. The interviews were recorded and transcribed. The theoretical essays were submitted at intervals throughout the semester. Three of the essays were about scientific theories of translation (Nida's theory of translation, the Leipzig School and functionalist translation theory), and for the fourth, students were invited to explain their own theory of translation. Two commentaries, in which students were asked to comment on their decision-making processes in the translation of two advertisements, were elaborated in October and November. Finally, students' translations of four different children's stories (400–500 words) in the space of one hour were recorded using Translog. Except for the interviews, which were conducted one to one, all the other tasks were carried out at the same time, in a group, in order to ensure conditions were the same for all students alike.

The use of questionnaires about translation and about students' own theoretical models was aimed at standardizing the data collection process and orienting answers towards a set of topics or a specific referential plane (the metaphor). The questionnaire soliciting sociolinguistic data was designed to help neutralize the effect of conditions that were not the object of study (such as prior training in translation) but which could have a marked effect on the construction and, in particular, the evolution of students' theories. It goes without saying that the use of questionnaires should enable the findings of this study to be contrasted with those of future studies – which will serve to validate the analyses carried out.

Findings

In all, 1,046 metaphoric expressions were found and ascribed to 37 conceptual metaphors (Martín de León and Presas, 2011). More than half the metaphoric expressions (60 per cent) referred to the domain TRANSLATION in terms of other more concrete or better-structured domains: TRANSFER OF OBJECTS, CHANGE OF OBJECTS, MOVEMENT TOWARDS A GOAL, PUTTING ONESELF IN ANOTHER PERSON'S PLACE, MECHANICAL PROCESS, TREE THAT GROWS, CHEMICAL EXPERIMENT, PICTURE, CONSTRUCTION. Most of the metaphors used by the students are widely used in Spanish. Only three of the conceptual metaphors identified (4.3 per cent of the metaphoric expressions) were unique to three individual students (TRANSLATION IS LIKE A TREE WHICH GROWS, TRANSLATION IS A CHEMICAL EXPERIMENT and TRANSLATION IS A PICTURE). In some cases a new, creative metaphor was related to a more common conceptual one, for example, 'a translator is an electrical plug' was taken to be a metaphoric expression of the conceptual metaphor TO TRANSLATE IS TO CONNECT PEOPLE.

The framework theory: TRANSFER

The TRANSFER metaphor has been identified in different scientific discourses on translation (Chesterman, 1997; Martín de León, 2008, 2010; Tymoczko, 2010). This metaphor offers a simplified view of translation as the transport of meaning between texts, languages or cultures that are conceived of as containers. Just like the CONDUIT metaphor (Reddy, 1993), of which it may be considered an extension (Martín de León, 2008, 2010), the TRANSFER metaphor enables the communicative process to be conceived of as the sending of information through language, overshadowing the active participation of the interlocutors (and the translator) in the process of meaning-making. The task of the translator, according to this metaphor, consists in extracting the meaning of the source text and transferring it to the target text, if possible without making any changes. Its main assumptions are that form and content are separate entities and that meaning is an object that may be transferred from one text to another and from one mind to another without being subject to change. It is a naive, decontextualized view of translation which masks the complexity of the task, and may have a negative influence on the translation process. For example, students may give precedence to the 'transfer' of isolated meaning without paying attention to the possible interpretations of the target audience, thus, relegating the pragmatic, social and cultural aspects of the communicative situation to a secondary level (Martín de León, 2010, p. 89).

The TRANSFER metaphor was the one most often used during the semester (323 tokens, 30.6 per cent of the total number of tokens). Moreover, this metaphor and the CHANGE metaphor were the only two that were used by all students without exception. The fact that this metaphor was the one most frequently used in the questionnaires at the beginning of the semester would appear to indicate that it plays an important role in the structuring of implicit theories of novice translators; and the consistency with which it was used allows one to suppose that it constitutes the main framework theory of students. During interviews, when the researcher explicitly asked informants about their beliefs in relation to the TRANSFER metaphor, the consistent use of different Vehicles related to this metaphor was noted, as in the following example:

(1) R: Do you still think that when you translate you *transfer something that never changes*?
GHI: Mmm . . . yes, I think so, because *the message* must be *the same*
R: And what is *the message*? For example . . .
GHI: *The message* . . . what . . . the writer, what the producer of the text wants to *transfer to another person.*

Sometimes, even when the researcher tried to approach the question from a different angle in order to avoid the use of the TRANSFER metaphor, informants reformulated the new approach in terms of the metaphor they were familiar with, as in example (2):

(2) R: You mean, *the function* of the elements in both texts should be similar.
GHI: Yes, we have to *transfer the intention* of the author, the producer (I don't know the word) of the text . . .
R: Of the producer of the source text . . .
GHI: . . . *to the target text.*
R: You mean, you think the intention of the author of the text is very important.
GHI: Yes. It doesn't matter which words you use, or what . . . What is important is that *the idea is passed on and it stays the same.*

As a result of formal instruction, the use of the TRANSFER metaphor diminished during the semester: at the beginning the number of tokens of this metaphor was 54 per cent of the total number; at the end only 13 per cent. This evolution coincided with an increase in the number of conceptual metaphors used (from seventeen in October to thirty-three in February). Although this increase was not steady, it indicates a process of diversification of the domains initially used to talk about and reflect on translation. This may be seen as a move from spontaneous concepts to the development of scientific concepts of communication and translation. Moreover, an increase in the degree of complexity of the concepts used to explain the translation process was detected. In most cases new elements were added to the TRANSFER metaphor (feelings, cultural elements) or several concepts were combined to expand it (CHANGE, EQUIVALENCE, MECHANICAL PROCESS), that is, an additive mechanism was activated which led to a synthetic model. Only in a few cases did true restructuring take place with respect to the initial metaphor (GROWTH OF A TREE, EXPERIMENT and CREATION metaphors). Nevertheless, in all cases metaphoric expressions of TRANSFER continued to be used even when they were not consistent with the new model.

The synthetic theory: TRANSFER and CHANGE

Although reflection on the practice and the study of scientific theories of translation led to the evolution of metaphors and the use of the TRANSFER metaphor diminished as the semester progressed, students found great difficulty in replacing this metaphor with others. When they had to translate the two advertisements and the mere 'transfer of contents' was not enough to produce translations that fulfilled the translation brief, they tended to extend their initial theory to adapt it to their new experience using enrichment mechanisms. Extending their theories most often meant including a process of change in the transfer of elements of the source text to the target text thereby adapting the target text to the requirements of the translation brief and the target reader profile. The use of the CHANGE metaphor increased considerably during the months of November and December, coinciding with students' translations of advertisements. This would appear to indicate a certain degree of influence of translation practice on students' implicit theories of translation. The use of the CHANGE metaphor, however, did not lead to the development of a new model, but rather the TRANSFER metaphor was adapted to create a synthetic model in which some transferred elements changed and others remained the same (Martín de León and Presas, 2011, pp. 292–3), as in the following example:

(3) 'I decided to *keep* the strategy but *change* the story'. (Subject TUV, second translation commentary)

In some cases the TRANSFER metaphor was extended to include the transfer of feelings or cultural elements. In all cases the process involved preserving the initial theory to accommodate the new experiences with a minimum of effort.

The strategies used during the semester to get students to relativize the TRANSFER metaphor coincide with those proposed by Spiro et al. (1989). On the one hand, new analogies (taken from scientific theories) were introduced, and students were encouraged to develop their own metaphors. On the other hand, the limitations of each metaphor were explicitly discussed with students. In particular, the metaphors used by each informant in their questionnaires were discussed at interview with the teacher. This discussion sometimes gave rise to relexicalization of the metaphoric Vehicle in an interactive chain of negotiations of meaning. In the course of discussion, students were encouraged to decide which metaphors they thought were most useful to explain the decisions they had taken when translating the advertisements.

(4) R: Here what would have been *transferred from one story to another, from one advertisement to another*?
W: Well, I don't know . . . it's as if . . . I associate it more with a *chip, changing from one language to another.*
R: You mean, *chip, changing chip* makes more sense to you than *transfer*?
W: Yes, yes I do, because . . . it's like something *automatic*, in my case, I *don't control it.*
R: Ahah, OK.
W: And that's why I say 'change chip'.
R: OK, so you *automatically go from one language to another.* Almost without wanting to you translate the text, . . . that would be the process, let's say spontaneous, intuitive. And then you would have the more detailed part, the *tree.*
W: Yes.
R: Could we say something like that?
W: Yes, and *we can rub out transfer because it has nothing to do with it.*

In this example, in an attempt to connect the metaphoric expressions used by the student with her reflection on her translations, a process of evaluation of the metaphors in terms of their ability to explain phenomena was initiated. The student finally rejected the TRANSFER metaphor because it was no longer useful in describing the translation process, although she continued to be consistent in her use of expressions of this metaphor until the end of the semester, as did the rest of her peers.

Conclusions

In recent years, the concept of translation itself has been defined as culture-bound, not universal. Tymoczko (2003, 2010) sustains that current Western translation theories are markedly Eurocentric and based on conceptual metaphors 'embodying a limited and controlled type of transfer' (2010, p. 111). Chesterman (2006) analyses the terms used in different world languages to denominate what in English is called 'translation'. His most relevant conclusions in the context of our study are that most Indo-European languages seem to foreground the similarity or even the identity between source and target texts, and that the words they use to denominate translation are based on the TRANSFER metaphor. In fact, 'identity between source text and target text' and 'transfer' are core concepts in Western translation theories. They shape not only scientific approaches but also folk theories. Thus it comes as no surprise that the TRANSFER metaphor was the one most frequently used by our informants. Although the aim of our study was not to find out how the students had acquired their framework theories, this finding would suggest that they are a product of their process of enculturation. Thus, the process of conceptual change could be seen as part of an acculturation process.

In his study of the memes of translation, Chesterman (1997, p. 20) claims that 'a modern theory of translation needs to draw on many such metaphors', since the use of only one metaphor would limit the perception of translation and communication to a single point of view. This idea coincides with that of Spiro et al. (1989), who suggest the use of a variety of metaphors to counterbalance the strength of the initial metaphor, since it is not enough to draw students' attention to the limitations of this metaphor. In order to problematize the spontaneous concept of translation implicit in the TRANSFER metaphor and facilitate the development of scientific concepts, various metaphors used in different theoretical perspectives were explicitly studied during the semester (e.g. the TRANSFER model implicit in the theories of Nida and the Leipzig School, the TARGET model of the German functionalists and other communication models implicit in different cognitive approaches).

Specialized language has its own metaphoric expressions; learning to use them is part of the process of integration into the group of specialists that results from formal learning (Cameron, 2003, p. 112). Moreover, learning to use linguistic metaphors in a specialist field may also mean learning to establish the corresponding conceptual mappings and as a result adopting a particular point of view. For example, adopting the linguistic terminology of the functionalist approach ('skopos', 'goal-oriented') increases the probability that the translation process will be conceived of as a road to a specific destination so that, as a result, greater importance will be given to the end-purpose of the translation and to the pragmatic, social and cultural aspects of communication (Martín de León, 2008, 2010).

Musolff (2004, p. 70) highlights two factors that may be vital for the 'survival' of a metaphor over time: '1) experiential grounding, which ensures that an essential meaning consistency is preserved, and 2) sufficient conceptual flexibility that allows for use in differing or even contrasting scenarios'. In our study of the 'micro-history' of the TRANSFER metaphor, the coincidence of both factors could explain students' difficulties in distancing themselves from the metaphor, even when explicit information is provided to demonstrate its inadequacy for the analysis of the complexity of the translation and communication processes. The basic experience of transporting objects provides a simple explanation for a complex process by which 'ideas are sent to others' just like an 'object' or an audible or written 'message' can be sent to them (in this case a metonymic shift is produced between different meanings of 'message' which are increasingly abstract [Martín de León, 2004; Reddy, 1993]). Moreover, the TRANSFER metaphor has sufficient conceptual flexibility to adapt itself to different situations, such as a combination with the CHANGE metaphor or when feelings are included among the transported elements.

Another reason for the survival of the TRANSFER metaphor may be that it provides a simplified, all-encompassing vision of the translation process which may contribute to an erroneous sensation that the process has been understood (Cameron, 2003, p. 39). As we have seen, the TRANSFER metaphor is the structural equal to the CONDUIT metaphor; both are based on an analogy in which ideas are equivalent to objects which are transferred in linguistic parcels between texts, people and cultures – the latter being conceived of as containers. This view of communication is so pervasive in our culture that it is difficult to recognize its metaphoric nature because it is seen to be a literal description of fact.

From the perspective of the theory of conceptual change, the factors that Musolff (2004) considers essential for the survival of a metaphor coincide with the defining features of framework theories: they are coherent structures of knowledge based on experience and are sufficiently flexible to be able to adapt to new situations by integrating new elements. In this study we have shown some evidence of the fact that students possess *framework theories* (in particular, theories based on the TRANSFER metaphor) and use them to construct *synthetic theories*. The pedagogical method which combines verbalization of initial theories with the study of scientific theories and hands-on experience of translation seems appropriate to effect conceptual change. An in-depth study of translation processes should provide evidence of the transfer of conceptual change to the practice of translation (e.g. the solution of problems) which would indicate that the implicit theories are not merely rote knowledge but are among the resources used in authentic processes of communication and translation. Determining the impact of subjective theories and conceptual change on translation processes could be an essential element for the design of learning programmes that would make students aware of the complexity and potential difficulties of translation and intercultural communication. The Western folk model based on the TRANSFER metaphor hides this complexity by depicting translation and intercultural communication as mechanical processes that do not require special knowledge or effort by the translator.

Notes

1 The authors wish to acknowledge the assistance of Dr Olivia Fox in the translation and proofreading of this text and the Department of Translation, Universitat Autònoma de Barcelona, for its financial support.

2 Proyecto CODIGO (Caracterización objetiva de la dificultad general de los originales) founded by the Spanish Ministry for Science and Innovation.

3 The quotations from the students' texts and discourses have been translated from the Spanish.

4 Translog is a software program that has been developed specifically to record all keyboard actions during the execution of translation tasks (Jakobsen and Schou, 1999).

References

Black, M. (1962), *Models and Metaphors*, New York: Cornell University Press.

Cameron, L. (2003), *Metaphor in Educational Discourse*, London: Continuum.

—(2007), 'Patterns of Metaphor Use in Reconciliation Talk', *Discourse and Society*, 18(2): 197–222.

Cameron, L. and Deignan, A. (2006), 'The Emergence of Metaphor in Discourse', *Applied Linguistics*, 27(4): 671–90.

Cameron, L. and Stelma, J. H. (2004), 'Metaphor Clusters in Discourse', *Journal of Applied Linguistics*, 1(2): 107–36.

Chesterman, A. (1997), *Memes of Translation*, Amsterdam: John Benjamins.

—(2006), 'Interpreting the Meaning of Translation', in M. Suominen, A. Arppe, A. Airola, O. Häinämäky, M. Miestamo, U. Määttä, J. Niemi, K. K. Pitkänen and K. Sinnemäki (eds), *A Man of Measure. Festschrift in Honour of Fred Karlsson on His 60th Birthday*, Turku: Linguistic Association of Finland, pp. 3–11.

Clement, J. J. (2008), *Creative Model Construction in Scientists and Students: The Role of Analogy, Imagery and Mental Simulation*, Dordrecht: Springer.

D'hulst, L. (1992), 'Sur le Rôle des Métaphores en Traductologie Contemporaine', *Target*, 4(1): 33–51.

DiSessa, A. A. (1993), 'Toward an Epistemology of Physics', *Cognition and Instruction*, 10: 105–225.

Hönig, H. G. (1997), *Konstruktives Übersetzen*, Tübingen: Stauffenburg.

Jakobsen, A. L. and Schou, L. (1999), 'Translog Documentation Version 1.0', in G. Hansen (ed.), *Probing the Process in Translation. Methods and Results*, Copenhagen: Samfundslitteratur, pp. 1–36.

Kövecses, Z. (1986), *Metaphors of Anger, Pride and Love: A Lexical Approach to the Structure of Concepts*, Amsterdam: John Benjamins.

—(2005), *Metaphor in Culture: Universality and Variation*, Cambridge: Cambridge University Press.

—(2009), 'The Effect of Context on the Use of Metaphors in Discourse', *Iberica*, 17: 11–24.

Krings, H. P. (1986), *Was in den Köpfen von Übersetzern vorgeht. Eine empirische Untersuchung zur Struktur des Übersetzungsprozesses an fortgeschrittenen Französischlernern*, Tübingen: Gunter Narr.

Lakoff, G. (1987), *Women, Fire and Dangerous Things*, Chicago: University of Chicago Press.

—(1993), 'The Contemporary Theory of Metaphor', in A. Ortony (ed.), *Metaphor and Thought* (2nd edn), Cambridge: Cambridge University Press, pp. 202–51.

Lakoff, G. and Johnson, M. (1980), *Metaphors We Live By*, Chicago: University of Chicago Press.

Lakoff, G. and Kövecses, Z. (1987), 'The Cognitive Model of Anger Inherent in American English', in D. Holland and N. Quinn (eds), *Cultural Models in Language and Thought*, Cambridge: Cambridge University Press, pp. 195–226.

Mandl, H. and Huber, G. L. (1983), 'Subjektive Theorien von Lehrern', *Psychologie in Erziehung und Unterricht*, 30: 98–112.

Martín de León, C. (2004), 'Metonymic Motivation of the CONDUIT Metaphor', *metaphorik.de*, 6: 79–90.

—(2008), 'Skopos and Beyond. A Critical Study of Functionalism', *Target*, 20(1): 1–29.

—(2010), 'Metaphorical Models of Translation: TRANSFER VS. IMITATION and ACTION', in J. St. André (ed.), *Thinking through Translation with Metaphors*, Manchester: St. Jerome Publishing, pp. 75–108.

Martín de León, C. and Presas, M. (2011), 'Metaphors als Ausdruck subjektiver Theorien zum Übersetzen', *Target*, 23(2): 272–310.

Musolff, A. (2004), 'Metaphor and Conceptual Evolution', *metaphorik.de*, 7:55–75.

Musolff, A. and Zinken, J. (2009), *Metaphor and Discourse*, Basingstoke: Palgrave Macmillan.

Núñez, R. (2000), 'Conceptual Metaphor and the Embodied Mind: What Makes Mathematics Possible?', in F. Hallyn (ed.), *Metaphor and Analogy in the Sciences*, Dordrecht: Kluwer Academic Publishers, pp. 125–45.

Posner, G. J., Srike, K. A., Hewson, P. W. and Gertzog, W. A. (1982), 'Accommodation of a Scientific Conception: Toward a Theory of Conceptual Change', *Science Education*, 66: 211–27.

Potvin, P., Mercier, J., Charland, P. and Riopel, M. (2012), 'Does Classroom Explicitation of Initial Conceptions Favour Conceptual Change or Is It Counter-productive?', *Research in Science Education*, 42: 401–14.

Pozo, J. I. (2003), *Adquisición de Conocimiento*, Madrid: Morata.

Pragglejaz Group (2007), 'MIP: A Method for Identifying Metaphorically Used Words in Discourse', *Metaphor and Symbol*, 22(1): 1–39.

Reddy, M. (1993), 'The Conduit Metaphor: A Case of Frame Conflict in our Language about Language', in A. Ortony (ed.), *Metaphor and Thought* (2nd edn), Cambridge: Cambridge University Press, pp. 164–201.

Scheele, B. and Groeben, N. (1998), 'Das Forschungsprogramm Subjektive Theorien', *Fremdsprachen Lehren und Lernen*, 27: 12–32.

Spiro, R., Feltovitch, P., Coulson, R. and Anderson, D. (1989), 'Multiple Analogies for Complex Concepts: Antidotes for Analogy-Induced Misconception in Advanced Knowledge Acquisition', in S. Vosniadou and A. Ortony (eds), *Similarity and Analogical Reasoning*, Cambridge: Cambridge University Press, pp. 498–531.

Toury, G. (1995), *Descriptive Translation Studies and Beyond*, Amsterdam: John Benjamins.

Tymoczko, M. (2003), 'Enlarging Western Translation Theory: Integrating Non-Western Thought about Translation'. <http://www.soas.ac.uk/literatures/satranslations/tymoczko.pdf> (accessed 23 December 2012).

—(2010), 'Western Metaphorical Discourses Implicit in Translation Studies', in J. St. André (ed.), *Thinking through Translation with Metaphors*, Manchester: St. Jerome Publishing, pp. 109–43.

Vosniadou, S. (2008), 'Conceptual Change Research: An Introduction', in S. Vosniadou (ed.), *International Handbook of Research on Conceptual Change*, New York and London: Routledge, pp. xiii–xxviii.

Vosniadou, S., Vamvakoussi, X. and Skopeliti, I. (2008), 'The Framework Theory Approach to the Problem of Conceptual Change', in S. Vosniadou (ed.), *International Handbook of Research on Conceptual Change*, New York and London: Routledge, pp. 3–34.

Vygotsky, L. (1962), *Thought and Language*, Cambridge: MIT Press.

Wiser, M. and Smith, C. L. (2008), 'Learning and Teaching about Matter in Grades K-8: When Should the Atomic-Molecular Theory Be Introduced?', in S. Vosnadiou (ed.), *International Handbook of Research on Conceptual Change*, New York: Routledge, pp. 205–39.

Wittgenstein, L. (1953), *Philosophical Investigations*, Oxford: Blackwell.

2

Translation of Metaphor in Popular Technology Discourse

Dafni Papadoudi

Introduction

Traditionally, translation studies address the issue of metaphor as a translation problem, a purely linguistic phenomenon with mainly ornamental function, while much attention is paid to two themes in particular: approaches to translating metaphor and the (un)translatability of metaphor. In very broad terms, metaphor translation seems to be influenced by a number of factors, such as the structure of the source language, cultural specificity, the text type, the metaphor's structure and function in the text and the new communicative context (e.g. Dobrzyńska, 1995, pp. 596, 598; Kittay, 1987, p. 82; Newmark, 1981, p. 84). Thus, from a linguistic and prescriptive model of translation, a metaphor should be translated in the target text (TT) as close to the source text (ST) as possible; while from a descriptive and culture-based model of translation, a metaphor cannot have any existing 'equivalence' in the target language (Dagut, 1976, pp. 21–33) and so it cannot (or even should not) be translated. In search of (ideal) approaches to translating metaphor, both prescriptive and descriptive models of translation have proposed a number of procedures to assist the translator in providing adequate translations of metaphor (Dobrzyńska, 1995; Newmark, 1981; Toury, 1995; Van Den Broeck, 1981). Their approaches seem to converge on a number of translation strategies, such as providing the 'same' metaphor in the TT, providing a 'different' metaphor in the TT, omitting the metaphor in the TT, providing a literal paraphrase of the metaphor in the TT or providing additional information to the metaphor in the TT in order to render it more comprehensible.

Since the mid-1990s, a number of research projects within translation studies, metaphor studies and English-language teaching (e.g. Deignan et al., 1997; Fuertes-Olivera and Pizarro-Sánchez, 2002; Mandelblit, 1995; Schäffner, 2004) have examined metaphor translation from a cognitive linguistics perspective, mainly influenced by Lakoff and Johnson's (1980/2003) study of conceptual metaphors. Their findings show that metaphor translation is a 'conceptual-cum-linguistic-cum-cultural phenomenon'

(Maalej, 2008), and metaphors are also examined as cognitive and cultural constructs rather than as exclusively linguistic entities.

These studies point to several valuable conclusions regarding metaphor translation. First, metaphors may entail 'cultural differences in conceptual structures' (Schäffner, 2004, p. 1267), which can surface during the translation process. Second, although conceptual metaphors and their expressions may sometimes be different in the source and the target cultures, this does not necessarily mean that they are translation errors, but rather they indicate a shift in perspective (Deignan et al., 1997; Schäffner, 2004). Third, cultural specificity is located mainly in metaphorical expressions and less in conceptual metaphors (Schäffner, 2004, pp. 1264–5). Fourth, metaphorical expressions can be translated literally, thereby giving rise to 'similarity-creating metaphors'[1] (Indurkhya, 1992), as a way to make the metaphors more direct and easily comprehensible to readers, and as solutions for filling in conceptual gaps (Fuertes-Olivera and Pizarro-Sánchez, 2002). Last, these studies point to several types of variation in translating metaphors, which are summarized as follows:

1. Same conceptual metaphor and equivalent linguistic expression.
2. Same conceptual metaphor but different linguistic expression. The following special cases are also observed:
   a. Linguistic expressions in target language make entailments explicit.
   b. Linguistic expressions in target language make the metaphor more elaborate.
   c. Linguistic expressions in target language reflect a different aspect of the metaphor.
3. Different conceptual metaphor preferred, although similar conceptualisation exists in both the source and target languages.
4. Different conceptual metaphor used but cognitive equivalence is achieved. This case differs from case 3 in that it refers to different conceptualisations occurring from cultural specificity.
5. Literal rendition that produces similarity-creating metaphors.
6. Literal rendition due to culture-bound metaphors in the source language.
7. Omission of conceptual metaphor in the TT. (Papadoudi, 2010, pp. 65–6)

Furthermore, another feature that seems to be central to metaphor translation is the notion of the main meaning focus (Kövecses, 2002). Kövecses states that when a source domain is applied to a number of target domains, this source domain 'is designated to play a specific role'. In his words:

> Each source is associated with a particular meaning focus (or foci) that is (or are) mapped onto the target. This meaning focus is conventionally fixed and agreed-on within a speech community; it is typical of most cases of the source; and it is characteristic of the source only. The target inherits the main meaning focus (or foci) of the source. (p. 110)

In view of this, when a particular source domain is selected to conceptualize a target domain, this selection is not random; it is made based on certain prominent features inherent in the source domain that render it plausible for use. In this manner, we may infer the main meaning focus from the most prominent conceptual material that the source domain carries over to the target domain. This seems to be particularly useful for metaphor translation, given that if we look at the main meaning focus of a metaphor in one language (L1), it may be possible to provide a corresponding metaphor in another language (L2), regardless of whether the two languages use the same or different source domains. For instance, if L1 conceptualizes time as money and L2 conceptualizes time as food, and their source domains share a common main meaning focus of regarding money and food as equally valuable commodities, we may deduce that the metaphors TIME IS MONEY and TIME IS FOOD are corresponding metaphors. Accordingly, these metaphors may produce corresponding linguistic expressions, regardless of their source domains being similar or different. Thus, the L1 expression *you wasted my time* would be equivalent to the L2 expression *you ate up my time*.

Accordingly, we can deduce that (un)translatability does not involve so much linguistic equivalence as 'cognitive equivalence' (Al-Zoubi et al., 2006, pp. 232–3) and 'cognitive restrictions' (Tabakowska, 1993, p. 69). In addition, it seems that translatability can be achieved by shifting the focus from reproducing the linguistic expressions per se to identifying and reproducing the conceptualization behind particular expressions. By such an approach, the issue of (un)translatability is associated with 'level of convergence and/or divergence between the conceptual systems of source and target cultures, and the amount of common experiential basis shared between the languages' (Papadoudi, 2010, p. 64).

The objectives of the study

The present study has two main objectives. The first is to examine the ways that conceptual metaphors of technology and their expressions are translated from English into Greek in four English popular technology magazines. The second is to identify similarities and differences in the ways technology is conceptualized, and consider possible motivations that may account for these similarities and differences.

Methodology

The research methodology utilizes elements of disourse approaches to metaphor research (Deignan, 2005). It involved two stages of analysis. The first stage involved the English data, and the second stage the Greek data. In particular, the analysis of the English data involved identifying metaphorical expressions in the texts by hand, and grouping them semantically under broad conceptual domains. The manual search for metaphorical expressions followed the Metaphor Identification Procedure (MIP; Pragglejaz Group, 2007), which consists of the following steps: reading the texts and identifying the lexical units; examining each lexical unit to determine if it has a more basic contemporary meaning in other contexts; last, marking the lexical unit as metaphorical if the contextual meaning contrasts with the basic meaning but can be understood in comparison with it (p. 3). It should be noted that in the present study, I consider as lexical units words, phrases, polywords, idioms, collocations or a chain of words that convey a single meaning.

In addition, in distinguishing metaphorical expressions, reliable sources of information on contemporary language use were also consulted. For this reason, the British National Corpus (BNC)[2] and the Corpus of Contemporary American English (COCA)[3] were used to determine the existence and frequency of occurrence of English expressions in the corpora. For determining the metaphoricity of the translated Greek expressions, the Hellenic National Corpus (HNC)[4] was consulted.

In terms of organizing the metaphorical expressions under broad conceptual domains, the process that was followed was based on the intention to provide consistent and clear categories of metaphors. This process resulted in a wide range of source domains, including specific cases of more generic conceptual domains, thereby classifying them under more generic-level domains. For instance, I identified the source domains of human activity, age, emotions, gender, human body, kinship, personality, physical appearance and role/occupation that I regarded as specific-level source domains and grouped them under the generic-level source domain of person. I chose to use a unified target domain, the domain of technology, regarding the conceptualization of technology applications and products, and the target domain of virtual space regarding the conceptualization of space on the internet, computer systems and the like.

The analysis of the Greek data involved a series of steps. The first step was to identify the metaphorical expressions in the Greek texts and match them to the English ones. Second, I looked at similarities and differences between the metaphor categories, and between the metaphorical expressions in the two languages. This entailed examining whether the metaphor categories were preserved, omitted or whether new categories emerged in the Greek translations. In terms of the metaphorical expressions, I examined whether they were retained, developed, explicated, paraphrased or omitted in the Greek translations. The last step was to identify translation patterns arising from the similarities and differences between metaphor categories and their expressions in the English and Greek texts.

Data

The study starts with the hypothesis that technology is such an integral part of everyday life that people as users of technology may have developed certain beliefs, attitudes and values towards it which may be expressed through language in technology texts. As a series of products and advancements, technology may be considered as global, but particular uses and perceptions of it may have more of a local character, which may surface in the ways technology is communicated. Given the fact that the English language has a near monopoly in creating computer language, it can be argued that English-speaking countries not only develop technology as devices, hardware and software, but they also develop particular ways of perceiving it through the use of metaphors. Thus, through the translation of technology metaphors, the target language and culture may also import particular ways of conceiving and talking about technology.

This study focuses on popular technology magazines as reliable, widespread, specialized media that produce, reproduce and diffuse up-to-date information on computer technology to a mass audience. They communicate complex technology issues such as computer security; provide updates on the latest developments in hardware and software products and on recent and forthcoming advancements in the area; and test new technologies and provide reviews of their effectiveness.

The data under investigation come from forty-eight articles from four English popular technology magazines, namely, *PC Magazine*, *PC World*, *Computer Active* and *T3*, published between January 2006 and December 2007 in the United Kingdom and the United States and their respective editions in Greece. The articles were selected in terms of their centrality to three themes: the internet, personal computing and popular technology devices. The data under investigation produced a corpus of 262,338 words, while a total of 6,773 English expressions and 3,657 translated Greek expressions were identified and analysed (Papadoudi, 2010, p. 72).

Results

Translation strategies

The analysis of 6,773 English expressions produced fourteen main metaphor categories and twenty-nine sub-metaphor categories, as can be seen in Table 2.1. The metaphor categories are quite diverse including animate and inanimate entities, such as PERSON and TOY, as well as abstract and concrete concepts, such as REVOLUTION and PHYSICAL SPACE.

The analysis of 3,657 translated Greek expressions produced the following seven translation strategies that are described here along with examples[5] and back translations in brackets.

1. Metaphors common to the ST and the TT
2. Metaphorical expressions elaborated in the TT
3. Shift of sub-metaphor category in the TT
4. Shift of metaphor category in the TT
5. Non-figurative rendition of metaphorical expressions in the TT
6. Omission of metaphorical expressions in the TT
7. No translation provided in the TT

The first translation strategy involves metaphors common to the ST and the TT. It is the most prominent category and accounts for more than half (58 per cent) of all the translated data. The fourteen main metaphor categories are preserved in the Greek texts, and the metaphorical expressions are translated either at the micro- or at the macro-level,[6] or by a literal translation of the English expression, otherwise referred to as similarity-creating metaphors (Indurkhya, 1992). It seems that the objective of

Table 2.1 Categories of conceptual metaphors in the English texts

Main source domains	Secondary source domains	Main source domains	Secondary source domains
1. PERSON	1.1 Human activity	5. SECURITY	5.1 Fortress
	1.2 Human lifecycle		5.2 Combat
	1.3 Emotions		5.2 Defence
	1.4 Gender		5.3 Attack
	1.5 Human body		5.4 Espionage
	1.6 Kinship		5.5 Invasion
	1.7 Personality	6. LIFESTYLE	6.1 Ideal
	1.8 Physical appearance		6.2 Fashion
	1.9 Roles/occupations		6.2.1 Clothing
2. LIVING ORGANISM	2.1 Animal	7. REVOLUTION	
	2.2 Plant	8. PROGRESS	
	2.3 Health/illness	9. OBJECT OF DESIRE	
	2.4 Life/death	10. TOY	
	2.5 Function	11. FOOD/COOKING	
3. MACHINE	3.1 Vehicle	12. SUPERNATURAL	
	3.1.1 Automobile	13. EXPERIENCE	
	3.1.2 Bus	14. PHYSICAL SPACE	14.1 Physical process
	3.1.3 Ship		14.2 Physical movement
4. COMPETITION	4.1 Race		14.3 Image-schemas
	4.2 Battle		14.3.1 Surface
	4.3 Boxing match		14.3.2 Container
			14.4 Highway

this translation strategy is to provide an equivalent conceptualization to the English expression along with a similar conceptual effect. For example:

(1) chasing **the holy grail** of artificial intelligence
ψάχνουν το **Άγιο Δισκοπότηρο** της Τεχνητής Νοημοσύνης
(searching for the **Holy Grail** of Artificial Intelligence)

This is an example of the metaphor TECHNOLOGY IS LIFESTYLE, and particularly the sub-metaphor of TECHNOLOGY IS AN IDEAL. The English expression 'chasing the holy grail of artificial intelligence' is translated at the micro-level, where both the conceptualization and the linguistic expression are carried over to the Greek language.

It should be noted that the cultural level plays an important role in the TECHNOLOGY IS LIFESTYLE metaphor because it contains symbols that may be specific to the English-speaking culture. In this case, the translation of the expression 'the holy grail' to Greek is easy since both cultures share views of the Christian religion, but also because a symbol like the Holy Grail is widely known to numerous cultures.

In the following example, the English expression is translated at the macro-level:

(2) the video games industry has **grown up**
έχει **'ωριμάσει'** η βιομηχανία ψυχαγωγίας
(has **'matured'** the industry of entertainment)

In example (2), both English and Greek expressions belong to the metaphor TECHNOLOGY LIFECYCLE IS HUMAN LIFECYCLE, and stress the aspect of technological sophistication. The difference is that while the English expression highlights the aspect of physical development, the Greek expression emphasizes the aspect of mental development. Last, it should be noted that the Greek expression is signalled as metaphorical by quotation marks.

The second translation strategy involves metaphorical expressions elaborated in the Greek translations, and this accounts for 2 per cent of all the data. Elaboration is employed to make the metaphor more explicit by adding metaphorical expressions of the same metaphor or of another source domain for explanatory purposes. For example:

(3) Despite dozens of cell-phone carriers, we've got countless **dead** spots.
Παρά τους αρκετούς παροχείς κινητής τηλεφωνίας, υπάρχουν αμέτρητα **νεκρά** σημεία (*δηλαδή*, σημεία **χωρίς κάλυψη** από τα αντίστοιχα δίκτυα).
(Despite the several providers of mobile phones there are countless **dead** spots [*that is*, spots **without coverage** from the respective networks].)

This is an example of the metaphor TECHNOLOGY IS A LIVING ORGANISM, and particularly the sub-metaphor of THE CONDITION OF TECHNOLOGY IS THE LIFE/DEATH OF A LIVING ORGANISM. The English expression 'dead' is translated as '*νεκρά*' (dead) and elaborated by the expression '*χωρίς κάλυψη*' (without coverage). Here we have elaboration with the use of another metaphorical domain, and in particular the domain of PHYSICAL SPACE (VIRTUAL SPACE IS PHYSICAL SPACE). In addition, the Greek expression '*δηλαδή*' (that is) signals that the expression in brackets serves as an explanation of the metaphorical expression 'dead', given that the expression 'dead' is a loan translation from the English language, and it is possible that it will not be understood without clarification.

The third category involves a shift from one sub-metaphor category to another, while the main metaphor category in the ST is preserved in the TT. It accounts for 2 per cent of all the data and includes only those metaphors which comprise sub-metaphors: TECHNOLOGY IS A PERSON, TECHNOLOGY IS A LIVING ORGANISM, TECHNOLOGY IS A MACHINE, TECHNOLOGY IS COMPETITION, TECHNOLOGY IS SECURITY, TECHNOLOGY IS A LIFESTYLE and VIRTUAL SPACE IS PHYSICAL SPACE. For example:

(4) The tech was **tired** [. . .] Nintendo needed to up its game.
Η τεχνολογία του **είχε αρχίσει να δείχνει σημάδια γήρανσης** [. . .]
(its technology **had started to show signs of oldness.**)

This example demonstrates a shift from the sub-metaphor of TECHNOLOGY IS A PERSON WITH PERSONALITY to TECHNOLOGY LIFECYCLE IS HUMAN LIFECYCLE. The common main metaphor category in the ST and TT is TECHNOLOGY IS A PERSON. While the English expression 'tired' conceptualizes technology as lacking energy, the Greek expression 'had started to show signs of oldness' conceptualizes it as lacking youth. By taking into consideration the main meaning focus of the English and Greek expressions, we arrive at the conclusion that these expressions are corresponding at the conceptual level, since both provide a representation of technology as old-fashioned and well-worn.

The fourth category involves a shift from one metaphor category to another in the TT, and accounts for 5 per cent of all the data. For example:

(5) The Playstation badge reminds us that this comes from a **stable** of unmatchable **pedigree** in its field.
Το σήμα του Playstation φαντάζει σαν **οικόσημο**, όπως το άλογο στη Ferrari.
(the badge of Playstation seems like a **blazon**, as the horse in Ferrari.)

The example demonstrates a shift from the TECHNOLOGY IS A LIVING ORGANISM to the TECHNOLOGY IS LIFESTYLE metaphor, and particularly from the sub-metaphor TECHNOLOGY IS AN ANIMAL to the sub-metaphor TECHNOLOGY IS AN IDEAL. The English expression 'pedigree' here refers to a line of ancestors of purebred animals which is further supported by the expression 'stable'. In the TT, the expression 'pedigree' is transferred as '*οικόσημο*' (blazon), a symbol of aristocratic lineage. This shift from the domain of animals to the domain of humans is quite common in the Greek translations, probably because technology is considered as a manifestation of intelligence and progress, so it may have seemed more appropriate to associate it with humans since they are viewed as superior to all living beings. By looking at the main meaning focus of the English and Greek expressions, we may deduce that these expressions are corresponding at the conceptual level, as they both refer to lines of descent and represent technology as having excellent qualities.

The fifth category includes English metaphorical expressions that are rendered non-figuratively in the TT, and accounts for 6 per cent of the data. The translated Greek expressions are either paraphrases that explain the information implied by the English expression, or constitute the actual referent. For example:

(6) Windows Defender is hardly **best-of-breed**.
Ο Windows Defender δεν είναι σε καμία περίπτωση **αρκετός**.
(Windows Defender is better than nothing, but in no way **sufficient**.)

The English expression 'best-of-breed' is translated literally as '*αρκετός*' (sufficient), thereby guiding the readers' interpretation of the English expression that the particular technology does not suffice to protect the computer system.

The sixth translation strategy involves English metaphorical expressions that were omitted in the TT, and accounts for 5 per cent of the data. This strategy is observed in the following cases: (1) when the metaphorical expressions can be implied by the reader, (2) when the metaphorical expressions are substituted by pronouns, thus avoiding repetition in the TT, (3) when the ST was freely adapted in the TT and (4) when the metaphorical expressions seemed as redundant in the TT. For example:

(7) with a couple of **mouse** clicks
με λίγα μόνο κλικ
(with just a few clicks)

(8) Similarly, you'd have to log on every time you visited a password-**protected** site.
Παρομοίως, θα έπρεπε να συνδέεστε κάθε φορά που επισκέπτεστε ένα site.
(Similarly, you would have to log on each time you visit a site.)

In example (7) The English expression 'mouse' is omitted in the TT, because it can be implied by the expression 'clicks', which is often used as short for mouse clicks in Greek. In example (8) the English expression 'protected' is omitted in the TT, because it may have been regarded as redundant based on the previous knowledge that a user only logs onto sites that are protected by a password.

The last category arises from the fact that numerous segments from the ST were not translated into the TT. These segments include English metaphorical expressions for which no type of equivalent, metaphorical or non-figurative, was provided in the TT. This category accounts for 22 per cent of the data. Given that I cannot provide a sound justification for this complete absence of translation, I can only make the following three assumptions. The first is that these metaphorical expressions were excluded from the TT, not because they presented difficulties in being translated into Greek, but because they served mainly aesthetic purposes, and/or their function was not constitutive in the text. For example, the expression 'The Fix: You'll have to play Sherlock Holmes to figure out **what's dead**' (THE CONDITION OF TECHNOLOGY IS THE LIFE OF A LIVING ORGANISM), which entertains the reader, but does not provide any (helpful) information on how to fix the computer system.

The second assumption is that these segments were not translated into the TT because they included metaphorical expressions that may have seemed particularly challenging to translate. For example:

(9) PSP didn't just **break the mould** of portable gaming. **It put it through a garbage compactor, set fire to the resultant electro-mechanical block, then did a little dance on the still-smouldering ashes.**

In example (9), the English author plays with the expression 'break the mould' (TECHNOLOGY IS REVOLUTION) on both metaphorical and literal levels, by exploiting the literal breaking to provide a description of complete destruction and celebration as a manifestation of revolutionary innovation. The particular expression would have been quite challenging to translate in Greek especially with regard to the wordplay of 'break the mould', but could have been adequately adapted in the TT. Thus, its absence points to the fact that there is certain reluctance in translating such expressions possibly due to a certain degree of difficulty in finding corresponding expressions and concepts.

The third and final assumption is that the Greek translators had to refrain from translating certain 'unnecessary' segments of the ST – in the sense of being challenging, not constitutive, or culture-specific – due to a strict word limit set for each article.

Translation effects

During the analysis of the Greek data, I also observed a number of translation effects that had arisen as by-products of the translation strategies, and in particular of the shift of sub-metaphor and shift of metaphor category. I identified the following four effects (Papadoudi, 2010, p. 223):

1. *Downplaying the metaphor in the TT*. This effect minimizes (obscures) the source domain used to conceptualize technology in the TT and keeps the focus on the content of the information rather than on the linguistic form used to present the information.
2. *Accentuating the metaphor in the TT*. In contrast to the previous one, this effect intensifies the source domain used to conceptualize technology in the TT and draws attention to the linguistic form used in the presentation of information. Whereas downplaying makes the metaphor unnoticeable, accentuation renders it clear and eye-catching.
3. *Explanation*. This makes the metaphor of the ST more explicit. If an ST metaphorical expression can be interpreted in more ways than one, the translation selects one of its possible interpretations and transfers the selected interpretation to the TT, thus causing the ST metaphor to change category in the TT.
4. *Adaptation*. Adaptation is in line with reproducing conceptually the metaphorical expressions of the ST, and reconstructing the original metaphorical expressions of the ST by using different creative linguistic means in the TT, thus resulting in a shift of metaphor.

In order to make these effects more clear, consider the following examples:

(10) Prevx1 easily scans your system for, finds, and **destroys** malware and suspicious files.
To Prevx1 μπορεί εύκολα να εντοπίσει και να **διαγράψει** κακόβουλα προγράμματα από τον υπολογιστή σας.
([. . .] and **delete** malicious programs from your computer.)

Example (10) demonstrates a case of downplaying the metaphor in the TT by shifting from the sub-metaphor TECHNOLOGY IS COMBAT to the sub-metaphor of TECHNOLOGY ACTIVITY IS HUMAN ACTIVITY. The Greek expression '*διαγράψει*' (delete) merely describes what the program actually does, thus obscuring the aspect of physical fighting in the English expression 'destroys'.

(11) Problem: Your trusty hard drive has **crashed**.
Το πρόβλημα: Ο «αξιόπιστος» σκληρός δίσκος μου **τα . . . τίναξε**!
(the problem: My 'trustworthy' hard disk **kicked the bucket**!)

Example (11) demonstrates a case of accentuating the metaphor in the TT by shifting from the sub-metaphor TECHNOLOGY IS AN AUTOMOBILE to the sub-metaphor of THE CONDITION OF TECHNOLOGY IS THE LIFE OF A LIVING ORGANISM. The English expression 'crashed' relates to the malfunction of a technology, while the Greek expression '*τα τίναξε*' (kicked the bucket) is a colloquial expression that means 'to die'. This shift from a crashing automobile to the dying of a living being not only elevates technology from an inanimate to an animate entity, but also aggravates the situation at hand, given that a living being dying is a serious and irreversible condition in relation to automobiles breaking down.

(12) The **snazziest** graphics cards are like miniature computers [. . .].
οι **σύγχρονες** κάρτες γραφικών διαθέτουν δικό τους επεξεργαστή [. . .].
(the **modern** graphic cards have their own processor [. . .].)

Example (12) demonstrates a case of explaining the metaphor in the TT by shifting from the sub-metaphor TECHNOLOGY IS FASHION to the sub-metaphor of TECHNOLOGY IS PROGRESS. The English expression 'snazziest' is translated as '*σύγχρονες*' (modern), which explains that usually the most current technologies are also the most fashionable innovations.

(13) **Wring Out** More Power
'Ξεζουμίστε' την ισχύ
('squeeze-out-the-juice' from the power)

Example (13) demonstrates a case of adapting the metaphor in the TT by shifting from the sub-metaphor VIRTUAL PROCESS IS PHYSICAL PROCESS to the metaphor TECHNOLOGY IS FOOD/COOKING. Both the English and Greek expressions conceptualize the production of more processing power as squeezing out liquid. The difference that produces the shift of metaphor category is that the Greek expression refers to extracting juices as if from a fruit.

Discussion

The previous section addressed the first objective of the study, namely, to identify the ways that conceptual metaphors of technology and their expressions are translated from English into Greek. The present section addresses the second objective and discusses the similarities and differences in the ways technology is conceptualized, and considers possible motivations that may account for these similarities and differences.

Similarities and differences

The first similarity is identified in the categories of metaphors. We find that the source domains identified in the English data are preserved and reproduced in the Greek texts. This can be explained by the fact that similar source domains exist in both languages/cultures, and that these source domains reflect similar socio-cultural experiences that are shared and valued by both languages/cultures (Gannon, 2001).

Apart from the metaphor categories, we find a second similarity in the metaphorical expressions. Although initial expectations pointed towards greater differences between the two languages, we find that there is a strong tendency to reproduce the English metaphorical expressions in the Greek translations, by providing conceptually and often linguistically corresponding expressions. This is quite evident in the translation strategies where the main metaphor category is unaffected: metaphors common to the ST and TT, metaphorical expressions elaborated and shifts of sub-metaphors.

Finally, we find similarities in the frequency, preference for and use of metaphors in the ST and TT. Table 2.2 provides a comparative view of the metaphors in the English and Greek texts, and shows that the categories of PHYSICAL SPACE, PERSON and MACHINE rank higher in frequency with relatively similar percentages, whereas the categories of SECURITY, LIVING ORGANISM, COMPETITION, FOOD/COOKING, EXPERIENCE, LIFESTYLE, PROGRESS, SUPERNATURAL, TOY, OBJECT OF DESIRE and REVOLUTION rank lower in frequency for both languages with relatively similar percentages.

On the other hand, we identified differences in the translated expressions that shifted from one metaphor category to another and from one sub-metaphor category to another. It should be noted that the third translation strategy, shift of sub-metaphor, indicates similarity between generic-level metaphors, given that the main metaphor category is preserved in both ST and TT. However, it also indicates difference between two specific-level metaphors (example [4]), or between a generic and a specific-level metaphor (example [12]). In addition, these shifts seem to reveal the use and usefulness of the main meaning focus of the source domain in producing conceptually corresponding expressions, and in achieving cognitive equivalence by identifying and rendering the conceptualization behind particular expressions, rather than focusing on the expressions per se. On the part of the researcher, the main meaning focus also provides assistance in comprehending and justifying the shifts.

A second difference relates to the more frequent use of signalling in the Greek translations than in the English texts, either by quotation marks, as in example (2), or by particular expressions, as in example (3). This suggests that the Greek translators felt the need to clarify metaphoricity and guide the readers' interpretations. It can be

Table 2.2 Comparison of metaphors between English and Greek texts

Metaphor	Metaphorical expressions (English)	(%)	Metaphor	Metaphorical expressions (Greek)	(%)
PHYSICAL SPACE	2373	36	PHYSICAL SPACE	1470	40
PERSON	2100	31	PERSON	1057	29
MACHINE	678	10	MACHINE	255	7
SECURITY	364	5	SECURITY	226	6
LIVING ORGANISM	336	5	LIVING ORGANISM	165	4.5
COMPETITION	247	3	COMPETITION	105	3
FOOD/COOKING	183	3	FOOD/COOKING	105	3
EXPERIENCE	138	2	PROGRESS	76	2
LIFESTYLE	138	2	EXPERIENCE	59	2
PROGRESS	83	1	LIFESTYLE	58	2
SUPERNATURAL	62	1	OBJECT OF DESIRE	23	1
TOY	30	0.4	SUPERNATURAL	21	1
OBJECT OF DESIRE	22	0.3	REVOLUTION	20	1
REVOLUTION	19	0.3	TOY	17	0.5
TOTAL	6773	100	TOTAL	3657	100

argued that this may be in line with the process of explicitation in translation studies (Vinay and Darbelnet, 1995), but it may also point to a certain uneasiness about using or translating such metaphors into Greek. For example, one may regard the metaphor TECHNOLOGY IS A PERSON as extreme, given that it not only personifies technology, but also attaches a whole array of human attributes, such as personality, physical traits and even sexual appeal, for example, PSP's 'voluptuous flanks'.

Motivations

Similarities between the English and Greek metaphorical expressions seem to be motivated by two factors: a common experiential basis shared between the two languages/cultures and 'translated experience' (Papadoudi, 2010, pp. 41, 276).

Similarities based on common experiences derive from experiential co-occurrence or experiential similarity (Haser, 2005). For example, experiential co-occurrence, which is based on the co-occurrence of different experiences, is quite evident in the TECHNOLOGY IS PROGRESS metaphor. The conceptualization of progress as forward motion is shared by both languages, and it is grounded in the co-occurrence of the experience that the more steps we take, the closer we get to our destination. Moreover, experiential similarity is based on perceived similarities between different experiences. An example of this is the TECHNOLOGY IS A PERSON metaphor, which is based on perceived similarities between the computer and ourselves as a way of developing a closer relationship with the computer system (Peele, 1983, p. 92), as well as trying to understand how it functions in order to use it more effectively.

Another kind of motivation is what I have termed as 'translated experience' which refers to the influence of the English language and culture at the conceptual level. Translated experience refers to particular experiences inherent in the ST metaphors that could be transferred into the TT, first because the target language/culture has knowledge of that experience from other contexts, and second because these metaphors refract beliefs and values which are common to both languages/cultures. For instance, the metaphor TECHNOLOGY IS LIFESTYLE is successfully transferred into the Greek texts because (1) the Greek culture has knowledge of the concept of lifestyle from the domains of fashion, the film industry, the automobile industry and so forth; and (2) because the concept of lifestyle and its symbolism are equally valued by the Greek culture.

Moreover, the differences identified in relation to the expressions that shifted from one sub-metaphor category into another and from one metaphor category into another seem to be motivated by three factors: alternative conceptualizations of terminology, cultural specificity and preferential conceptualizations. The first factor involves alternative conceptualizations of terminology. Consider, for example, the English expression 'internet backbone' (TECHNOLOGY PARTS ARE HUMAN BODY PARTS) and the corresponding Greek translated expression 'the trunk of the internet' (TECHNOLOGY IS A PLANT). The expression 'backbone', which is the supporting basis of the human body, is transferred to the domain of computing to refer to the main communications network that carries data to other smaller networks (Microsoft Press, 1997). In Greek, it was decided to use the trunk of a plant by analogy to the backbone of the body as the central feature that provides support.

The second factor is cultural specificity. For example:

(14) Game Boy the handheld-gaming **messiah**
το Game Boy τον **εξάγγελο της επανάστασης** του φορητού gaming
(the Game Boy the **messenger of the revolution** of the portable gaming)

The English expression 'messiah' refers to a quite prevalent symbol from the domain of religion, and conceptualizes Game Boy as the 'saviour' of traditional handheld gaming. The Greek expression 'messenger of the revolution' conceptualizes Game Boy as the ultimate innovation, although a corresponding expression is available in Greek. However, the expression 'messiah' is used metaphorically in Greek to conceptualize usually men whose work and contributions are considered quite extraordinary. Therefore, many readers may regard it as outlandish or even hubris if an inanimate object was conceptualized as a messiah. But since technology and revolution are closely related concepts, the domain of revolution is considered a more suitable candidate. Thus, this shift from the LIFESTYLE to the REVOLUTION metaphor seems to be motivated by cultural specificity, due to the fact that religion and its symbols are highly valued in the Greek culture.

The third factor involves preferential conceptualizations. For example:

(15) **Go to** Settings.
Ανοίξτε το Settings
(**Open** the Settings.)

This example demonstrates a shift from the sub-metaphor of VIRTUAL MOVEMENT IS PHYSICAL MOVEMENT to the sub-metaphor of VIRTUAL SPACE IS A CONTAINER, while the main metaphor of VIRTUAL SPACE IS PHYSICAL SPACE is common to the ST and TT. The English expression 'go to' denotes that the start menu in Windows is a static location and the user is moving to that location, while the Greek expression '*ανοίξτε*' (open) denotes that the start menu is a closed space that needs to be opened by the user. Both types of conceptualization are used interchangeably in the data in both the ST and TT. Therefore, such shifts seem to be motivated by the English authors' and the Greek translators' personal preferences of talking about virtual space in terms of how they perceive it each time.

Conclusion

The present study set out to observe how conceptual metaphors of technology and their expressions are translated from English into Greek in popular technology discourse. The translation strategies identified here seem to add to the variations and range of options for achieving equivalence in translation, as well as corroborating many of the strategies observed in previous research mentioned in the Introduction. These translation strategies along with the translation effects proved to be quite useful in the study in that they helped to consider similarities and differences between the English and Greek texts and provide possible motivations for these similarities and differences. Moreover, the translation effects could be further investigated as complementary features to translation procedures. They may be examined as markers for assessing the quality of translation, and as tools for making translation decisions in conjunction with particular text types, stylistics, textual functions, socio-cultural frameworks and so forth.

Returning to the issue of the (un)translatability of metaphor, this seems to be connected to the amount of common experiential basis shared between the languages, and the level of convergence or divergence between the conceptual systems of the source and target languages/cultures involved in translation. In the present study, we observed that there is greater convergence than divergence in translating technology metaphors, which can be explained by the fact that both languages/cultures share the same target concept of technology, and both languages/cultures share the same source domains.

Within a cognitive approach to translating metaphor, the notion of the main meaning focus of the source domain is considered significant to both the translation process and the translation product. Though this feature merits further research, I hope to have shown how the main meaning focus can provide insight into the core meaning of the metaphor and its use in the text, and so it may work as a tool in the hands of the translator for making translation decisions, as well as in the hands of the researcher for drawing conclusions on equivalence and intercultural communication.

A last point to be made is regarding the significance of the results for intercultural communication in conjunction with translation. Given the fact that the most dominant translation strategy involves metaphors common to the ST and TT, it may be argued that by translating metaphors of technology, the various beliefs, attitudes, values and ideologies about technology of the English-speaking culture are imported to the Greek language/culture, thus influencing and/or contributing to the shaping of the Greek socio-cultural environment regarding the domain of technology. On the other hand, translating metaphors of technology may be also regarded as a manner of 'keeping up with the Joneses', in terms of being informed about current technologies as well as current ideologies about them. This gives rise to the question whether these ideologies are shared by the Greek language/culture, thereby retaining the metaphors in the TTs, or whether they are not shared, thereby altering the metaphors to present a different perspective of technology in the TTs.

Notes

1 Similarity-creating metaphors are not based on known similarities between source and target domains, but they create the similarities and make the target look similar to the source (Indurkhya, 1992, p. 275). Such metaphors have also been identified in the literature as a basis for developing computer design and terminology (Colburn and Shute, 2008).

2 The BNC is a corpus of written and spoken language of one hundred million words that are collected from a variety of sources, and represents a wide range of current spoken and written British English (British National Corpus, 2007).
3 The COCA is a corpus of contemporary American English containing more than 385 million words of text including 20 million words each year from 1990 to 2008; it is equally divided among spoken word, fiction texts, popular magazines, newspapers and academic texts (Davies, 2008).
4 The HNC contains more than forty-seven million words of written text and is constantly being updated (ILSP, 2009).
5 It should be clarified that in some examples certain metaphorical uses of words have not been signalled as metaphorical. This is because I would like to draw attention to the particular highlighted expressions.
6 The term 'micro-level' refers to the translation of metaphors that correspond both conceptually and linguistically, and the term 'macro-level' refers to the translation of metaphors that correspond at the conceptual level but are expressed by different linguistic means (Schäffner, 2004, p. 1260).

References

Al-Zoubi, M. Q., Al-Ali, M. N. and Al-Hasnawi, A. R. (2006), 'Cogno-cultural Issues in Translating Metaphors', *Perspectives*, 14(3): 230–9.

British National Corpus, version 3 (BNC XML Edition) (2007), distributed by Oxford University Computing Services on behalf of the BNC Consortium. <http://www.natcorp.ox.ac.uk/> (accessed 31 December 2012).

Colburn, T. R. and Shute, G. M. (2008), 'Metaphor in Computer Science', *Journal of Applied Logic*, 6(4): 526–33.

Dagut, M. (1976), 'Can Metaphor Be Translated?', *Babel*, XXII(1): 21–33.

Davies, M. (2008), *The Corpus of Contemporary American English* (COCA). <http://www.americancorpus.org> (accessed 31 December 2012).

Deignan, A. (2005), *Metaphor and Corpus Linguistics*, Amsterdam and Philadelphia: John Benjamins.

Deignan, A., Gabrýs, D. and Solska, A. (1997), 'Teaching English Metaphors Using Cross-Linguistic Awareness-Raising Activities', *ELT Journal*, 51(4): 352–60.

Dobrzyńska, T. (1995), 'Translating Metaphor: Problems of Meaning', *Journal of Pragmatics*, 24(6): 595–604.

Fuertes-Olivera, P. A. and Pizarro-Sánchez, I. (2002), 'Translation and "Similarity-Creating Metaphors" in Specialised Languages', *Target*, 14(1): 43–73.

Gannon, M. J. (2001), *Understanding Global Cultures: Metaphorical Journeys through 23 Nations* (3rd edn), Thousand Oaks, CA: Sage Publications.

Haser, V. (2005), *Metaphor, Metonymy, and Experientialist Philosophy: Challenging Cognitive Semantics*, Berlin: Mouton de Gruyter.

ILSP (2009), *Hellenic National Corpus*. <http://hnc.ilsp.gr/en/default.asp> (accessed 31 December 2012).

Indurkhya, B. (1992), *Metaphor and Cognition: An Interactionist Approach*, Dordrecht: Kluwer Academic Publishers.

Kittay, E. F. (1987), *Metaphor: Its Cognitive Force and Linguistic Structure*, Oxford: Clarendon Press.

Kövecses, Z. (2002), *Metaphor: A Practical Introduction*, New York: Oxford University Press.

Lakoff, G. and Johnson, M. (1980/2003), *Metaphors We Live By*, Chicago: University of Chicago Press.

Maalej, Z. (2008), 'Towards a Cognitive Theory of Metaphor Translating: An Exercise in Comparative Culture', Presentation at 7th International Conference on Researching and Applying Metaphor, University of Extremadura, Cáceres, Spain, 29–31 May. <http://faculty.ksu.edu.sa/zmaalej/Documents/9%20Translating%20metaphor.pdf> (accessed 18 August 2012).

Mandelblit, N. (1995), 'The Cognitive View of Metaphor and Its Implication for Translation Theory', in M. Thelen and B. Lewandowska-Tomaszczyk (eds), *Translation and Meaning, Part 3*, Maastricht: Maastricht University Press, pp. 482–95.

Microsoft Press (1997), *Microsoft Press Computer Dictionary* (3rd edn), Redmond Washington: Microsoft Press.

Newmark, P. (1981), *Approaches to Translation*, Oxford and New York: Pergamon Press.

Papadoudi, D. (2010), 'Conceptual Metaphor in English Popular Technology and Greek Translation', unpublished PhD thesis, University of Manchester.

Peele, H. (1983), 'Computer Metaphors: Approaches to Computer Literacy for Educators', *Computers and Education*, 7(2): 91–9.

Pragglejaz Group (2007), 'MIP: A Method for Identifying Metaphorically Used Words in Discourse', *Metaphor and Symbol*, 22(1): 1–39.

Schäffner, C. (2004), 'Metaphor and Translation: Some Implications of a Cognitive Approach', *Journal of Pragmatics*, 36(7): 1253–69.

Tabakowska, E. (1993), *Cognitive Linguistics and Poetics of Translation*, Tübingen: Gunter Narr.

Toury, G. (1995), *Descriptive Translation Studies and Beyond*, Amsterdam and Philadelphia: John Benjamins.

Van Den Broeck, R. (1981), 'The Limits of Translatability Exemplified by Metaphor Translation', *Poetics Today*, 2(4): 73–8.

Vinay, J.-P. and Darbelnet, J. (1995), *Comparative Stylistics of French and English: A Methodology for Translation* (trans. Juan C. Sager and M.-J. Hamel), Amsterdam and Philadelphia: John Benjamins.

3

Revisiting the Function of Background Information in Sight Translating Metaphor: An Analysis of Translation Product and Process

Xia Xiang and Binghan Zheng

Introduction

Metaphor, as a typical feature of utterance expression, is 'treated as illustrating the entire complexity of language communication' (Dobrzyńska, 1995, p. 595). It presents a particular challenge for interlingual and intercultural communication, as confirmed by Dobrzyńska: '[D]ifficulties in interpreting metaphors are particularly conspicuous in the case of a contact between two languages in a situation when a metaphorical utterance is translated into another language' (p. 598). The difficulties, according to translation scholars, lie in the fact that 'transferring (metaphors) from one language and culture to another may be hampered by linguistic and cultural differences' (Schäffner, 2004, p. 1253).

A number of cross-linguistic studies (e.g. Dobrzyńska, 1995; Newmark, 1988; Schäffner, 2004; Tirkkonen-Condit, 2002) have at a theoretical or empirical level investigated this translation problem and its corresponding solutions, providing valuable contributions both to the study of translation and to metaphor processing in general. In this research, however, our focus lies not on what strategies should be applied to translate metaphors, but rather on the impact of introducing relevant materials to help bridge the cultural gap and thus assist translators in translating metaphorical expressions (MEs). Empirical in its nature, this research builds on a between-subjects experiment in which background information (BI) serves as the only independent variable, and aims to explore whether the acquisition of BI influences the product and process of metaphor translation. Before proceeding to a detailed analysis, we feel it is necessary to clarify some of the basic concepts underlying this research.

Some basic concepts

Sight translation

Sight translation (STR) is modelled by Gile (1995, p. 183) as a process consisting of the 'reading effort' (understanding a message written in one language) and the 'production effort' (reformulating the message orally in another language). Despite the various differences compared with consecutive and simultaneous interpreting (Agrifoglio, 2004, p. 44), it has been treated as being closer to interpreting than to written translation, because sight translators 'are able to apply largely the same strategies that they use when they perform oral-to-oral interpreting' (Dragsted and Hansen, 2007, p. 254). For many scholars, STR is just a pedagogical exercise for getting started on the techniques of interpreting; however, researchers have shown that the cognitive demands it exerts on the interpreter are no less than those of consecutive and simultaneous interpreting (Agrifoglio, 2004; Shreve et al., 2010). Hence, in this study, STR was adopted as the vehicle for examining the effect of BI on metaphor translation.

Background information

Gile (2002) suggests that professional behaviour in real-life interpretation should include the study of relevant materials, the clarification of terminological doubts and the preparation of a glossary. The acquisition of BI in advance is 'regarded unanimously as an important part of working conditions' (Gile, 1995, p. 147). In practice, in training or in experimental research, interpreters expect to be provided with BI in various forms: speech transcripts, drafts of papers, abstracts, outlines, headings, information on the setting, the topic and the participants and so on (Díaz-Galaz, 2011, p. 176; Gile, 1995, p. 147). In this research, BI refers to the cultural context of the source text (a speech), or more specifically, the social and historical background to the time in which the speech takes place, as an example of the internal manifestations of a culture.

Linguistic metaphors

The groundbreaking work *Metaphors We Live By* (Lakoff and Johnson, 1980) revived interest in metaphor, or more exactly, conceptual metaphor, redefining it as 'a cross-domain mapping in the conceptual system' (Lakoff, 1993, pp. 202–3). Despite the public enthusiasm for metaphor at a conceptual level in the field of Translation Studies (e.g. Andersen, 2000; Jensen, 2005; Schäffner, 2004; Tirkkonen-Condit, 2002), our study chooses to focus on metaphor at the linguistic level, distinguished by Lakoff (1993, pp. 202–3) as 'individual linguistic expressions (words, phrases or sentences) that are the surface realization of cross-domain conceptual mappings'. We feel it is equally important to investigate MEs in language use, since a study of them 'may provide a good clue to finding the systematic conceptual correspondences between domains (i.e. to conceptual metaphors)' (Kövecses, 2005, p. 32).

Background

The function of background information in translation and interpreting

The function of BI, which can be operationalized as 'speech transcripts', 'summary of the speech' or 'prior topic knowledge', has attracted great interest among translation and interpreting researchers. A number of studies have designed empirical experiments to explore whether BI has a significant impact on the results and processes of translation and interpreting.

Griffin (1995) measured the production times, correctness and appropriateness of the word translations in two different conditions, that is, with relevant or irrelevant BI. The results supported the viewpoint that relevant BI had a positive effect on the quality of translation, though it might consume more time.

Lamberger-Felber (2003) examined the impact of a transcript of a speech on interpreters' performance, revealing that transcripts had a positive impact on interpreting performance. A similar study by Kim (2006) focused on the effect of BI on translators' performance. Results indicated that having access to BI had a more significant influence on translation quality than prior English reading proficiency. Díaz-Galaz (2011) examined the effect of previous preparation on the process and product of simultaneous interpreting as performed by advanced interpreting students. The author concluded that 'preparation supports a more efficient processing, as students who prepared were able to produce more accurate, complete and correct target speeches within a similar period of time than students who did not prepare' (p. 186).

The function of background information in translating metaphor

Although very few studies have investigated the effect of BI on translating MEs in texts, there has been interest in exploring the function of BI in understanding metaphors in sentences. In these studies, the construct of BI has been operationalized as 'context', be it linguistic or cultural.

A series of empirical studies were designed by Ortony and his colleagues (1978; Ortony, 1983) to observe their subjects' different responses to sentences containing MEs by manipulating prior sentential context. One of the major findings was that 'the thematic relatedness of the idea expressed to the preceding context makes a big difference to the ease with which a metaphor can be understood both by adults and by children' (Ortony, 1983, p. 28). This observation was echoed by Martin (2006). His examination of the subjects' comprehension of sentences containing MEs after having processed a short span of the text gave clear evidence of the predictive value of contextual cues for future metaphors.

This branch of research is not confined to monolingual settings. McDonald and Carpenter (1981), for example, explored cross-linguistic communication. Their experiment, in which the subjects were engaged in a simultaneous translation task, revealed that the identification and interpretation of an ambiguous phrase (an idiom or an ME) was closely connected with the preceding context.

Other studies have focused on the effect of cultural background on metaphor comprehension, which naturally deals with subjects who do not share the same first language (L1) as the speaker or writer. Littlemore (2003) asked a group of Bangladeshi students to explain the metaphors used by their British lecturers, and found that a disparity in value systems was a stumbling block for the students in trying to make sense of the metaphors. Jensen (2005) examined the translation process of metaphorical and metonymic expressions by expert translators and concluded that knowledge of the cultures of both the source and target domains was essential for the translation of such expressions.

Our research attempts to assess the impact of BI on the product and process of sight translating of MEs in texts rather than in sentences, as this mode is much closer to real-life practice. To that end, we designed a between-subjects experiment which included an STR task and a post-task interview. The two groups of subjects were asked to sight translate a source speech containing ten MEs, but only the experimental group was given time in advance to read materials introducing related BI.

Experiment

Subjects

The research was conducted with sixty-eight fourth-year English major undergraduates at a Chinese university. All the subjects were of a similar age (around twenty-two) and had a similar language background (Chinese as L1, English as L2). They had all passed Test of English Major Band 4, and were taking an intermediate interpreting course when they participated in the experiment. We cross-grouped the subjects into an experimental group (EG) and a control group (CG) based on their scores in the most recent interpreting exam to ensure that both groups' interpreting abilities were as near equal as possible.

Materials

Source speech

A source text that contained expressions with figurative elements was specifically chosen. It was an excerpt from Bill Clinton's 2001 farewell speech (see Appendix 3.1), since modern political discourse is permeated with metaphors for their communicative and persuasive effect. Feedback from our previous pilot study indicated that the text was of acceptable length (241 words) and difficulty, and would be unfamiliar to the subjects.

Metaphorical expressions

The identification of MEs should 'not be based on our own intuition, but on the definitions provided by dictionaries' (Krennmayr, 2008, p. 113) and the linguistic context. In our effort to identify the MEs in the source speech, we used several dictionaries for reference and double-checking, among which *The Macmillan English Dictionary for Advanced Learners* (MED) and the *Oxford Advanced Learner's English-Chinese Dictionary* (OALD [E-C]) were the most frequently consulted. In the end, ten metaphors were identified within the source speech (see Appendix 3.2).

Preparation material

The EG was given ten minutes to read a topic-related text[1] as a form of BI before the STR task. They were supplied with pens and markers so that they could take notes, mark the document or write comments. However, they were not given access to any external source of information, such as the internet or dictionaries. The text given was mainly about Clinton's approach to dealing with other countries, and his aim of harnessing the benefits of globalization to advance America's objectives of spreading democracy and achieving shared prosperity and peace. While it offered a glimpse of the social background during the Clinton presidency, the passage was not directly related to the source text of the experiment.

Experimental procedure

Both the pilot and formal experiments were carried out in a simultaneous interpreting lab, an environment familiar to the subjects. The experimental procedure included the following steps:

1. The chief examiner described the task and briefed the subjects on the circumstances of Clinton's speech, as in a real-life translation scenario.
2. The examiner distributed questionnaires asking about the subjects' knowledge of the speech and its social background[2].
3. The CG left the lab for ten minutes while the EG was offered the preparation material.
4. The CG re-entered the lab and was assigned a warm-up task together with the EG.
5. Both groups completed the STR task while the source text was displayed using moving window presentations monitored by the examiner (Macizo and Bajo, 2009). The subjects read the screen in front of each of them and sight translated each paragraph within a defined time span (150 per cent of normal reading time).
6. After the STR was completed, all the subjects were asked to retrospectively report on their processing of the ten metaphors during the STR. Both the STR sessions and retrospective reports were recorded and transcribed afterwards.

Data collection

The answers to pre-test questionnaires revealed that four out of sixty-eight subjects had some knowledge of the Clinton presidency and three had heard about this speech before the experiment. Out of concern that their long-term background knowledge might be activated and thus give them an advantage over the other subjects, we decided to remove these seven samples. A further random sample from the CG was dropped to ensure the numbers would be even. In all, there were a total of sixty valid samples employed in the ensuing data analysis, thirty for each group.

The study triangulated the following three streams of data: (1) transcriptions of the recordings, based on which the translation errors were classified and assessed; (2) recordings of the subjects' acoustic outputs, which were then imported into the open-source program Audacity (2.0.3) so that both silent and filled pauses when dealing with the MEs could be calculated; and (3) the subjects' retrospective interviews, from which was obtained a clearer picture of how each subject coped with the metaphors.

Data presentation and discussion

The evaluation of the translation products consists of 'macro assessment' and 'micro error analysis', while the investigation into the translation process is presented through the analyses of silent and filled pauses. A qualitative analysis will be incorporated to help explain the quantitative results.

Analysis of the translation products

Our attempt to evaluate the contribution of BI to the translation performance is complicated by the absence of a clear-cut definition of 'translation quality'. 'Quality is an elusive concept, if ever there was one' (Shlesinger, 1997, p. 123), and quality assessment in translation and interpreting 'immediately raises the question of quality for whom and from which perspective' (Dragsted and Hansen, 2009, p. 592). The evaluation of metaphor translations in our research was carried out on the basis of 'error observation', as recommended by Agrifoglio (2004) and Lambert et al. (1995).

Assessment score – a global picture

First, we defined three categories of performance as the basis for evaluating each ME STR product, namely, 'successful translations', 'faulty translations' (or 'translation with minor errors') and 'failed translations' ('translation with major errors' and 'omissions'). Two external assessors were asked to group all metaphor translations into the three designated categories, without attempting to evaluate or grade the performances. When discrepancies occurred, they discussed them until agreement was reached.

The second step was to give each unit of translation (i.e. a metaphor translation) a score ranging from 1 to 5. 'Successful translations' were given a score of 5, while 'failed translations' were given a score of 1. 'Faulty translations' were given a score between 2 and 4 depending on the number of minor errors. As the majority of translation units in this category contained no more than three minor errors, we gave a score of 4 to the unit with one minor error, 3 to the one with two minor errors and 2 to the one with more than two minor errors. The operational definition for each marking category, together with some specific examples, can be found in Table 3.1, and the results of the assessment are listed in Table 3.2.

Table 3.1 Operational definition for marking categories used in quality assessment

Category	Operational definition	Examples: M4. (ST: a powder keg); M9. (ST: weave the threads . . . into the fabric of one America)
Failed translations (a score of 1)	The translation of the ME displays 'a high degree of explicit divergence from the source text' (Al-Qinai, 2000, p. 500) or sounds 'alien to the target language recipients' (p. 507), or the ME was completely omitted.	M4. was translated as '面粉盒' (a box used to contain flour); M9. was translated as '把各种材料融进一个美国的纤维' (to weave all materials into an American fabric).
Faulty translations[a] (a score from 2 to 4)	The translation of the ME displays errors including 'missing information' and 'added mistakes' (Lambert et al., 1995, p. 42)	M4. was translated as '是一个，是一个，**(6. RE)** 火药，额，导火线 **(12. CC)**' (a, a powder, well, a blasting fuse); M9. was translated as '将. . . (7 seconds' pause) **(10. LH)** 各种人融合成一个美国 **(3. IM)**' (to . . . melt all people into one America)
Successful translations (a score of 5)	The translation of the ME has successfully achieved functional equivalence (Nida and Taber, 1969, p. 12) as it operates in the source text	M4. was translated as '火药桶' (powder keg), '炸药包' (explosive cartridge); M9. was translated as '将美国境内，所有人团结在一起'(to unite all people within the United States)

[a] Faulty translations include twelve types of errors based on Lambert et al. (1995, p. 42) with some adjustments. They are errors of lexis (abbr. as 1. EL), partial omissions (2. PO), imperfections (3. IM), calques (4. CA), additions (5. AD), repetitions (6. RE), morphosyntactic mistakes (7. MM), slips of the tongue (8. ST), false starts (9. FS), long hesitations[b] (10. LH), wrong corrections (11. WC) and correct corrections (12. CC).

[b] We counted those pauses lasting longer than five seconds as minor errors of long hesitation. This is supported by Aguilar (2000, p. 107) who proposes that silences should not be too long, to avoid losing the attention of the audience, and suggests that on the radio, for example, a silence of over five seconds can have a negative effect on listeners' attention.

Table 3.2 Assessment of translation products based on error observation (full score = 50)

Subject code	Metaphor STR score	Subject code	Metaphor STR score	Subject code	Metaphor STR score	Subject code	Metaphor STR score
EG1	36	EG16	32	CG1	27	CG16	18
EG2	25	EG17	15	CG2	16	CG17	31
EG3	42	EG18	23	CG3	16	CG18	25
EG4	25	EG19	22	CG4	24	CG19	27
EG5	35	EG20	18	CG5	18	CG20	22
EG6	23	EG21	27	CG6	25	CG21	22
EG7	17	EG22	22	CG7	21	CG22	17
EG8	26	EG23	20	CG8	28	CG23	19
EG9	28	EG24	21	CG9	25	CG24	31
EG10	19	EG25	20	CG10	27	CG25	24
EG11	33	EG26	34	CG11	25	CG26	17
EG12	35	EG27	26	CG12	25	CG27	12
EG13	26	EG28	17	CG13	18	CG28	21
EG14	32	EG29	21	CG14	21	CG29	18
EG15	32	EG30	28	CG15	11	CG30	20

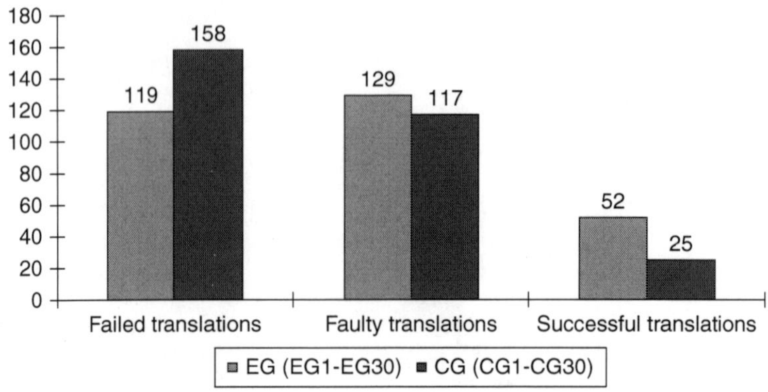

Figure 3.1 Number of metaphor translations in each category.

Figure 3.1 reveals that the EG produced more than twice as many successful metaphor translations as the CG, while having fewer failed translations than the CG. The tabular presentation of the individual subjects' scores and the t-test results serve as reinforcing indicators of the EG's superior performances. As Table 3.3 indicates, the mean score for the EG's metaphor translations was 26, which was much higher than that of the CG (21.7). The two-tailed t-test result (t = 2.79, p = 0.007) reveals that the difference is statistically significant. The quantitative results lead to the conclusion that the provision of BI enabled the EG members to come up with better metaphor translations than CG members within the same time span. The subjects' retrospective reports echo this conclusion: the majority of the EG members were keenly aware of the assistance afforded by the BI when trying to decipher M2, M3, M6, M7, M9 and M10, the six expressions on which they performed better, with more instances of successful translation and fewer major errors.

Table 3.3 t-Test comparing EG and CG metaphor STR scores

t-Test: Two-Sample Assuming Unequal Variances		
	Variable 1(EG)	Variable 2(CG)
Mean	**26**	**21.7**
Variance	45.44827586	25.73448276
Observations	30	30
Hypothesized Mean Difference	0	
df	54	
t Stat	**2.79152599**	
p(T = t) one-tail	0.003619146	
t Critical one-tail	1.673564907	
p(T = t) two-tail	**0.007238291**	
t Critical two-tail	2.004879275	

Error analysis – a closer investigation

Major errors and omissions

Our focus in this section is on the failed translations, represented by a detailed analysis of 'major errors' and 'omissions'. Based on the transcriptions of the subjects' recordings and their retrospective reports, we analysed the reasons for failed translations in Table 3.4. As is clear from the table, most failed translations were caused by divergent understanding (in the reading phase) rather than alienated expressions (in the production phase). This result echoes one of our previous findings (cf. Zheng and Xiang, 2013) that the origin of failed ME translations in STR does not lie in the intrinsic difficulty of the expression, but rather in the incomplete or incorrect understanding of the source language and the resultant imbalanced distribution of processing capacity.

The t-test results reveal that the differences between the EG and the CG in terms of 'divergent understanding' ($t = -2.84$, $p = 0.006$) and 'omitted translation' ($t = -2.78$, $p = 0.008$) are statistically significant, supporting the argument that the provision of BI exerts some facilitating impact on reading effort, as it would be revealed later that omission was largely caused by insufficient understanding. This finding is supported by a well-established dynamic view of comprehension: '[P]rocessing new information requires the active construction of some form of mental representation by integrating the input with various kinds of pre-existing knowledge—lexical, syntactic, pragmatic, encyclopedic, etc.' (Pöchhacker, 2004, p. 119).

Taking as our examples the translations of M2 ('the cutting edge') and M3 ('the knife's edge'), Table 3.5 surveys the number and distribution of major errors in the translations of these two units by the EG and the CG. It is clear that the EG members had similar numbers of divergent understanding and alienated expression errors, while the CG members made more errors in understanding than in expression. When

Table 3.4 Number and distribution of major errors in STR of the MEs

	Divergent understanding (percentage)	Alienated expression (percentage)	Omitted translation (percentage)	Total
EG(1–30)	65 (54.62%)	44 (36.97%)	10 (8.40%)	119 (100%)
CG(1–30)	91 (57.59%)	41 (25.95%)	26 (16.46%)	158 (100%)
Two-tailed t-test	t = -2.84, p = 0.006	t = 0.46, p = 0.64	t = -2.78, p = 0.008	

Table 3.5 Number and distribution of major errors in STR of M2 and M3

		Divergent understanding	Alienated expression	Omitted translation	Total
M2 STR	EG(1-30)	6	5	1	12
	CG(1-30)	11	6	4	21
M3 STR	EG(1-30)	3	3	1	7
	CG(1-30)	11	3	2	16

vertically comparing the number of divergent understandings, the CG failed in as many as twice, or even three times, the number of cases as the EG. The quantitative data indicate that the availability of BI provided the EG members with positive support in grasping the metaphorical meaning when translating. The retrospective data collected soon after the STR task reveal that 70 per cent of the EG members were instantly aware that both metaphors were describing the chasm between developed and developing countries when they read the words 'trade' and 'gap' in the first sentence of the source text. This instant reaction was greatly facilitated by relative BI such as 'economic integration advances both our interests and our values, but also accentuates the need to alleviate economic disparity'. The activation of the BI steered their comprehension of M1 ('close the gap') along the correct path; at the same time, it served to generate expectations which guided the comprehension process of M2 and M3. By contrast, with no BI in mind as cognitive schemata, the CG members often had to make arbitrary associations in decoding MEs. For example, eleven of them constructed wrong mental representations in interpreting 'the knife's edge'. Some connected the image of a 'knife' to 'Western-style cuisine' and then inferred 'being rich', while others jumped from 'edge' to 'bordering areas'.

Meanwhile, omissions as an indicator of semantic loss that can be attributed to the complexity of the task (Pöchhacker, 2004; Pym, 2009) are calculated and presented in Table 3.4. The figures show that omitted translations were much more frequent in the CG (16.46 per cent) than in the EG (8.40 per cent). The t-test result ($t = -2.78$, $p = 0.008$) shows that the difference between the two groups was statistically significant. When it comes to the specific cases of M2 and M3, the ratio of omitted translations was also higher for the CG than for the EG. The retrospective reports reveal that most omitted translations were the result of failures to activate proper mental representations when decoding metaphorical meanings. Hence, the 'omitted translation' observations lead to the conclusion that the availability of BI has an effect in reducing the degree of information loss.

Minor error analysis

In this section, a comparative analysis of minor errors focuses on the most frequent errors made by the EG and the CG in their metaphor STRs. It is worth noting that minor errors included in failed translations were not counted, since such translations had already been identified as failures; and there might be more than one minor error found in each faulty ME translation.

As can be seen from Figure 3.2, there are some overlaps between the EG and the CG in terms of the top five minor errors (Table 3.6), that is, repetitions, false starts and long hesitations, all of which can be identified as symptoms of disfluency, 'phenomena that interrupt the flow of speech and do not add propositional content to an utterance' (Gósy, 2007, p. 93). These linguistically detectable faults are considered as manifestations of the (cognitive) efforts of reasoning and formulation which accompany linguistic production (Goffman, 1981, p. 172).

Non-overlaps in Figure 3.2 drew our attention as well, and the results of a closer investigation proved them worthy of attention (Table 3.7). 1. Errors of lexis (EL) and 12.

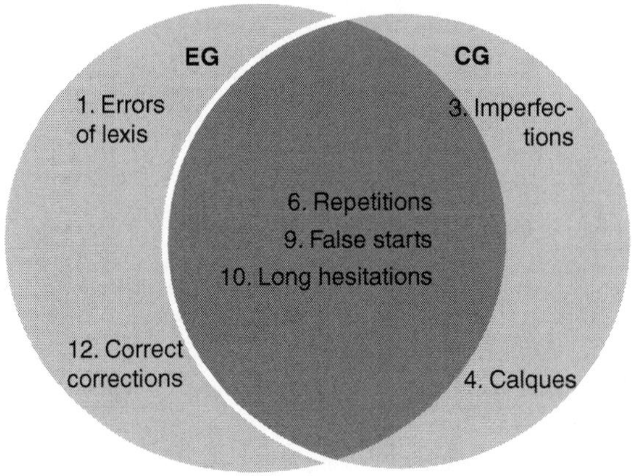

Figure 3.2 Top five minor errors made by the EG and the CG.

Table 3.6 Number (percentage) of top five minor errors (bold) for EG and CG in metaphor STR

	1. EL	3. IM	4. CA	6. RE	9. FS	10. LH	12. CC
EG	**16 (7.84%)**	15 (7.35%)	8 (3.92%)	**62 (30.39%)**	**21 (10.29%)**	**36 (17.65%)**	**32 (15.69%)**
CG	7 (3.59%)	**17 (8.72%)**	**21 (10.77%)**	**56 (28.72%)**	**31 (15.90%)**	**19 (9.74%)**	16 (8.21%)

Table 3.7 Examples of non-overlapping minor errors in Figure 3.2

Error type	Source text	Subjects	Translation scripts
12. Correct corrections	M9 & M10: weave the threads of our coat of many colors into the fabric of one America	EG5	额，用，用各种颜色来编织，编织我们的衣服 ... 那，那就是作为一个整，作为一个整体 (well, to use all colors to weave our coat ... that is, that is, we as a united entity)[a]
		EG23	我们一起...除非所，额，所有种族的人来一起编织美国，美国...抛弃种族观念，一起来创建美国 (we together ... unless, all races together weave America, America ... discard the race prejudice, join hands and build up America)
4. Calques	M3: live on the knife's edge	CG2	在幸存，嗯，刀刃边缘的，很贫穷的 (live on the edge of the knife, being very poor)
		CG4	生活在存活边缘，嗯，挣扎的刀刃上 (live on the edge of survival, well, the knife's edge of struggling)

[a] Back translations in brackets were provided by the authors

Correct corrections (CC) are more frequently made by the EG, while 3. Imperfections (IM) and 4. Calques (CA) occur are more common with the CG.

'Because of the time constraints present in interpreting, including sight translation, interpreters have to start producing TL output simultaneously with comprehending SL input' (Gile, 1995, p. 169). Sight translators' flow of production can be viewed as a mirror of their mental processing of the source language input. In this sense, 12. CC mirrors the latter two STR passes suggested by McDonald and Carpenter (1981, pp. 236–7): 'verbal translating' and 'error recovery'. EG5 and EG23 are typical examples. At the first stage, 'weave', 'colors' and 'coat' were combined into a configuration, and thus the initial translations were delivered. BI intervened soon after the first step, and a discrepancy was consequently detected. The subjects hesitated for a few seconds, reread the phrase, and from the phrases 'many colors' and 'one America', activated the two BI components: 'America is a melting pot with many nationalities and diversified cultures' and 'people of all nationalities are united'. At that point, a complete and accurate understanding was achieved. By contrast, with no helpful BI available, the CG could only resort to bottom-up processing and became entrapped in the 'weaving a coat' schema or introduced some irrelevant or erroneous sayings from Chinese culture, such as '闭门造车' (work behind closed doors; CG12), or '自扫门前雨' (sweep the snow from one's own doorstep; CG22). Major errors were seen in 60 per cent of their translations of M9 and M10.

The percentage of calques (4. CA) for the CG is higher than that for the EG. Calques are assumed to be more common in STR than in other branches of interpreting, since the sight translators are constantly distracted by the continuous presence of the source text. Both the EG and the CG were exposed to this risk, but as indicated earlier, the provision of BI could help translators arrive at a meaning-driven understanding so that the EG members were more likely to de-verbalize the derived message in a flexible way. Thus, some were able to think outside the 'edge' component and seek different metaphorical images in the target language which could express a similar meaning, such as '水深火热' (in deep water and scorching fire; EG2 and EG13) and '勒紧裤带' (tighten one's belt; EG20). By contrast, the CG processing was more superficial; thus they were more likely to produce a rigid word-for-word translation with obvious residue from the source language, which was not 'adequate vis-à-vis the "normal" standard usage of native speakers in a given situation' (House, 1997, p. 18). An example is '挣扎的刀刃上' (the knife's edge of struggling; CG4).

In short, our error analysis leads to the conclusion that for subjects with equal translation capability, the provision of BI brought about a perceptible difference in the ME translation products, especially in the reading phase. The EG members used the BI as 'frames' to predict, select, absorb and assimilate the input message, in all, to 'make inferences and build mental models of message content' (Pöchhacker, 2004, p. 120). There is no doubt that the interplay of input message and the BI enabled subjects to get closer to the true meaning of the MEs than with lexical processing alone.

Analysis of translation process – an investigation into pauses

This section presents a process-oriented investigation of the ME STR based on a pause analysis of the subjects' acoustic recordings. As McDonald and Carpenter (1981) point out:

> [U]nlike oral interpreters, (sight) translators are starting from written text. They can control the rate of input and determine their own junctures in the material. It will be shown that where the translators pause and what they reread indicates the component processes of translation. (p. 233)

Pauses have long been considered a 'window' on the cognitive planning activity intrinsic to speech production in psycholinguistic research on spontaneous speech and interpreting (Erman, 2007; Goldman-Eisler, 1967). Furthermore, it is quite common to operate with a distinction between filled and unfilled/silent pauses (Duez, 1982). Filled pauses typically consist of hesitation markers ('ums and ahs'), while unfilled pauses are defined as silence intervals (Dragsted and Hansen, 2007, p. 261).

In our study, both categories were counted and analysed. To start with, we imported the subjects' recordings into Audacity (2.0.3) so that they could be digitally processed, and the pauses counted. Since the ten MEs were scattered throughout the source text, we had to determine the beginning and ending of the processing of each of them before the pauses could be identified and calculated. The segmentation was conducted by two external assessors, who reached a consensus after referring to Jakobsen et al. (2007, p. 236): '[P]auses appearing in the production stream at the point of entry to an idiom being formulated are in fact reflections of processing targeted at producing the downstream idiom' and thus were included in the production process; whereas pauses immediately after the processing of MEs (if there were any) were not included.

Our operational definition of a silent pause is an interruption in the speech process of one second or more. Not every pause was viewed as a fault or imperfection, because of the dual roles they play: 'as a positive element of fluency and as a negative element if their presence is "abundant or frequent"' (Macías, 2006, p. 27).

For a detailed comparison, we grouped the silent pause measurements into three different ranges of duration: short pause (one–two seconds), medium pause (two–five seconds) and long pause (over five seconds). The short pause was described as perceivable but not negative, 'as 1–2 seconds have been shown to indicate some translation task-related cognitive processing' (Dragsted and Hansen, 2007, p. 260). The medium and long pauses were described as having a negative impact on the listeners' perceptions (Macías, 2006, p. 31). Silent pause frequencies (in three duration ranges) and filled pauses indicated by Chinese hesitation markers (such as 呃 'er' and 嗯 'en') were calculated and are presented in Table 3.8. As shown in the table, the CG produced many more medium pauses and filled pauses than the EG. The t-test results show that both differences are statistically significant. By contrast, the CG produced slightly more short pauses and long pauses than the EG, but the t-test results show that neither difference is statistically significant.

Table 3.8 Silent pauses (in three duration ranges) and filled pauses: number and t-test result

	Short pause (1–2 sec)	Medium pause (2–5 sec)	Long pause (>5 sec)	Filled pause
EG (EG1–EG30)	47	32	67	86
CG (CG1–CG30)	54	81	69	149
two-tailed t-test	t = −1.4, p = 0.17	t = −8.24, p = 0.00	t = −0.28, p = 0.78	t = −6.18, p = 0.00

The number of long pauses includes the number of long hesitations (pauses of over five seconds) occurring in both 'faulty translations' and 'failed translations', which explains why the number listed here exceeds the 'long hesitations' classification in the minor error analysis. While the number of long pauses was almost equal for both the EG and the CG, we discovered another interesting difference from the STR recordings. The majority of long pauses for the EG members occurred at the initial phase of metaphor processing, which indicates that these long pauses were used for planning and structuring their subsequent translation outputs. We tend to attribute this observation to the 'trade-off between the resource cost of holding and using a schema, and the benefit of using the schema to predict the incoming text' (Britton et al., 1985, p. 241). However, on the whole, we witnessed a prevalence of pros over cons in the schemata activated by the BI, as the processing of the downstream ME was characterized by fewer silent and filled pauses. In contrast, for the CG members, most of the long pauses were inserted in their fragmentary speech, indicating that they were searching for solutions as they were suddenly struck by 'the disharmony between lexical access and articulatory planning' (Tóth, 2011, p. 29). The different positions of the long pauses indicate that access to relevant BI might influence subjects' approach to ME-related translation problems.

The CG produced many more filled pauses than the EG. This result is closely related to our previous observation that the EG utilized long pauses (more than five seconds) in planning for metaphor translations. According to Yin (2011, p. 464), '[W]ith a lack of adequate planning (in consecutive interpreting), a rushing start may lead to the abuse of fillers and repeated words'.

Medium pauses (two–five seconds) were not identified as errors in the present study in consideration of the audience's 'charity principle' (Bühler, 1990, p. 541); thus they were regarded as 'tolerable yet negative' pausing behaviour, and could serve as one of the indicators of painstaking cognitive efforts spent in searching for equivalents. Our data reveal that the CG produced significantly more medium pauses than the EG. This result, from the perspective of pause study, supports the argument that the availability of BI could to some extent alleviate cognitive effort in ME STR. However, as the understanding and reformulation of metaphors involve a complex cognitive system, a more specific research project should be designed to investigate the relationship between the availability of BI and the cognitive effort cost.

Conclusion

The preceding quantitative and qualitative analyses indicate that the acquisition of BI impacts the quality of sight translating metaphor products. The number of translation errors and the mean scores for metaphor translations reveal that the quality of the EG's translations were, in general, greatly superior to those of the CG. Further analysis of the major error features shows that BI exerts a positive effect largely on the reading phase, helping the EG members to apprehend the metaphorical meaning much more quickly and accurately. Furthermore, analysis of the omitted translations tells us that BI functions by reducing the proportion of information loss. Such an observation is further substantiated by the comparison of the numbers of minor errors made by the two groups.

In addition, the acquisition of BI has a significant impact on the processing of sight translating metaphors, as indicated by the numbers of silent and filled pauses. Our data show that, supported by BI, the EG produced significantly fewer medium and filled pauses than the CG. There was no major difference in the number of long pauses between the two groups. However, the different positions of the long pauses reveal that BI might have influenced the subjects' approach towards translation problems, helping the EG members to plan their metaphor translations at the beginning of each unit. Concomitantly, such planning for metaphor translations led to a reduction in filled pauses. Based on our preliminary analysis of medium pauses, the availability of BI might be helpful in alleviating the cognitive effort in STR; however, the exact relationship between BI and cognitive effort awaits further examination through a specific research project targeting this aspect.

The present empirical study revisits the function of social-cultural BI in sight translating metaphor with the aim of providing new insights into the cross-lingual and cross-cultural study of metaphor. Although the ten metaphors identified for observation were strictly based on linguistic metaphor definitions, a complex cognitive system was broadly involved in the process of understanding and reformulating metaphors from one language to another. This is explicitly discussed from the perspectives of translation product and process. Even so, more effort could, and should, be devoted to this topic, such as further examining the impact of BI on the translation of 'congruent metaphors' and 'alternative metaphors' based on their cross-cultural variations (Boers, 2004; Kövecses, 2006). This will mark our next step in endeavouring to advance the study of metaphor from the perspective of the discipline of Translation Studies.

Appendix 3.1 Source texts: excerpts from Clinton's farewell speech (2001)

Slide 1 The expansion of trade hasn't fully closed the gap between those of us who live on the cutting edge of the global economy and the billions around the world who live on the knife's edge of survival. This global gap requires more than compassion. It requires action. Global poverty is a powder keg that could be ignited by our indifference.

Slide 2 In his first inaugural address, Thomas Jefferson warned of entangling alliances. But in our times, America cannot and must not disentangle itself from the world. If we want the world to embody our shared values, then we must assume a shared responsibility.

Slide 3 If the wars of the 20th century, especially the recent ones in Kosovo and Bosnia, have taught us anything, it is that we achieve our aims by defending our values and leading the forces of freedom and peace. We must embrace boldly and resolutely that duty to lead, to stand with our allies in word and deed, and to put a human face on the global economy so that expanded trade benefits all people in all nations, lifting lives and hopes all across the world.

Slide 4 Third, we must remember that America cannot lead in the world unless here at home we weave the threads of our coat of many colors into the fabric of one America. As we become ever more diverse, we must work harder to unite around our common values and our common humanity.

Appendix 3.2 The identification of linguistic metaphors in the source text[3]

Linguistic metaphors	Source semantic domain	Target semantic domain	Identification method
M1. close the gap/ global gap	cover the opening or break in something or between two things	bridge the separation between two parts	OALD (E-C)
M2. the cutting edge	the cutting surface of a blade	the most modern and advanced point in the development of something	MED
M3. the knife's edge	cutting edge of the blade of a knife	at a critical point	OALD (E-C)
M4. a powder keg	a small barrel for holding gunpowder	potentially dangerous or explosive situation	OALD (E-C)
M5. be ignited by our indifference	a powder keg be ignited by fuse	global poverty be triggered by indifference	Definition and context
M6. entangling alliances	becoming twisted, tangled or caught (in something)	involving somebody/oneself (in difficult or complicated circumstances)	OALD (E-C)
M7. disentangle itself from the world	free something/somebody from something that impedes it/him	free something/somebody from a relationship with something/somebody	OALD (E-C)
M8. put a human face on the global economy	connect things to an actual person	make something seem more real and easier to understand	MED
M9. weave the threads . . . into the fabric of one America	weave threads into a fabric	make America into a melting pot with many nationalities and diversified cultures	Definition and context
M10. coat of many colors	the name for the multicoloured garment that Joseph owned (in the Hebrew Bible)	people of all ethnic groups	Definition and context

Notes

1 The passage 'The Clinton Presidency: A Foreign Policy for the Global Age' is excerpted from 'Record of Progress' on a website launched by Bill Clinton himself. <http://clinton5.nara.gov/WH/Accomplishments/eightyears-10.html> (accessed 16 January 2012).

2 The questionnaire was composed of one closed-ended and two open-ended questions: (1) Have you ever heard about this speech? (2) Would you make a list of whatever you know about Bill Clinton? (3) How much do you know about Clinton's achievements in his presidency?

3 The ten metaphors are encoded from M1 to M10 ('M' stands for metaphor).

References

Agrifoglio, M. (2004), 'Sight Translation and Interpreting: A Comparative Analysis of Constraints and Failures', *Interpreting*, 6(1): 43–67.

Aguilar, Lourdes. (2000), 'La Prosodia', in Santiago Alcoba (ed.), *La Expresión Oral*, Barcelona: Ariel, pp. 89–146.

Al-Qinai, Jamal. (2000), 'Translation Quality Assessment: Strategies, Parameters and Procedures', *Meta*, 45(3): 497–519.

Andersen, M. S. (2000), *Metaforkompetence – En empirisk undersøgelse af semi-professionelle oversætteres metaforviden*, unpublished PhD thesis, Copenhagen Business School

Boers, F. (2004), 'Cross-Cultural Variation as a Variable in Comprehending and Remembering Figurative Idioms', *European Journal of English Studies*, 8(3): 375–88.

Britton, B. K., Glynn, S. M. and Smith, J. W. (1985), 'Cognitive Demands of Processing Expository Text: A Cognitive Workbench Model', in B. K. Britton and J. B. Black (eds), *Understanding Expository Text: A Theoretical and Practical Handbook for Analysing Explanatory Text*, Hillsdale, NJ: Erlbaum, pp. 227–48.

Bühler, H. (1990), 'Orality and Literacy – Theoretical and Didactic Considerations in the Context of Translation Studies', in R. Arntz and G. Thomé (eds), *Übersetzungswissenschaft: Ergebnisse und Perspektive*, Tübingen: Gunter Narr Verlag, pp. 537–44.

Díaz-Galaz, S. (2011), 'The Effect of Previous Preparation in Simultaneous Interpreting: Preliminary Results', *Across Languages and Cultures*, 12(2): 173–91.

Dobrzyńska, T. (1995), 'Translating Metaphor: Problems of Meaning', *Journal of Pragmatics*, 24(6): 595–604.

Dragsted, B. and Hansen, I. G. (2007), 'Speaking Your Translation: Exploiting Synergies between Translation and Interpreting', in F. Pöchhacker, A. L. Jakobsen and I. M. Mees (eds), *Interpreting Studies and Beyond*, Copenhagen: Samfundslitteratur, pp. 251–74.

—(2009), 'Exploring Translation and Interpreting Hybrids: The Case of Sight Translation', *Meta*, 54(3): 588–604.

Duez, D. (1982), 'Silent and Non-silent Pauses in Three Speech-Styles', *Language and Speech*, 25: 11–28.

Erman, B. (2007), 'Cognitive Processes as Evidence of the Idiom Principle', *International Journal of Corpus Linguistics*, 12(1): 25–53.

Gile, D. (1995), *Basic Concepts and Models for Interpreter and Translator Training*, Amsterdam and Philadelphia: John Benjamins.

—(2002), 'The Interpreter's Preparation for Technical Conferences: Methodological Questions in Investigating the Topic', *Conference Interpretation and Translation*, 4(2): 7–27.

Goffman, E. (1981), *Forms of Talk*, Philadelphia: University of Pennsylvania Press.

Goldman-Eisler, F. (1967), 'Sequential Temporal Patterns and Cognitive Processes in Speech', *Language and Speech*, 10(3): 122–32.

Gósy, M. (2007), 'Disfluencies and Self-Monitoring', *Govor*, 26: 91–110.

Griffin, J. S. (1995), *The Role of Context, Background Knowledge, Language Skill and Translation Training and Experience in Lexical Choice in French-English Translation*, unpublished PhD thesis, Kent State University.

House, J. (1997), *Translation Quality Assessment: A Model Revisited*, Tübingen: Gunter Narr Verlag.

Jakobsen, A. L., Jensen, K. T. H. and Mees, I. M. (2007), 'Comparing Modalities: Idioms as a Case in Point', in F. Pöchhacker, A. L. Jakobsen and I. M. Mees (eds), *Interpreting Studies and Beyond*, Copenhagen: Samfundslitteratur, pp. 217–49.

Jensen, A. (2005), 'Coping with Metaphor: A Cognitive Approach to Translating Metaphor', *Hermes, Journal of Linguistics*, 35: 183–209.

Kim, H. (2006), 'The Influence of Background Information in Translation: Quantity vs. Quality or Both?', *Meta*, 51(2): 328–42.

Kövecses, Z. (2005), *Metaphor in Culture: Universality and Variation*, Cambridge: Cambridge University Press.

—(2006), *Language, Mind and Culture: A Practical Introduction*, Oxford and New York: Oxford University Press.

Krennmayr, T. (2008), 'Using Dictionaries in Linguistic Metaphor Identification', in N.-L. Johannesson and D. C. Minugh (eds), *Selected Papers from the 2006 and 2007 Stockholm Metaphor Festivals*, Stockholm: Department of English, Stockholm University, pp. 97–115.

Lakoff, G. (1993), 'The Contemporary Theory of Metaphor', in A. Ortony (ed.), *Metaphor and Thought*, Cambridge: Cambridge University Press, pp. 202–51.

Lakoff, G. and Johnson, M. (1980). *Metaphors We Live By*, Chicago: University of Chicago Press.

Lamberger-Felber, H. (2003), 'Performance Variability among Conference Interpreters: Examples from a Case Study', in A. Collados Aís, M. M. Fernández Sánchez and D. Gile (eds), *La evaluación de la calidad en la interpretación: Investigación*, Granada: Comares, pp. 147–68.

Lambert, S., Darò, V. and Fabbro, F. (1995), 'Focalized Attention on Input vs. Output during Simultaneous Interpretation: Possibly a Waste of Effort!', *Meta*, 40(1): 39–46.

Littlemore, J. (2003), 'The Effect of Cultural Background on Metaphor Interpreting', *Metaphor and Symbol*, 18(4): 273–88.

Macías, M. P. (2006), 'Probing Quality Criteria in Simultaneous Interpreting: The Role of Silent Pauses in Fluency', *Interpreting*, 8(1): 25–43.

Macizo, P. and Bajo, M. T. (2009), 'Schema Activation in Translation and Reading: A Paradoxical Effect', *Psicológica*, 30: 59–89.

Macmillan English Dictionary for Advanced Learners (2nd edn) (2007), Oxford: Macmillan Publishers.

Martin, J. H. (2006), 'A Corpus-Based Analysis of Context Effects on Metaphor Comprehension', in A. Stefanowitsch and S. T. Gries (eds), *Corpus-Based Approaches to Metaphor and Metonymy*, Berlin and New York: Mouton de Gruyter, pp. 214–36.

McDonald, J. L. and Carpenter, P. A. (1981), 'Simultaneous Translation: Idiom Interpretation and Parsing Heuristics', *Journal of Verbal Learning and Verbal Behavior*, 20: 231–47.

Newmark, P. (1988), *Approaches to Translation*, Englewood Cliffs, NJ: Prentice-Hall.

Nida, Eugene A. and Taber, Charles R. (1969). *The Theory and Practice of Translation*. Leiden: E. J. Brill.

Ortony, A. (1983), 'Theoretical and Methodological Issues in the Empirical Study of Metaphor', *Reading Education Report 38*, Champaign, IL: University of Illinois at Urbana-Champaign, Center for the Study of Reading, pp. 2–38.

Ortony, A., Schallert, D. L., Reynolds, R. E. and Antus, S. J. (1978), 'Interpreting Metaphors and Idioms – Some Effects of Context on Comprehension', *Journal of Verbal Learning and Verbal Behavior*, 17: 465–77.

Oxford Advanced Learner's English-Chinese Dictionary (4th edn) (1997), Beijing: The Commercial Press.

Pöchhacker, F. (2004), *Introducing Interpreting Studies*, London and New York: Routledge.

Pym, A. (2009), 'On Omission in Simultaneous Interpreting: Risk Analysis of a Hidden Effort', in G. Hansen, A. Chesterman and H. Gerzymisch-Arbogast (eds), *Efforts and Models in Interpreting and Translation Research: A Tribute to Daniel Gile*, Amsterdam and Philadelphia: John Benjamins, pp. 83–105.

Schäffner, C. (2004), 'Metaphor and Translation: Some Implications of a Cognitive Approach', *Journal of Pragmatics*, 36(7): 1253–69.

Shlesinger, M. (1997), 'Quality in Simultaneous Interpreting', in Y. Gambier, D. Gile and C. Taylor (eds), *Conference Interpreting: Current Trends in Research-Proceedings of the International Conference on 'Interpreting: What Do We Know and How?'*, Amsterdam and Philadelphia: John Benjamins, pp. 123–31.

Shreve, G. M., Lacruz, I. and Angelone, E. (2010), 'Cognitive Effort, Syntactic Disruption, and Visual Interference in a Sight Translation Task', in G. M. Shreve and E. Angelone (eds), *Translation and Cognition*, Amsterdam and Philadelphia: John Benjamins, pp. 63–84.

Tirkkonen-Condit, S. (2002), 'Metaphoric Expressions in Translation Processes', *Across Languages and Cultures*, 3(1): 101–16.

Tóth, A. (2011), 'Speech Disfluencies in Simultaneous Interpreting: A Mirror on Cognitive Processes', *SKASE Journal of Translation and Interpretation*, 5(2): 23–31.

Yin, K. (2011), 'Disfluencies in Consecutive Interpreting among Undergraduates in the Language Lab Environment', in H. H. Gao and M. Dong (eds), *Proceedings of the 25th Pacific Asia Conference on Language, Information and Computation*, Singapore: Nanyang Technological University, pp. 459–66.

Zheng, B. and Xiang, X. (2013), 'Processing Metaphorical Expressions in Sight Translation: An Empirical-Experimental Research', *Babel*, 59(2): 160–83.

4

Conceptual Metaphors in Translation: A Corpus-Based Study on Quantitative Differences between Translated and Non-translated English

Claudia Förster Hegrenæs

Introduction

To translate, that is, to transfer meaning from one language into another, establishes contact not only between different languages but also between different cultures. The translation process creates new texts (target texts) which exist independently from their source texts (ST) not only as products of the target language but also within the target culture. Early on, scientific fields such as comparative literature and contrastive analysis (Munday, 2001, pp. 8–9) investigated differences and similarities between source and target texts in order to be able to make statements about semantic and linguistic differences between these texts and thus between languages. However, translated texts were widely treated as inferior texts and 'the study of translation . . . [was] relegated to the periphery of other disciplines and sub-disciplines' (Baker, 1993, p. 234). Interestingly, Baker also points to an important issue with this demotion of translated texts by stating that 'this traditional view of translation implies, in itself, an acknowledgement of the fact that translational behaviour is different from other types of linguistic behaviour' (p. 234). Following Baker, investigations into the relationship between source (the text to be translated into another language) and target texts (the translated text) were incorporated into Translation Studies (TS), the scientific discipline dealing with theoretical and practical aspects accompanying the process of rendering one language into another.

One linguistic feature that is the object of comparative investigations between source and target texts is metaphor. Non-literal language in the form of metaphors can be found not only in literary language use but in language use in general and in different registers in particular (see, e.g., Fuertes-Olivera and Nielsen [2011] on the translation of metaphorical terms in accounting between English and Spanish). Given conceptual differences between languages and cultures, metaphors pose an extra challenge to the translator. To ensure understanding of the target text in the target culture and thus successful communication of the source text, the translator needs to be aware of those conceptual differences. Studies on translational processing of non-literal language (e.g. how translators deal with linguistic expressions realizing conceptual metaphors) and on the equivalence of metaphors in source and target expressions (Al-Hasnawi, 2007; Schäffner, 2004) have accompanied the transformation of TS from a purely normative discipline to an academic one. The importance of the translator as a mediator not only between languages but also between cultures has been shown, and these studies have concluded that the translation of metaphor is mainly influenced by conceptual cultural similarities and/or differences. But what does that mean for the target text and its place in the target culture?

Among the features that Baker (1993, p. 243) identified as one of the 'universal features of translation' is that translated text is marked by '[a] general tendency to exaggerate features of the target language' (p. 244), which is characterized by quantitative differences between translated and non-translated texts (p. 245). While Baker refers to the distinct features of translated texts as 'linguistic features', studies on universals are confined to lexical/semantic language patterns (see, e.g., Olohan [2000] on the use of the optional *that* in translated English). The aim of the present study was to investigate whether or not Baker's universal of explication and exaggeration can be applied to cognitive phenomena (i.e. conceptual metaphorical expressions). To my knowledge, no research has yet ventured to apply translation universals to the translation of conceptual linguistic phenomena like metaphors.

It should be pointed out that this investigation was by no means intended to be exhaustive. Due to the massive number of conceptual metaphors identified in the literature so far and the methodological approach (corpus studies), the study concentrated on linguistic expressions of the conceptual metaphor TIME IS MOTION as it is represented in metaphorical expressions such as *time flies by* or *as the day goes on*. TIME and MOTION are basic concepts of the English language and the respective conceptual mapping widely used. Lexical expressions of the mapping were thus expected to be quite a prevalent feature of original English.

Using a quantitative approach, the study aimed to answer the following research questions:

1. Are there quantitative differences between the occurrences of metaphorical expressions of the conceptual metaphor TIME IS MOTION in translated and non-translated English?
2. What do possible differences look like? Are metaphorical expressions over- or underrepresented in translated text compared to non-translated text?

The chapter is structured as follows. After introducing the theoretical approach, I present the methods and the material employed to extract, organize and analyse the data. The results of the analysis are then described according to quantitative distributions between translated and non-translated categories of a number of variables. Thus, I establish interrelations between the members of these variables and their affiliation to the translated or non-translated category. The results are discussed in relation to the research questions before I summarize the findings, place the study into the prospect of further research and discuss possible limitations of the methodology and the analysis.

Theoretical approaches

Within translation theory as proposed by Mona Baker (1993) and Gideon Toury (1995), for example, the translated text is treated as independent both from the source text and from similar texts in the target culture. Research in the field moved from studies of word-to-word translations to research including the context of the translation situation, such as source and target culture, the employment situation of the translator and so on. The translator assumes the task not only of transferring one language into another but of transferring meaning from one culture into another. Sense, not only in terms of lexical semantic sense, but also in terms of the intended communicative aim of the source texts, comes to the fore. Thus, intercultural communication through translation is not reduced to the meaning of a single text (i.e. words, phrases and sentences), but includes a comprehensive communicative situation where the text is placed in a larger context. This amplifies the notion of a distinction between source and target text as two independent texts with only a semantic connection.

Since translations are no longer carried out on a word-to-word equivalence basis, they do 'not simply . . . reproduce the formal structures of the source text but also give some thought, and sometimes priority, to how similar meanings and functions are typically expressed in the target language' (Baker, 1993, p. 236). Thus, the target text becomes detached from the source text not only in terms of lexis (choice of lexical expressions) and syntax (sentence structure), but also by disguising the source culture. Baker (1993, p. 239) states that '[t]he source text is a source of information and . . . it may be exploited in a variety of ways to meet the expectations of an envisaged audience', that is, the audience in the target culture. However, with its own independent status, one would expect the target text to blend into the target culture by imitating its cultural, social and textual norms. On the contrary, Baker finds that 'the need to communicate in translated utterances, operates as a major constraint on translational behaviour and gives rise to patterns which are specific to translated texts' (p. 242). Hence, translated texts can be distinguished from target language texts, and it is possible to identify these texts on the basis of translation universals. Baker further claims that these distinguishing patterns can be found in the complete translated variety of a language irrespective of the source language, and that they differ qualitatively as well as quantitatively from the non-translated variety of that same language (p. 245). Hence, even though translation is assumed to be profoundly target text and target culture orientated, and Munday (2001, p. 144) refers to the invisibility of the translator to the target text reader, Baker notes that there are significant differences between translated and original texts in one language on a number of levels (lexical, syntactic, semantic etc.).

As has been stated, this study was motivated by one of Baker's (1993, pp. 244–5) universals which states that translated texts have '[a] general tendency to exaggerate features of the target language' and that they are marked with 'a specific type of distribution of certain features in translated texts vis-à-vis source texts and original texts in the target language'. These features originate in the target language and are not necessarily also a feature of the source language. To exaggerate these features means to overuse them quantitatively in comparison to non-translated (original) texts in the target language. In this study, lexical expressions of conceptual metaphors are the linguistic patterns that are assumed to deviate between translated and original English. Baker claims that universal patterns are detectable by comparing the translated and the non-translated variety of English (p. 245) and proposes so-called comparable corpus studies (i.e. studies of translated and non-translated texts in the same language) to investigate translational universals (p. 237). This chapter follows this proposal insofar as several different corpora for the English language are used to extract data. Texts translated into English from any given language as well as original English texts are investigated regarding the quantitative use of lexical expressions realizing the conceptual metaphor TIME IS MOTION. Such an investigation into quantitative deviations of lexical (and thus conceptual) representations between translated and non-translated English texts aims to describe the nature of translated English regarding metaphors.

On the other hand, corpus studies on conceptual metaphors in translation of the type carried out by Christina Schäffner (2004) on political discourse in English and German or by Al-Hasnawi (2007) in English and Arabic are characterized by qualitative descriptions of translations leading to internal generalizations on translational strategies (Schäffner) or the existence of culture-overlapping and culture-specific conceptual metaphorical mappings (Al-Hasnawi). Schäffner analyses different English translations of one and the same German political metaphor, thus aiming to reveal different translation strategies. Al-Hasnawi's analysis of Arabic translations of English metaphorical expressions aims to establish similar mapping conditions (i.e. translation equivalence) on the basis of similar conceptualizations of reality within two cultures. Both studies are performed on language pairs (English/German and English/Arabic), thus approaching conceptual metaphors from both the source and the target text/language. In contrast, the present study aims to describe quantitative differences *within* two varieties of the target language (English), ignoring the source languages of the single tokens by including texts translated from various source languages.

In short, previous corpus-based studies on metaphor explored qualitative equivalence and difference between two languages. My aim was to study quantitative deviations between the translated and the non-translated varieties of English.

Methodology

There are several different methods to investigate conceptual linguistic phenomena within translation studies. The introspective method as used by Lakoff and Johnson (2003), for example, produces examples by the goodness-of-fit principle without considering actual language use. Then there are surveys (e.g. questionnaires), experiments (e.g. eye tracking, keystroke-logging) and corpus studies (Tummers et al., 2005, p. 229). With the BNC (British National Corpus) and the COCA (Corpus of Contemporary American English) there are two large general corpora available that are assumed to be representative of their respective language variety (British and American English) and therefore to be illustrative of what I call 'original English'. As of August 2011, the COCA consisted of a total number of 425 million words while the BNC consisted of 100 million words. According to their composition (i.e. different sections/genres and time periods), they are general corpora supposed to reflect current everyday language use in the United Kingdom and the United States. Just like the COCA and the BNC, the TEC (Translation English Corpus) belongs to the category of general corpora constructed to describe the general aspects of translational English and is not 'domain (e.g. medicine or law) or genre (e.g. newspaper text or academic prose) specific' (McEnery et al., 2006, p. 15). Undeniably, the composition (only written texts) and size (10 million words) of the corpus makes it somewhat different from the other two corpora. But since the TEC exemplifies translational English, which is a relatively minor variety of English, this is not crucial. All three corpora are available online.[1]

In many respects, corpora were the only choice possible to generate a sufficient amount of data to answer my research questions. Availability, accessibility, electronic processability and representativeness were major factors determining my choice for this method. The TEC is the only available source for translated English and in many aspects is comparable to the COCA and the BNC. However, choosing corpus studies for this analysis does not automatically exclude the other three research methods mentioned. Indeed, a combination of two or more different methodological approaches might complement the results and support (or even refute) them, thus strengthening the scientific approach.

Approaching linguistic topics through corpora has become a common practice within many linguistic disciplines (see Gilquin and Gries, 2009), but what about cognitive linguistic phenomena? How can corpora be exploited at the level of concrete language use (i.e. syntactic, morphological, semantic and phonological issues)? Musolff (2004, p. 8) states that 'metaphors cannot be identified by external features, because they do not belong to the "expression" side of linguistic signs but to their conceptual side'. Investigating conceptual metaphors means investigating their linguistic manifestation in actual language use. Thus, one has to distinguish 'between "underlying" metaphorical concepts (domain mappings) and linguistic "surface" text features' (p. 8). The latter refers to actual language use as represented in corpora whereas the former refers to the conceptual level. All scientific description and statistical evaluation of corpus data are first and foremost valid for the empirical data drawn from corpora and not for the conceptual level. However, empirical data constitute the basis for the conceptual level and 'any claims about specific metaphorical concepts "underlying", "informing" or "organizing" the discourse and thinking of larger social groups need to be related to empirical discourse data before any significant conclusions can be drawn' (p. 9).

The corpus search

Language data extracted from corpora are called tokens (e.g. words, phrases, sentences etc.). Regarding metaphor, tokens represent individual manifestations (metaphorical expressions, e.g. *time flies*) of conceptual metaphorical mappings (e.g. TIME IS MOTION). To extract such tokens for a certain conceptual metaphor from a corpus, the underlying requirement is to assign the particular metaphorical mapping certain lexical items that are searchable within the corpus. Semantically, the mapping TIME IS MOTION can presumably be realized in a number of different ways with an even higher number of different nouns and verbs. Musolff (2004, p. 11) proposes the following procedure: '[grouping] the conceptual elements into source domains by using lexical fields (as exemplified in standard thesaurus categories) as well as patterns of collocation and relative frequencies in the emerging corpus'. I employed this procedure as a model for my own approach to corpora.

Stefanowitsch (2006, p. 66) refers to metaphorical expressions that 'contain both source and target domain lexemes' as metaphorical patterns. Following this definition, the metaphor was divided into its two constituent parts: the source domain (MOTION) and the target domain (TIME). To achieve maximum comparability between the corpora and a manageable search string as well as a manageable set of tokens, I exclusively used verbs of motion as lexical items representing the source domain. The target domain TIME, out of necessity, consists only of nouns. Starting with the target domain, I compiled a list of nineteen nouns based on my own understanding of the domain TIME. This included nouns referring to time periods, references to points in time as well as units of time. The nineteen nouns were then entered into the online database WordNet.[2] Every entry for every noun was examined individually for hyponyms, which in turn were chosen if their respective hypernyms were either defined as *time*, *time unit*, *unit of time*, *time period* or *time interval*. Using this procedure for all nineteen nouns, the list was extended to fifty-one nouns. The seven days of the week and the twelve months were added, bringing the total to seventy lexical items. In a next step, it was necessary to rank the nouns to decide which could be used in a corpus search and which would most likely not produce any suitable tokens. It proved most beneficial to sort them by frequency according to the two corpora that were representing original English in this study, the COCA[3] and the BNC (Leech et al., 2001). Raw frequencies from both corpora were added up and normalized frequencies per ten million words generated. The nouns were then ranked from highest to lowest. The top two month nouns (May and March) and days of the week (Sunday and Friday) were taken as representatives for their respective categories.

The list of searchable lexical items for the domain MOTION originates in Levin's (1993) work on English verb classes and alternations. I incorporated all the verbs Levin categorizes as verbs of inherently directed motion (p. 263) plus all *run* verbs (p. 265) for three reasons. First, they are fairly large categories containing a substantial number of verbs. Second, I assume the verbs in these two categories to be basic verbs (in contrast to more specific verbs like *chase* and *waltz*). Thus, I expected these verbs to be highly frequent. Third, metaphorization is assumed to be more likely with basic lexical items than with highly specific ones. This way I compiled a list of 133 verbs. I performed the same operations on the frequency lists for COCA and BNC as described earlier: (1) the verbs were searched for in the frequency lists of the COCA and the BNC; (2) the raw frequencies were added up, and normalized frequencies generated per ten million words; and (3) the verbs were ranked by their normalized frequencies. Thus, I ended up with two frequency lists of lexical items for the domains TIME and MOTION to be used as search words in the corpus search. It became quite obvious that I could not – at least not in the course of this study – search the corpora for all 48 nouns in combination with every single one of the 133 verbs in their respective grammatical forms. This would have resulted in an enormous number of different queries which in turn would most likely have produced a huge amount of data. In consequence, I decided to take the 15 most frequent verbs and their respective forms for the present, the past and the infinitive and search for them in combination with the 20 most frequent nouns in singular and plural. This appeared to be the right number of nouns and verbs to generate both a manageable number of queries in the three different corpora and a manageable amount of data resulting from the queries.

In all three corpora, every noun in its singular and plural form was searched for in combination with every verb in the infinitive, the present tense and the past tense form. Since I was looking for lexical expressions of the metaphor TIME IS MOTION, a pure quantitative search simply including all the tokens resulting from a query was not possible. Every token was in fact examined individually to disregard instances where the noun-verb combination did not fit the conceptual mapping TIME IS MOTION, as in the phrase *I don't have much time left*, where *left* is not the past tense form of the verb *leave* but an adjective, and *time* is not an object or substance in motion but an entity to keep. Another example is the noun *May*, which occurred several times as a proper name instead of referring to the particular month. As a result of the data extracting process from all three corpora, I ended up with n = 6,850 tokens, of which 5,570 came from the COCA, 709 from the BNC and 571 from the TEC.

To determine possible relations between the tokens in my data set, I conducted statistical analyses using the computer program Statistical Package for the Social Sciences (SPSS). Regarding the research questions about whether and how the usage of metaphorical expressions of the conceptual metaphor TIME IS MOTION differs between translated and non-translated English, five variables were chosen to be investigated further: **noun**, **verb**, **tense**, **genre** and **translated**. Since the variable **translated** is assumed to be the influencing factor (i.e. whether a token originates in original or translated English), it constitutes the independent variable while the other four are dependent variables which are assumed to be influenced by the independent variable. Every variable was coded for several different classifications (values). For the first variable **noun**, for example, there are twenty values denoting the twenty TIME nouns used in the corpus search. The same applies for the variable **verb** which includes fifteen values denoting the different verbs of motion. The variable **tense** is represented by the three values *infinitive*, *present* and *past*. **Genre** indicates whether the token is taken from a *fictional* or a *non-fictional* text; and the independent variable **translated** indicates whether the token was translated into English or not. In statistical analyses, one always assumes that the relevant variables do not have any relation whatsoever and thus 'the . . . distributions are the same' (Hinton, 2004, p. 29). This is the so-called null hypothesis. Significance testing is supposed to prove or refute this null hypothesis. For my data, the null hypothesis states that the distribution of the tokens for every dependent variable (i.e. **noun**, **verb**, their affiliation to a certain **genre** or their grammatical **tense**) is not associated with their being translated into English or not. This automatically presupposes that the distribution for every variable between translated and non-translated tokens in the data set is the same, that is, there are as many translated tokens as there are non-translated ones for every variable. The chi-square/Fisher's exact test was employed to determine the validity of assumed associations between the dependent variables and the independent one. The chi-square test 'examines . . . proportions and presents the probability of obtaining this pattern when there is no difference in the choices' (p. 275). The result of the chi-square test and Fisher's exact test, which is valid for variables with only two categories (see **genre**), is presented as the *p*-value and assesses how well the observed data fit the expected results.

Data and results

The compiled data set is relatively large (n = 6,850 tokens). Every token represents a phrase extracted from one of the three corpora, that is, a phrase containing a metaphorical pattern of a noun representing the target domain TIME and a verb form representing the source domain MOTION. Table 4.1 shows the distribution of the tokens among the three corpora.

The tokens from the COCA and the BNC represent original English and the tokens from the TEC constitute the translated category. The COCA, which is also the biggest of the three corpora with 410 million words, is represented with 5,570 tokens in the data set. This is followed by the BNC (100 million words) with 709 tokens and the TEC (10 million words) with 571 tokens. The distribution between translated and non-translated tokens within the data set is given in Figure 4.1.

Without a doubt, the distribution between translated and non-translated tokens within the data set is highly disproportional. The bar for the translated tokens ('yes') is significantly lower than that for the non-translated ones ('no'). There are 571 translated and 6,279 non-translated tokens. This large divergence is mainly due to the aforementioned difference in size between the corpora. Hence, the distribution of the tokens for the dependent variables in the next four sections is given in normalized figures per ten million words to acknowledge this difference and to generate better comparability.

Translated is the independent variable which I considered to influence the usage of metaphorical expressions in one way or another. In other words, I considered quantitative differences between the distributions of the tokens to be due to their affiliation to either the translated or the non-translated category of a variable. Thus, the variable was tested against the four dependent variables. The distribution of these four

Table 4.1 Observed token distribution per corpus

Corpus	Observed frequencies	%
COCA	5,570	81.3
BNC	709	10.4
TEC	571	8.3
Total	6,850	100.0

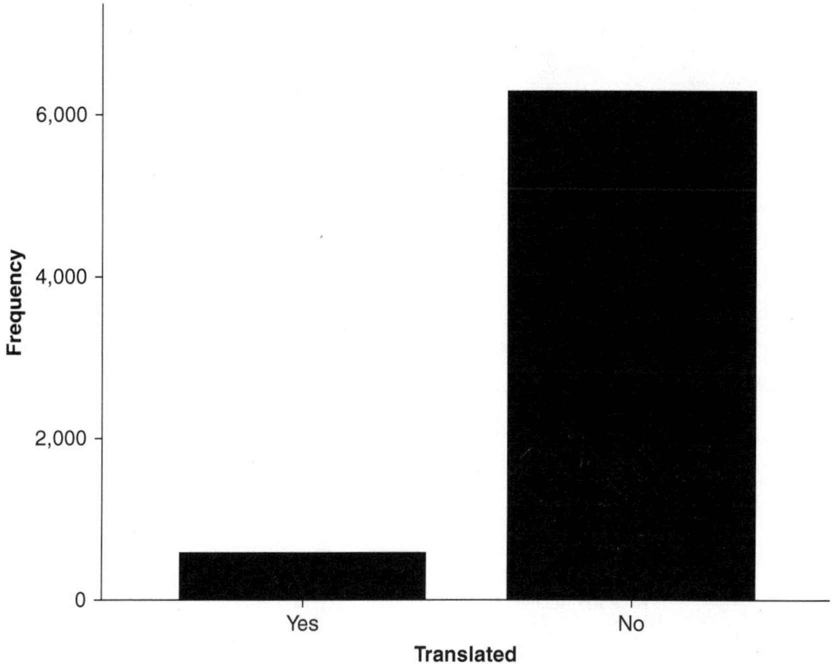

Figure 4.1 Observed token distribution for the variable **translated**.

variables within the data set and the results of their interrelation with the independent variable are described in the following sections.

Noun

The descriptive analysis of the variable **noun** reveals that the usage of nouns in metaphorical expressions of TIME IS MOTION differed significantly between the translated and non-translated categories. As Table 4.2 shows, translated tokens outnumber the respective non-translated tokens of a noun in almost all of the cases.

The noun *time*, for example, occurs 157 times per ten million words in translated texts but only 39.9 times in non-translated texts. Phrases containing a metaphorical usage of the noun *night* are used approximately 7 times more per ten million words in translated (70) than in non-translated texts (10.9). Only the nouns *season*, *future*, *century* and *decade* are less frequent in translated than in non-translated metaphorical expressions. Thus, sixteen out of the twenty nouns tested are overrepresented in translated English.

Statistically, the association between the variables **noun** and **translated** is significant and the divergence between translated and non-translated uses of the nouns not random. For fourteen of the twenty nouns, there is either a positive or a negative (statistically relevant) divergence from the expected count (if the null hypothesis were true) as displayed in Table 4.3.

Table 4.2 Cross-tabulation normalized distribution per ten million words for **noun/translated**

Noun	Translated		Noun	Translated	
	Yes	No		Yes	No
time	157.0	39.9	evening	21.0	2.8
day	121.0	15.9	hour	27.0	2.5
life	38.0	12.5	minute	5.0	1.7
night	70.0	10.9	end	5.0	1.6
year	40.0	8.8	age	1.0	0.8
moment	23.0	8.3	Sunday	3.0	0.6
season	4.0	4.8	future	0	0.4
week	18.0	4.4	century	0	0.4
morning	11.0	3.3	decade	0	0.2
month	25.0	3.0	May	2.0	0.1

Table 4.3 Chi-square test **noun/translated**

	Value	df	*p*-value
Pearson chi-square	94.398	13	.000
No. of valid cases	6,715		

The test of the null hypothesis stating that the nouns are equally distributed between translated and non-translated tokens shows significance beyond the .05 level: x^2 (13) = 94.398; $p < .001$. Since the chi-square test is not valid for categories with an expected count of less than 5 tokens per value, the data had to be cleared of such instances in advance. There remain fourteen nouns in the data set, given as the degree of freedom (df) in Table 4.3 (fourteen minus one). These fourteen nouns are represented in 6,715 tokens of the data set. Thus, the excluded nouns account for 135 tokens, which is a rather small number, and the exclusion is not expected to alter the results of the study significantly.

Verb

The descriptive analysis reveals divergence between the translated and non-translated categories for the variable **verb** as well, as displayed in Table 4.4.

Two verbs did not produce any metaphorical tokens in any of the corpora. Ten of the thirteen remaining verbs in the data set produce more metaphorical instances per ten million words in translated than in original language. The verb *go*, for example, appears 236 times per ten million words in translated English while it only occurs in 49.5 times per ten million words in non-translated English. Three other verbs (*rise*, *travel* and *jump*) did not produce any translated tokens in the corpus search of the TEC and the respective normalized frequencies for the non-translated tokens are close to zero. This might be for different reasons. First, the TEC might not contain the necessary number of words to include instances of these three verbs used in metaphorical expressions

Table 4.4 Cross-tabulation normalized distribution per ten million words for **verb/translated**

Verb	Translated		Verb	Translated	
	Yes	No		Yes	No
go	236.0	49.5	return	10.0	1.0
come	208.0	49.5	rise	0	0.4
fall	49.0	8.5	enter	2.0	0.3
run	6.0	4.6	leave	1.0	0.2
arrive	30.0	3.6	travel	0	0.1
roll	7.0	3.2	jump	0	0.1
fly	22.0	2.0			

Table 4.5 Chi-square test **verb/translated**

	Value	df	*p*-value
Pearson chi-square	45.849	7	.000
No. of valid cases	6,789		

in combination with one of the twenty nouns. Second, these verbs might not be used in metaphorical expressions in translated language. The latter reason is interesting insofar as an additional qualitative analysis of the tokens including source languages might reveal relations between the source language and English regarding culture-overlapping and culture-specific conceptual metaphorical mappings. In the present data set, the majority of verbs are overrepresented in translated language compared to the corresponding non-translated verbs.

Statistically, the association of the variables **verb** and **translated** in the data set is significant, as can be seen in Table 4.5.

The test of the null hypothesis that the verbs are equally distributed between the translated and the non-translated category shows significance beyond the .05 level: x^2 (7) = 45.849; $p < .001$. Hence, the distribution of the tokens between the translated and the non-translated category is not due to random dissemination but to their affiliation to one of the categories.

Tense

In line with the two preceding variables **noun** and **verb**, the variable **tense** also exhibits a considerable divergence of normalized instances between translated and non-translated tokens. In all three verb forms (infinitive, present and past tense), translated language contains far more metaphorical instances of the conceptual metaphor TIME IS MOTION per ten million words than non-translated language (see Table 4.6).

Undeniably, there is a considerable divergence between the translated and non-translated categories. In translated language, there are 389 occurrences per ten million words in past tense, but only 65 usages per ten million words in non-translated

Table 4.6 Cross-tabulation normalized distribution for **tense/translated**

Verb form	Translated	
	Yes	No
Past	389	65
Present	161	52
Infinitive	21	6

Table 4.7 Chi-square test **tense/translated**

	Value	df	*p*-value
Pearson chi-square	48.478	2	.000
No. of valid cases	6,850		

language. The same applies for the other two verb forms with 161 to 52 instances per ten million words in present tense and 21 to 6 occurrences per ten million words in any of the infinitive forms. The chi-square analysis in Table 4.7 revealed that the association between the variable **tense** and the variable **translated** is statistically significant. The test of the null hypothesis that the tenses of the verb forms are equally distributed between the translated and the non-translated category shows significance beyond the .05 level: x^2 (2) = 48.478; p <.001. The distribution of past tense, present tense and infinitive verb forms between translated and non-translated tokens is not random but somehow influenced by the fact that the tokens are either translated or not. In line with the previous two variables, the divergence between translated and non-translated cases within the data set indicates a difference between translated and original English in relation to the use of the conceptual metaphor TIME IS MOTION.

Genre

The variable **genre** consists of only two classifications: fiction and non-fiction. The distribution of fictional and non-fictional tokens between the translated and the non-translated category reveals that translated fictional and non-fictional tokens are more frequent than their non-translated counterparts. Thus, the translated category outnumbers the non-translated category (see Table 4.8).

Within the fictional category, there are 469 translated tokens per ten million words and 57 non-translated tokens. In contrast, the non-fictional tokens do not exhibit that big a difference. The data set contains 102 translated and 66 non-translated tokens per ten million words. The non-fictional part of the translated category ('yes') is considerably smaller than the fictional part. Only 102 tokens per ten million words originate in non-fictional texts while 469 were extracted from fictional texts. In contrast, the non-translated category ('no') exhibits a much more balanced distribution of fictional and non-fictional tokens. A total of 66 tokens per

Table 4.8 Cross-tabulation normalized distribution per ten million words for **genre/translated**

Genre	Translated	
	Yes	No
Non-fiction	102	66
Fiction	469	57

Table 4.9 Fisher's exact test for **genre/translated**

	Value	df	*p*-value
Pearson chi-square	266.327	1	.000
Fisher's exact test			.000
No. of valid cases	6,850		

ten million words are non-fictional and 57 tokens are fictional. The difference (11 tokens) is considered to be minimal in relation to the 367 tokens per ten million words that distinguish non-fictional translated tokens from fictional translated tokens. There is a considerable overrepresentation of fictional tokens in translated language. This suggests that within translated English, fictional texts are more likely to contain metaphorical expressions of TIME IS MOTION than found in original English language. However, this finding has to be treated with caution since this divergence might be due to the quantitative overrepresentation of fictional tokens within the translated category of the data set. The question remains whether this is due to an imbalance between fictional and non-fictional texts within the TEC or if it actually points towards different usage of metaphorical expressions within translated and non-translated texts. Unfortunately, the TEC does not provide any information on the frequency distribution of words between the different sub-corpora; hence, I cannot make any claims about a possible imbalance in the corpus. I can only refer to the findings that result from the data set and acknowledge that these findings are highly dependent on the composition of the corpus, which I am not sufficiently familiar with. Further studies on the same or other data material would have to take a closer look at the influence of the variable **genre** on the distribution of metaphorical expressions within translated language.

Statistically, the association between the variables **genre** and **translated** is significant and the divergence of the tokens from the expected distribution considerably large as can be seen from Table 4.9.

Fisher's exact test also evaluates the possibility that the two variables are associated as highly significant. The exact *p*-value is less than 0.001. Hence, the distribution is noticeably different from purely random distribution and determined by the variable **translated**, that is, dependent on whether the token is translated or not. The two variables are related and the descriptive analysis reveals overrepresentation in the translated category for both fictional and non-fictional texts, indicating that with regard to metaphorical expressions of TIME IS MOTION translated language differs from non-translated language regarding genre as well.

Conclusion

Translation is an important constituent of cross-cultural communication. Metaphors as instances of non-literal language are part of every register and pose extra challenges to the translator due to conceptual differences between languages and cultures. Previous studies on conceptual metaphors in translation have been concerned with the qualitative analysis of source and target text expressions, mainly investigating semantic equivalence or deviation (Al-Hasnawi, 2007; Schäffner, 2004). They aim to investigate translational processes and strategies and draw conclusions about the nature of translation or even about empirical theories of other scientific disciplines (linguistics, psychology etc.). However, to my knowledge, there has not yet been a study investigating possible quantitative deviation between original and translated English texts concerning the usage of conceptual metaphorical expressions.

My hypothesis in this study was that there are quantitative differences concerning the usage of metaphorical expressions realizing conceptual metaphors in texts that are originally produced in English and texts that are translated into English. This hypothesis was investigated in relation to metaphorical expressions representing the conceptual metaphor TIME IS MOTION. Researchers within translation studies (e.g. Baker, 1993) claim that translated texts (i.e. target texts) distinguish themselves from comparable non-translated texts through a number of features such as the overuse of conventional grammar and exaggeration of target language features (p. 244).

Approaching translations quantitatively using the comparable corpus method helped to establish that there is indeed a divergence between the translated and non-translated varieties of English. Regarding four different variables (i.e. **noun**, **verb**, **tense** and **genre**) there is a significant deviation between the translated and non-translated tokens per ten million words. Thus, regarding my research questions, I can conclude that:

1. Translated language differs quantitatively from non-translated language regarding the use of metaphorical expressions of the conceptual metaphor TIME IS MOTION.
2. Translated text exhibits overrepresentation of metaphorical expressions of the conceptual metaphor TIME IS MOTION per ten million words regarding the four variables investigated in this study.
   a. There are more instances of metaphorical expressions employing certain nouns and verbs per ten million words.
   b. The usage of the verbs in the three investigated verb forms (infinitive, present and past tense) within the translated tokens differs quantitatively from the respective non-translated tokens. In other words, the quantitative overrepresentation of the variable **verb** continues throughout the syntactically related variable **tense**.

c. The fourth variable **genre** also exhibits overrepresentation of the translated tokens. Interestingly, the translated category displays an inner quantitative deviation of the distribution of translated tokens between fictional and non-fictional tokens which the non-translated category does not.

The results of this study show that, with regard to Baker's (1993) translation universal of exaggeration, metaphorical expressions realizing the conceptual metaphor TIME IS MOTION appear in translated English language and are exaggerated by overuse.

Concerning the methodology employed in this study, it must be acknowledged that there are problems with the representativeness of at least one of the corpora employed to extract tokens representing the different varieties. First, the TEC is relatively small compared to the other two corpora. This in itself does not pose an overarching problem since the figures are compared on the basis of normalized frequencies per ten million words. However, the TEC does not provide enough information to assess whether the distribution of words between the different sub-corpora is as balanced as it should be for the corpus to be representative of a certain language or language variety. Thus, there might be a considerable imbalance between fictional and non-fictional texts in the corpus which gives rise to the respective deviation within the data set. I also recognize that the COCA and the BNC might contain translated texts. The sub-corpus NEWSPAPER, for example, might contain articles that are translated into English from other languages. Unfortunately, the corpora do not include any information in this regard, so I had to treat the language represented in the two corpora as non-translated. Further research on the subject is necessary to eliminate such potentially compromising factors, providing more empirical control over the setting of the investigation. Compiling one's own corpora of translated and non-translated English instead of the use of pre-prepared online corpora appears to be one solution to the problems and is recommended for future studies on the topic.

Further research on this subject could take a number of different directions to test the findings of this study. First of all, continuing with the four variables included in this investigation, a combination of two, three or even all four of them can be tested against the expected influence of the variable **translated**. Thus, one could examine how the distribution of the tokens evolves when they are treated as phrases including a noun and a verb (e.g. *time flies*) and not only phrases containing either a noun (e.g. *time*) or a verb (e.g. *flies*). At a later stage, these phrases could be studied regarding the verb forms and the genre of the texts they are extracted from. Thus, it can be investigated if the quantitative deviation of the tokens between translated and non-translated language changes when, for example, the phrase *time flies* is investigated as an instance of a present tense phrase from a non-fictional text. Are there significant differences between the two varieties? Is the translated category still overrepresented or does the merging of variables cause a different distribution? Second, different conceptual metaphors and their respective metaphorical expressions have to be examined to confirm the fact that the imbalance between translated and non-translated texts is not only due to the metaphor TIME IS MOTION but to conceptual metaphors in general. Third, when establishing a broader and more controlled source of data, other text types should be included. Since this study only included written texts in both the translated and the non-translated category, the inclusion of spoken texts (i.e. interpreting) is a possibility. This might, for example, be realized by the application of other research methodologies, like experimental settings, where interpreters are asked to interpret text prepared by the researcher. Furthermore, translated tokens representing particular values of the variables (certain nouns and verbs etc.) that differ significantly from the non-translated variety can be investigated regarding the information about the nature of the translation, that is to say the source language, the translation mode, the translator employment and so on. Are there certain source languages that produce more overrepresentation than others or are training or employment situation of the translator causing these deviations? Last but not least, a qualitative analysis of the tokens concerning the use of particular translation strategies from the source language to the target language might be investigated where possible.

Notes

1 BNC: <http://www.natcorp.ox.ac.uk/>; COCA: <http://corpus.byu.edu/coca/>; TEC: <http://www.monabaker.com/tsresources/TranslationalEnglishCorpus.htm>.
2 <http://wordnet.princeton.edu/>
3 Frequency lists are available on the corpus webpage.

References

Al-Hasnawi, A. R. (2007), 'A Cognitive Approach to Translating Metaphors', *Translation Journal* 11(3). <http://www.bokorlang.com/journal/41metaphor.htm> (accessed 30 January 2013)

Baker, M. (1993), 'Corpus Linguistics and Translation Studies. Implications and Applications', in M. Baker, G. Francis, J. Sinclair and E. Tognini-Bonelli (eds), *Text and Technology: In Honour of John Sinclair*, Amsterdam and Philadelphia: John Benjamins, pp. 233–50.

Fuertes-Olivera, P. A. and Nielsen, S. (2011), 'The Dynamics of Terms in Accounting. What the Construction of the Accounting Dictionaries Reveals about Metaphorical Terms in Culture-Bound Subject Fields', *Terminology*, 17(1): 157–80.

Gilquin, G. and Gries, S. T. (2009), 'Corpora and Experimental Methods: A State-of-the-Art Review', *Corpus Linguistics and Linguistic Theory*, 5(1): 1–26.

Hinton, P. R. (2004), *SPSS Explained*, London: Routledge.

Lakoff, G. and Johnson, M. (2003), *Metaphors We Live By*, Chicago: University of Chicago Press.

Leech, G. N., Rayson, P. and Wilson, A. (2001), *Word Frequencies in Written and Spoken English: Based on the British National Corpus*, Harlow: Longman.

Levin, B. (1993), *English Verb Classes and Alternations*, Chicago: University of Chicago Press.

McEnery, T., Xiao, R. and Tono, Y. (2006), *Corpus-Based Language Studies: An Advanced Resource Book*, London: Routledge.

Munday, J. (2001), *Introducing Translation Studies: Theories and Applications*, London: Routledge.

Musolff, A. (2004), *Metaphor and Political Discourse: Analogical Reasoning in Debates about Europe*, Basingstoke: Palgrave Macmillan.

Olohan, M. (2000), *Intercultural Faultlines: Research Models in Translation Studies I : Textual and Cognitive Aspects*, Manchester: St. Jerome Publishing.

Schäffner, C. (2004), 'Metaphor and Translation: Some Implications of a Cognitive Approach', *Journal of Pragmatics*, 36: 1253–69.

Stefanowitsch, A. (2006), 'Corpus-Based Approaches to Metaphor and Metonymy', in A. Stefanowitsch and S. T. Gries (eds), *Corpus-Based Approaches to Metaphor and Metonymy*, Berlin: Mouton de Gruyter, pp. 1–16.

Toury, G. (1995), *Descriptive Translation Studies and Beyond*, Amsterdam and Philadelphia: John Benjamins.

Tummers, J., Heylen, K. and Geeraerts, D. (2005), 'Usage-Based Approaches in Cognitive Linguistics: A Technical State of the Art', *Corpus Linguistics and Linguistic Theory*, 1(2): 225–61.

Part Two

Universal versus Culture-Specific Aspects of Metaphor

5

Variation within Universals: The 'Metaphorical Profile' Approach to the Study of ANGER Concepts in English, Russian and Spanish[1]

Anna Ogarkova and Cristina Soriano

Introduction

Few topics have received more elaboration within Conceptual Metaphor Theory (CMT) than emotions. Since the publication of seminal works by Lakoff and Johnson (1980) and Lakoff and Kövecses (1987) on English, many researchers in Cognitive Linguistics embarked on their own explorations of the conceptual 'scaffolding' of emotion talk, investigating both Indo-European (e.g. Apresyan and Apresyan, 1993; Athanasiadou, 1998; Chand, 2008; Soriano, 2005) and non-Indo-European language families (e.g. Emanatian, 1995; Krupa, 1996; Matsuki, 1995; Taylor and Mbense, 1998; Yu, 1995, 1998). These studies have addressed the so-called basic emotions (cf. Ortony and Turner, 1990), such as anger, fear or happiness, and the social emotions, including shame, guilt, pride or love. Research on emotion metaphor in present-day languages has been paralleled by considerable diachronic work (e.g. Geeraerts and Grondelaers, 1995; Gevaert, 2005). Investigations of the grammatical properties of metaphorical expressions (e.g. Glynn, 2002) have also co-evolved with the research on emotion metaphors in specific types of discourse (e.g. Beger and Jäkel, 2009).

In this rich research context, a particularly salient topic has been the dichotomy between universality and lingual or cultural specificity in emotion metaphor (e.g. Kövecses, 2000a,b), and this is exactly the issue at stake in the present study. The main objective of this chapter is to provide a very granular assessment of both the shared and the language-specific in the metaphorical representation of various ANGER[2] concepts in three of the most widespread languages of the world: English, Russian and Spanish. The broad emotion category of ANGER has been chosen for its alleged universality: anger is always included in the lists of universal (Hupka et al., 1999), basic (Ortony and Turner, 1990) or modal (Scherer, 2009) emotions. Additionally, this emotion is particularly interesting for our research goals because it is reported to vary considerably across cultures, especially as concerns its evaluation, expression and regulation in different cultural groups (cf. Ogarkova, 2013).

While the overarching research goal and the broad emotion category under consideration in our study is hardly new in the CMT domain (dozens of studies have focused on anger, and some had a comparative focus), our study is much more concerned with, and hopes to break new ground in, the methodological aspects pertinent to the research of emotion metaphor across languages. The study design and the method used in this chapter have arisen in response to several methodological concerns about past CMT work. Four of these concerns are most important, and are briefly outlined in the following sections.

Units of analysis in the study of emotion metaphor

Until recently, most emotion metaphor studies focused on 'basic-level' concepts (Rosch, 1978) such as ANGER, FEAR or HAPPINESS. Both linguistic expressions containing emotion nouns (such as *fury* or *rage*) and metaphorical expressions referring to the emotion without actually naming it (such as *exploding, stewing* or *fuming*) counted as linguistic evidence for the existence of a conceptual metaphor.

While this approach can be justified in the study of broad emotion categories, adopting it makes it impossible to determine which specific target domain (i.e. emotion) is at stake for any one single expression. For example, do the metaphorical expressions *He exploded* and *You make my blood boil* involve the English target domain of ANGER (Kövecses, 1998), or do they rather involve the target domains of FURY, RAGE or INDIGNATION?

The issue is not trivial in the light of the recent cross-cultural evidence showing that, although similarities are observable across cultures at the basic level of emotion categorization (cf. Ogarkova, 2013), considerable differences emerge at its subordinate level, that is, at the level of emotion subtypes (e.g. English GLEE, CHEERFULNESS, ELATION within the English category of HAPPINESS; cf. Shaver et al., 1987). Studies show that cross-lingual variation exists in the *degree of lexicalization* of the basic categories (e.g. the Chinese SHAME group is larger than the English one; Li et al., 2004) and in the features highlighted by the words within a category in one language compared to another (e.g. different typical features in English and Indonesian LOVE words; Shaver et al., 2001). Furthermore, languages are also reported to diverge in the features differentiating between lexemes within a category. For example, the English ANGER words form meaningful groups largely because of the *intensity* of the denoted varieties (e.g. an IRRITATION, ANNOYANCE and GRUMPINESS group emerges as distinct from an ANGER, FURY, WRATH and RAGE group; Shaver et al., 1987). However, in Cree (an indigenous American language) the lexicalization of ANGER is driven by the (culturally important) need to highlight different *types of anger-eliciting events*[3] (Watkins, 1938, pp. 284–5). Taken together, this evidence emphatically highlights the need to consider the metaphorical representation of subordinate-level emotion concepts within broader emotion categories.

Luckily, recent advances in corpus-based CMT research offer methodological possibilities relevant for the task. One such case is Metaphoric Pattern Analysis (MPA; Stefanowitsch, 2004, 2006). In MPA, the metaphorical expressions qualifying for metaphor analysis are exclusively multi-word expressions containing a specific emotion lexeme from a given target domain (e.g. *he gave vent to his fury* or *he unleashed his anger*). This resolves the ambiguity about which specific (or subordinate) target domain is at stake (in the previous examples FURY and ANGER, respectively). Although MPA does not consider linguistic expressions associated with the general emotion concept that do not contain a specific emotion lexeme (e.g. *she got all steamed up*), the method captures all conceptual mappings attributed to emotion concepts in the classical introspection-based literature (Stefanowitsch, 2006). Moreover, due to the use of distributional statistics, the method allows for the quantitative evaluation of the (dis)similarities in the metaphorical representation of subordinate-level emotion concepts, both within and across languages (cf. the analysis of *happiness/Glück* and *joy/Freude* in English and German in Stefanowitsch, 2004).

Analytical measures in CMT emotion research

Three further concerns arise with regard to the analytical measures typically employed in emotion metaphor studies. First, in the majority of past work the mere *existence* of similar emotion metaphors (or their entailments) across languages has been treated as evidence for universality. However, even when a metaphor is found in all of the compared languages, those metaphors need not be equal in their *saliency*. Emotion concepts can vary significantly across languages in their *degree of association* to a given source domain (see Stefanowitsch, 2004, 2006; Ding, 2011, for compelling evidence in this respect).

The second concern relates to the commonly used *types* of analytical measures. While the few studies on metaphor using quantitative measures employ only the most common distribution statistical analyses (such as chi-square and Fisher exact tests), recent developments in corpus cognitive semantics (Divjak and Gries, 2006, 2008; Janda and Solovyev, 2009) compellingly show the utility of a much wider spectrum of procedures for the research on near-synonyms (which applies to subordinate-level emotion labels, also near-synonyms). Particularly interesting in this respect is Hierarchical Cluster Analysis (HCA), which allows for a succinct representation of a category by highlighting subgroups (clusters) of words within it, united by similarity in their distributional behaviour.

The third and final concern is the general disregard for the *qualitative* (vs quantitative) elaboration of emotion metaphor in language. A rare exception is a recent study by Oster (2010) which proposes quantifying the relevance of the corpus-based results not only with regard to the absolute frequency of metaphorical patterns co-occurring with a specific emotion noun (also known as 'tokens'), but also with regard to the number of different linguistic expressions in which a particular mapping is realized in a corpus sample (also referred to as 'types').

Representativeness of the languages in emotion metaphor research

Another shortcoming of past comparative CMT work on emotion metaphor is the number of languages included in any single study. With very few exceptions (e.g. Kövecses, 2000a), most emotion metaphor studies consider the evidence from either one or at best two languages, which impacts the validity of the claims made about universality. This shortcoming is particularly obvious in comparison with other disciplines concerned with the study of emotion, where larger-scale studies considering evidence from many languages are much more common (e.g. Fontaine et al., 2013; Hupka et al., 1999).

Relating emotion CMT findings to a broader research context

Two final concerns relate to CMT emotion scholars' failure to contextualize their findings in a broader research context by comparing their results with those obtained in other disciplines studying emotions. First, although many CMT studies discuss their findings in the light of the so-called folk emotion theories, such as the European humoral theory (e.g. Geeraerts and Grondelaers, 1995; Gevaert, 2005) or the theory of five elements in Chinese medicine (e.g. Yu, 1995), hardly any attempt has been made to investigate whether the metaphorical representation of emotions coheres with (or diverges from) the scientific descriptions advanced by expert emotion theories and cross-cultural emotion psychology. The second (and related) concern here is methodological: although sometimes a posteriori interpretations are offered (e.g. Yu, 1998), there has been no serious attempt to formulate predictions on the patterns of metaphorical language use *before* the analyses are undertaken.

Notwithstanding these limitations, there are at least two areas of cross-cultural divergence in emotions that could be explored by CMT. The first has to do with the commonly held view that a fundamental way in which culture shapes human behaviour is through *self-construal style*, that is, the way in which people define themselves and their relation to others in their environment (e.g. Markus and Kitayama, 1991; Nisbett et al., 2001). Cultures deemed more individualistic (most prominently, the United States, United Kingdom and Australia; cf. Hofstede, 2001)[4] encourage the 'independent self' construal, where people think of others as independent of each other and where self-expression, self-autonomy and pursuit of individuality are emphasized. By contrast, more collectivistic countries, like Russia or Spain (Tower et al., 1997; Triandis and Gelfand, 1998), are characterized by the 'interdependent' self-construal style, which endorses thinking of people as highly interconnected to one another ('self-in-relation') and where maintenance of social harmony and one's belongingness to a group are favoured over the assertion of individuality. Cultural variance on the individualism/collectivism dimension has been robustly supported by empirical evidence on various types of appraisal, conceptualization, expression and regulation of emotions (e.g. Mesquita, 2001; Triandis, 2001; but see Voronov and Singer, 2002, for a critique).

Concerning anger, cross-cultural psychological research suggests that in collectivistic compared to individualistic cultures anger is predominantly viewed as more negative and socially disruptive, as an emotion that challenges social order and harmony, and thus, should be regulated with regard to its expression and one's acting on the feeling. The evaluation is relatively more positive in individualistic cultures, which are more favourable towards the open manifestation of intense emotional experience as affirmation of the self.

The second area of attested cultural differences in emotion conceptualization concerns somatization, that is, the degree to which the connection between the body and the emotions is elaborated in a culture. For example, the link between the body and emotions is reported to be more salient in cultures like the Chinese or Russian as compared to that of the United States. This has been shown by clinical research studies where, compared to American depressed patients, people with a comparable medical record but from Chinese and Russian cultural backgrounds were found to be more likely to somatize (i.e. represent in somatic rather than psychological terms) their emotional experiences (e.g. Kleinman and Kleinman, 1985; Shiroma and Alarcon, 2011). For Russian, comparable reports come also from a more anthropological and psycholinguistic line of work: Wierzbicka (1992) proposes that the connection between emotions and the body is emphasized in Russian to a higher degree than in English, and the results from a follow-up psycholinguistic study (Pavlenko, 2002) support the claim.

In sum, with regard to English, Russian and Spanish (the languages analysed in the present study), this psychological evidence allows us to expect the following: (1) metaphors emphasizing the negativity of ANGER, and, more specifically, its harm/disruption to the self and others would be more saliently represented in Russian and Spanish than in English, (2) metaphors emphasizing controlled expression and enhanced regulation of anger would be more salient in Russian and Spanish than in English, while conversely, metaphors emphasizing less/no control in the manifestation and experience of the emotion would be more salient in English than in Russian and Spanish; and (3) metaphors emphasizing the somatic/physiological component of anger would be more saliently represented in Russian than in English.

The present study: responding to the overviewed concerns

Our study attempts to improve current CMT practices on the four areas of concern discussed earlier. First of all, we focus on the metaphorical construal of ANGER concepts in three languages from different Indo-European families – English (Germanic), Spanish (Romance) and Russian (Slavic) – which expands the conventional two-language format of current CMT work on emotion metaphor. Second, we adopt a lexeme-specific approach largely comparable to (but not identical to) the MPA proposed by Stefanowitsch (2004, 2006), and investigate several types of anger in the three languages as instantiated by twenty salient lexemes relevant for the language groups in question. In doing so, we adopt an *emic* perspective (Helfrich, 1999), in that we rely on the emotion labels that have been empirically found to be relevant for cultural communities to talk about anger. Third, our study strictly adheres to the 'bottom-up' orientation in the corpus-based analyses of metaphorical expressions and pursues saliency-focused research. But, alongside conventional distribution statistics, we also employ several other data-mining techniques, and take into account the qualitative dimension of metaphor elaboration in language. Fourth and last, we explicitly start by formulating the hypotheses (derived from prior psychological research) for the expected similarities and differences to be found in the representation of ANGER, and test these hypotheses against the metaphor data. In the following sections, we detail the data and the method used, and report our findings on both universality and culture-specificity.

Data and method

Selection of emotion words

The emotion terms were selected on the basis of a situation-labelling study (Ogarkova et al., 2012), where native speakers of five European languages (Russian, N = 17; Spanish, N = 17; French, N = 12; German, N = 17; and English, N = 11) were presented with a varied set of ANGER situations and requested to provide an emotion label that would best describe the way they would feel in those situations. The most salient ANGER terms in the three languages – that is, the most frequently mentioned across all scenarios – are presented in Table 5.1.

Data and methodology

The corpora used are the British National Corpus (BNC), *Corpus del Español*, and the Russian National Corpus (all of them at least one hundred million words at the time of data collection). All genres and modes of text were included in the searches, but only examples from the twentieth century onwards were chosen. In several cases there were fewer than one thousand occurrences of a word in a corpus, in which case we complemented the samples with additional concordances from two additional corpora, the Bank of English (British section) and the *Corpus de Referencia del Español Actual* (CREA) for Spanish.

Table 5.1 Spanish, Russian and English ANGER terms elicited in an emotion situation labelling task

Spanish	Russian	English
rabia* [anger]	razdrazhenie* [irritation]	anger*
enfado ['small anger']	obida* [resentment/hurt]	annoyance
indignación*	zlost'* [anger]	rage*
cabreo [anger, colloquial term]	gnev* ['justified anger']	fury*
ira* [wrath]	dosada* [frustration/vexation]	frustration*
molesto [annoyed]	vozmuschenie* [indignation]	irritation*
frustración*	negodovanie [indignation]	indignation*
irritación *	jarost'* [fury]	resentment*
furia*	serdityj [cross]	

Note: In descending order of frequency of recall. For readability reasons, Russian terms are transliterated from Cyrillic.
* indicates the terms for which metaphorical profiles were obtained in the present study.
Source: Ogarkova et al., 2012.

The method for metaphor identification and classification derives from the MPA method proposed by Stefanowitsch (2006) and also used by other researchers (e.g. Ogarkova, 2007; Ding, 2011). However, our version has undergone several modifications (and extensions) in handling the data. Schematically, the method unfolds in seven successive steps (see Soriano and Ogarkova, submitted, for a more detailed account):

1. Retrieval of one thousand random KWIC (Key Word in Context) hits for each of the twenty ANGER words in the three languages.
2. Manual extraction of the metaphorical patterns, defined by Stefanowitsch (2006, p. 66) as 'a multi-word expression from a given source domain (SD) into which a specific lexical item from a given target domain (TD) has been inserted'. Determining whether the words surrounding anger lexemes in KWIC strings were used metaphorically (rather than literally) was facilitated by the use of the 'metaphor identification procedure' (MIP) proposed by the Pragglejaz Group (2007, p. 3).[5]
3. Classification of the metaphorical expressions into conceptual metaphors according to their source domains (see Tables 5.2–5.5).
4. Reanalysis of 10 per cent of the English sample with the help of another rater, and submission of results to inter-rater reliability testing. The re-analysis of 10 per cent of the English sample by both authors revealed a high degree of inter-rater agreement (Kappa value = 0.83, $p < .000$). Discrepancies were solved through discussion.
5. Quantifying the results both with regard to the overall *number* of metaphorical patterns instantiating a metaphor ('tokens'), and the number of different *types* of patterns in which this metaphor is realized ('types').
6. Conversion of the observed raw frequencies into relative frequencies (against the total number of metaphorical patterns identified for a word). Creation of a cross-table indicating the relative co-occurrence of each word with each metaphor. The vector of these co-occurrence percentages for a word is referred to in this chapter as the word's 'metaphorical profile'. Twenty metaphorical profiles of ANGER nouns in three languages constitute our database.
7. Data analyses for cross-lingual similarities and divergences in the distribution of metaphorical patterns (and types thereof), on both the raw and the relative frequencies. A series of Fisher exact tests was carried out on the raw frequencies. Pearson correlations were computed between the average ANGER metaphorical profiles computed for each language and between the best translation pairs. In each language, independent HCA (amalgamation strategy: Ward) were executed on all the ANGER metaphorical profiles, and *t*-scores[6] were calculated for the metaphors associated to each cluster. Finally, productivity indexes (PIs)[7] and creativity ratios (cf. Oster, 2010) were calculated for all metaphors in each sample. All analyses were done in SPSS (version 19).

Since metaphor identification and classification are admittedly among the most debated issues in CMT, a few words clarifying these stages in our study are due.

Unlike in previous work (e.g. Stefanowitsch, 2006), where all mappings are treated as independent from each other and thus equal in status, in our approach some of the metaphors were grouped into coherent clusters headed by a 'root' metaphor. The subtypes under each root metaphor were found to be of two kinds (cf. Soriano, 2005): *entailment sub-metaphors*, which constitute entailments of the root that receive extensive linguistic elaboration on their own (e.g. EXPLOSION/BURST in the root metaphor ANGER IS A PRESSURIZED FLUID IN A CONTAINER); and *special case sub-metaphors*, where the subtype specifies the scope of the source domain in the root metaphor (e.g. ANGER IS A SOLID OBJECT and ANGER IS A FLUID SUBSTANCE in the root metaphor ANGER IS A PHYSICAL ENTITY).

The metaphors in the resulting inventory fall into four categories (see also Soriano and Ogarkova, submitted, for an in-depth discussion). In the *specific metaphors* (Table 5.2) emotion concepts are metaphorically construed via specific-imagery source domains invoking fairly complex scenarios rich in detail and entailments: for example, in the FIRE metaphor ANGER is metaphorically construed as fire, ignited by some event; it burns the person who experiences the emotion and others nearby; like all fires, it is intense, prominently visible, consuming and damaging; it can last for a long time as embers, potentially to be reactivated at a later time.

In the case of *generic metaphors* (Table 5.3), the source domain is more generic than in the specific metaphors, and these metaphors can apply to almost any target, providing only a generic ontological nature to the source.[8]

Table 5.2 Specific metaphors and examples of metaphorical patterns (English)

Source domain	Subtype		Metaphorical patterns (examples)
PRESSURIZED FLUID IN THE BODY-CONTAINER	E	RISE	*rage rise in X, indignation well up in X*
	E	PRESSURE	*choke with rage, swell with indignation*
	E	COUNTERPRESSURE	*suppress irritation, swallow fury*
	E	CONTENTION	*contain anger, retain fury, bottle up frustration*
	E	COMING OUT	*vent anger, anger spill out, fury overflow*
	E	EXPLOSION/BURST	*outburst of resentment, explode with anger*
HOT FLUID			*simmering resentment, scalding rage*
FIRE			*anger burn, ignite fury, blazing indignation*
OPPONENT IN A STRUGGLE			*X wrestle with X's rage, X succumb to resentment*
	S	CONTROLLER/SUPERIOR	*X be obedient to rage, frustration dominate X*
FORCE OF NATURE			*avalanche of fury, volcano of resentment*
INSANITY			*fit of anger, frenzied rage, X be deranged with fury*
	S	ANGER IS BLINDNESS	*blind in fury/blind fury, blinding rage*
ILLNESS			*X be sick with rage, paroxysms of indignation*
ANIMAL			*leash/unleash anger, harness fury, ferocious rage*
	S	EMOTER IS ANIMAL	*X snarl in anger, X bellow with fury*
WEAPON			*turn, direct, cast anger/rage against (at, on) Y*

Note: E = entailment subtype metaphor, S = special case subtype metaphor, *X* = emoter, *Y* = third person.

Table 5.3 Generic metaphors and examples of metaphorical patterns (English)

Source domain	Subtypes	Metaphorical patterns (examples)
LOCATION		*in anger, lead/drive to rage*
	S CONTAINER	*drive/send/fly/[etc] X into fury*
FORCE		*anger sweep over X, rage grip X, fury take hold of X*
	S AGENT	*anger make X do/be something, anger causes X to [verb]*
MOVING ENTITY		*anger go, rage push through, fury return*
PHYSICAL ENTITY		*generate anger, produce rage, handle anger*
	E VISIBLE/HIDDEN OBJECT	*hide fury, show anger, conceal rage*
	E CONSISTENCY/TEXTURE	*resentment dissipate, irritation melt away/dissolve*
	E POSSESSION	*have irritation, keep rage, accumulate fury*
	E MOVED OBJECT	*bring rage, export anger, receive fury, steal anger*
	S SOLID OBJECT	*rage barrier, brick wall of indignation*
	– E INTENSITY IS SIZE	*enormous frustration, titanic rage, massive anger*
	S SUBSTANCE	*anger evaporate, reservoir of fury, irritation seep out*
	– E INTENSITY IS QUANTITY	*much anger, rage be in plentiful supply*
	– E MIXTURE	*mixture/blend of [emotion] and anger*
LIVING ORGANISM		*root of anger, seeds of resentment, rage ripen*
	S HUMAN	*suspicious anger, scheming fury*

Note: E = entailment subtype metaphor, S = special case subtype metaphor, *X* = emoter.

Table 5.4 Primary metaphors and examples of metaphorical patterns (English)

Source domain	Subtypes	Metaphorical patterns (examples)
INTENSITY IS HEAT		*heat of anger, hot rage, white-hot fury*
INTENSITY IS DEPTH		*deep anger, depth of resentment*
INTENSITY IS A SCALE		*anger is matched, degree of anger, level of anger*
MORE IS UP/LESS IS DOWN		*irritation mount, rage be at peak, anger drop away*
BAD IS DARK		*black fury, dark with rage*
THE BODY IS A CONTAINER		*anger be inside X, rage be within X*
FOR ANGER	S EYES	*resentment [verb] in X's eyes, anger [verb] from the eyes*
	S FACE	*anger [verb] in X's face, frustration be on X's face*
	S VOICE	*anger be in the voice, fill voice with anger*
	S SOUL	*indignation in X's soul*
	S CHEST/BREAST	*get anger off the chest, anger within the chest/the breast*
	S HEAD/MIND	*fury in X's head, fury fill X's brain*
	S OTHER	*anger on X's cheeks, indignation in X's spine*

Note: E = entailment subtype metaphor, S = special case subtype metaphor, *X* = emoter.

Table 5.5 Infrequent metaphors and examples of metaphorical patterns (English)

Source domain	Metaphorical patterns (examples)
DANGER/THREAT	*safe/save from anger, victim of fury, protect from anger, escape from frustration*
LIGHT/BRIGHT	*rage flashes, glint of anger, fury glow, glitter of indignation*
SOURCE OF ENERGY	*X be fuelled with/by indignation, anger keep X going, rage drive life into X*
TOOL	*turn fury to use, make use of indignation, exploit resentment*
BURDEN	*freighted with anger, carry resentment, indignation be heaped on X's shoulders*
COLD	*cold anger, icy rage, fury chill X*
SOUND	*muted anger, a note of irritation, crescendo of indignation, shrill fury*
BITTER	*bitter fury, acrid resentment, sour resentment*
MESSAGE/IDEA	*understand X's anger, explain anger, written fury, read resentment*
COSTLY	*pay for the irritation*
ENVIRONMENT	*atmosphere of resentment,, climate of resentment*

Note: *X* = emoter.

In the group of *primary metaphors* (Table 5.4), the target domain is not the emotion per se, but some salient aspects of the emotion – such as its INTENSITY, NEGATIVITY or THE BODY of the emoter – which are represented metaphorically too (as DEPTH, DARKNESS or CONTAINER).

Finally, we still observed a group of *infrequent/other metaphors* which includes mappings that were either not sufficiently robustly instantiated in the database for all the words, or were less conventionally referred to in the emotion metaphor literature (Table 5.5).

Results

Shared aspects in the metaphorization of ANGER in English, Russian and Spanish

Several findings suggest that the use of figurative language in talking about various ANGER concepts in the three languages bears considerable resemblance to one another. First of all, in order to have a general idea of how well the metaphorical representation of the entire ANGER domain coheres across the three languages, we computed an average ANGER profile per language (across all ANGER terms in that language for which metaphorical profiles were obtained). These average ANGER profiles were then correlated (Pearson). The correlations were found to be not only significant (*sig* < 0.000) but also very high, above 0.8 in all three cases (0.924, 0.921 and 0.852 for English vs Russian, English vs Spanish and Russian vs Spanish, respectively). Reasonably high correlations (ranging from 0.609 to 0.889, all significant at the 0.01 level) were also found for the best translation pairs across languages (e.g. English *indignation*, Spanish *indignación*, Russian *vozmuschenie*).

The three languages also cohered regarding the most frequent and productive metaphors in their average ANGER profiles (Table 5.6).[9]

Table 5.6 Relative frequency (%) and productivity indexes (*PIs*) of conceptual metaphors in the mean ANGER profiles in English, Russian and Spanish

Source domains	English		Russian		Spanish	
	%	PI	%	PI	%	PI
PHYSICAL ENTITY	24.25	618.13	18.79	352.55	30.3	681.93
LOCATION	13.81	40.16	14.41	25.73	6.58	31.51
PRESSURIZED FLUID	8.97	73.54	10.63	95.93	6.93	43.72
ANIMATE ENTITY	8.80	105.69	7.21	93.80	8.65	98.91
BODY IS CONTAINER	6.91	47.34	9.51	77.79	8.22	79.83
FIRE	3.81	16.7	3.77	17.08	3.27	13.55
ANIMAL	3.54	18.05	2.24	11.83	3.39	16.89
FORCE	3.25	21.41	4.86	24.88	6.12	61.01
ILLNESS	2.67	15.15	3.57	24.82	2.76	12.41
OPPONENT	2.61	10.22	2.23	11.02	3.78	21.13
MOVING ENTITY	2.48	10.36	2.64	10.43	2.73	10.2
FORCE OF NATURE	2.32	9.45	3.81	21.85	1.73	6.82
WEAPON	2.18	6.56	1.84	9.47	1.75	5.61
HOT FLUID	2.15	4.00	2.23	3.46	0.21	0.15
MORE IS UP	1.87	3.33	1.14	1.30	0.21	0.15
INSANITY	1.73	5.15	2.22	10.69	3.01	11.73
INTENSITY IS SCALE	1.39	4.10	0.80	1.21	0.79	1.31
INTENSITY IN DEPTH	0.81	0.41	0.50	0.28	0.82	0.54
INTENSITY IS HEAT	0.58	0.48	0.79	1.47	0.15	0.05
BAD IS DARK	0.34	0.27	0.22	0.25	0.25	0.21

Robust convergence was further observed in the internal structure of the ANGER categories in each of the languages. Hierarchical Cluster Analysis executed on the metaphorical profiles of all words yielded a two-cluster structure in each of the languages at the highest level of the dendrogram (Figures 5.1–5.3). The emerging clusters were highly comparable as well: in all three languages nouns denoting the most 'intense' ANGER varieties (such as English *rage* and *fury*, Russian *jarost* and *gnev* or Spanish *furia* and *ira*) invariably formed a cluster distinct from the remaining words.

Finally, strikingly similarities were also observed across languages for the metaphors underlying the obtained two-cluster solutions. The *t*-scores[10] of the metaphors for the words in each cluster (Table 5.7) show that the clusters with the most intense ANGER varieties were best characterized by conceptual metaphors highlighting the intensity (FIRE, FORCE OF NATURE), irrationality (INSANITY, BLINDNESS), uncontrollability (FORCE OF NATURE, EXPLOSION/BURST), aggression (ANIMAL), harm (DANGER/THREAT) and prominent visibility (EYES-CONTAINERS, FIRE) of the emotions. The remaining words were best characterized by a set of metaphors highlighting the idea of controllability, like the PHYSICAL ENTITY metaphor and many of its entailments (see Stefanowitsch, 2006; and Radden, 1998, on the relationship between the PHYSICAL OBJECT schema and controllability/manageability of emotions).

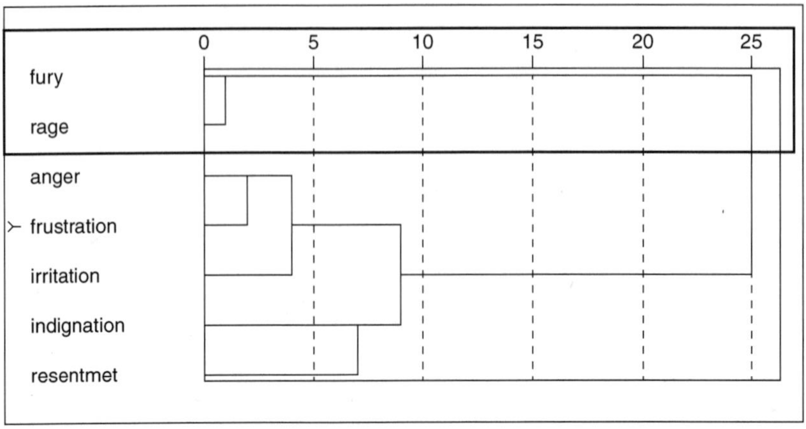

Figure 5.1 Hierarchical clustering of the metaphorical profiles of English ANGER words.

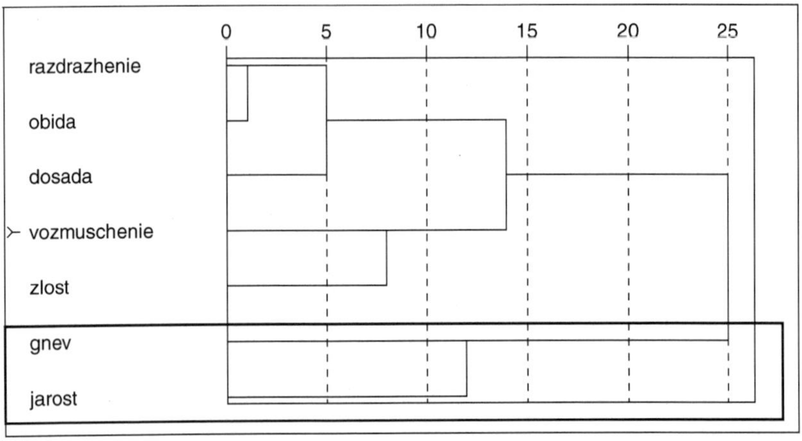

Figure 5.2 Hierarchical clustering of the metaphorical profiles of Russian ANGER words.

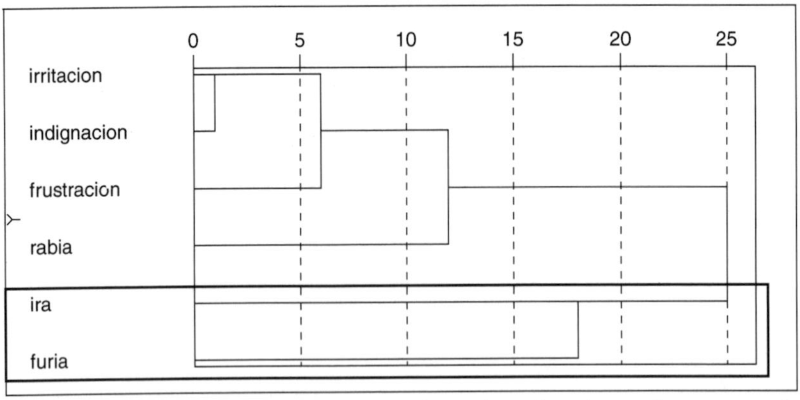

Figure 5.3 Hierarchical clustering of the metaphorical profiles of Spanish ANGER words.

Table 5.7 Most representative metaphors for each cluster of ANGER terms per language

Cluster 1: 'intense' ANGER words				**Cluster 2: other ANGER words**			
	En	Ru	Sp		En	Ru	Sp
FIRE	0.52#	1.21#	0.95#	ENTITY	1.23#	1.09#	1.21#
INSANITY	1.21#	0.65#	0.44#	visible/hidden object	0.88#	1.08#	0.87#
BLINDNESS	1.14#	0.91#	1.02#	physical entity	0.79#	0.32#	0.74#
ANIMAL	0.53#	0.72#	0.93#	consistency/texture	0.71#	0.78#	0.30#
DANGER/THREAT	0.41#	1.04#	1.12#	mixture	1.25#	0.65	0.67#
eyes are containers	0.94#	0.30#	0.96#	intensity is size	0.66#	0.84#	0.73#
FORCE OF NATURE	0.72#	0.07#	0.72#	intensity is quantity	1.37#	0.62#	0.45#
explosion/burst	0.72#	0.05#	0.79	possession	0.30	0.35	0.59#
				INTENSITY IS DEPTH	0.56#	0.57#	0.81#
				ILLNESS	0.62#	0.16#	0.78#
				ORGANISM	0.61#	0.88#	0.42#
				voice-container	0.72#	0.91#	0.44#

Notes: # indicates the cases when comparably high *t*-scores were also obtained for the different *types* of expressions instantiating the metaphor (rather than simply the tokens).

En = English, Ru = Russian, Sp = Spanish.

Language-specific aspects in the metaphorical representation of ANGER concepts

Language-specific aspects in the metaphorical representation of ANGER concepts in the three languages have been investigated through the prism of previously reported cultural divergences in the language groups at stake. The three specific predictions outlined earlier were tested using the notion of 'semantic focus' (see Soriano and Ogarkova, submitted, for an in-depth discussion). As suggested by several metaphor scholars (Kövecses, 2000b, pp. 40–6; Soriano, 2005, 2013; Ding, 2011, pp. 186–91), metaphors important for the characterization of an emotion concept can form meaningful groups highlighting semantic 'foci', or 'dimensions'. Among these semantic foci are intensity, evaluation (positive/negative), difficulty to cope, controllability or harm (Kövecses, 2000b; Soriano, 2005, 2013). The concept of semantic focus is valuable in two ways. First, it facilitates relating aspects of variation reported in cross-cultural research (such as appraisal, regulation or expression) to the CMT-based findings. Second, looking at differences in the distribution of metaphorical patterns in entire clusters of metaphors according to their focus (as opposed to individual metaphors) allows us to minimize the risk of misattribution of the observed differences to a specific case of metaphor when a more general pattern is at issue (cf. Stefanowitsch, 2004).

The procedure we followed in testing each of the predictions unfolded in three steps:

1. Identifying a set of metaphors highlighting the semantic focus related to the predicted area of variation (e.g. negativity [including harm/damage], regulation, expression and somatization).
2. Calculating the frequency of metaphorical patterns instantiating this semantic focus in a language (as a sum of the frequencies of the relevant individual metaphors across all terms in that language).

3. Cross-tabulating the obtained 'foci' frequencies against the number of all other metaphorical expressions observed in the language sample and running a series of Fisher exact tests. Significance levels were subjected to Bonferroni correction (i.e. divided by the number of tested semantic dimensions and their subtypes).

Cross-cultural differences in the appraisal of the negativity and harm/damage of anger

The perception of an emotion as positive or negative is a well-known characteristic of emotion concepts for both psychologists and laypeople (Fontaine et al., 2007; Russell, 2003). This bipolar dimension is commonly referred to as evaluation, pleasantness or valence. Although the valence of emotions has many readings (Solomon, 2006), most experts on emotions tend to agree that anger is essentially a negative emotion.

In our inventory (see Table 5.8), the source domains profiling negativity include the characterizations of anger in terms of physiological sicknesses or psychological disorders/impairments (ILLNESS and INSANITY), as enemies the emoter fights against (OPPONENT), or as WEAPONS used to harm others. Furthermore, FORCE OF NATURE and DANGER/THREAT both highlight the uncontrollable nature of anger, the powerlessness of the emoter in attempting to counteract/escape the emotion and its high potential for causing harm and damage to both the emoter and others. Also inherently negative are the conceptualizations of anger as an aggressive ANIMAL, a heavy BURDEN, an unpleasant taste (BITTER) and a COSTLY entity or phenomenon, depleting the resources of the person who experiences it and for the third parties who experience its consequences.

An appraisal of potential harm is a part of the general negativity of ANGER outlined earlier. This semantic focus is elaborated by metaphors in which the source domain invites the inference that the emotion can harm the person experiencing it and/or other people around. This focus is most prominent in four metaphors in our inventory (see Table 5.8), two of which highlight the harm/damage caused by the emotion to the emoter (ILLNESS and INSANITY), while the other two highlight the harm it inflicts on others (WEAPON and DANGER/THREAT).

Testing for the differences in the distribution of metaphorical patterns in these two semantic foci across the languages (Fisher exact) yields results that are entirely congruent with our expectations. As hypothesized, metaphors emphasizing the negativity of ANGER were more saliently represented in Russian and Spanish than in English (Table 5.9).

Table 5.8 Metaphors profiling Negativity and Harm/damage of anger

Semantic foci		Source domains
Negativity		FORCE OF NATURE, OPPONENT, WEAPON, ANIMAL, ILLNESS, INSANITY, BURDEN, BAD IS DARK, DANGER/THREAT, BITTER, COSTLY
Harm/damage	self	ILLNESS, INSANITY
	other	WEAPON, DANGER/THREAT

Table 5.9 Distribution of metaphorical patterns in the semantic foci of Negativity and Harm/damage (overall per language)

Semantic foci			En	Ru	Sp	$p_{en/ru}$	$p_{en/sp}$	$p_{sp/ru}$
Negativity		N	675	736	685			
		N_{total} -N	3,220	2,895	2,507	**	***	ns
Harm/damage	self	N	168	222	185			
		N_{total} -N	3,727	3,409	3,007	**	*	ns
	other	N	128	167	155			
		N_{total} -N	3,767	3,464	3,037	**	*	ns

Notes: N = number of metaphorical patterns (collapsing across words) in the metaphors of the focus; $p_{x/y}$ = p-value (Fisher exact) in comparing language X and language Y.
*/**/*** indicate $p < 0.05/0.01/0.001$ (corrected), respectively.
En = English, Ru = Russian, Sp = Spanish.

Table 5.10 Summary of comparisons between English vs Russian/Spanish translation equivalents where p-values (Fisher exact) reached the corrected levels of significance

Semantic foci		Ru and Sp		En	p
Negativity		gnev	>	anger	***
		ira			***
		rabia			*
		furia	>	fury	***
		obida	>	resentment	***
Harm/damage	self	zlost'	>	anger	***
		gnev			*
		ira			***
		rabia			***
		furia	>	fury	*
		jarost			***
	other	gnev	>	anger	***
		furia	>	fury	***

Notes: */**/*** indicate $p < 0.05/0.01/0.001$ (corrected), respectively.
En = English, Ru = Russian, Sp = Spanish. > shows the direction of the effect.

Further testing on the metaphorical profiles of typical translation equivalents of the English versus Russian and Spanish words (Table 5.10) shows that the tendency fares well for the subordinate-level concepts as well: again, for most translation pairs the English concepts are perceived as less negative and less harmful than their correlates in Russian and Spanish.

Cross-cultural differences in the regulation and expression of anger

Emotion expression and regulation are major emotion components (cf. Fontaine et al., 2007; Scherer, 2009) related to which emotions one has, when one has them and how

Table 5.11 Metaphors profiling expression and regulation of anger

Semantic foci		Source domains
Regulation	enhanced regulation	OPPONENT, COUNTERPRESSURE, PRESSURE, CONTENTION, COLD
	unrestrained anger	COMING OUT, EXPLOSION, EMOTER-ANIMAL
Expression	visible anger	EYES-CONTAINERS, FACE-CONTAINER, VOICE-CONTAINER, LIGHT
	'internalized' anger	HEART-CONTAINER, SOUL-CONTAINER, CHEST-CONTAINER, HEAD-CONTAINER, BODY-CONTAINER, INTENSITY IS DEPTH

one experiences, expresses and acts on these emotions (cf. McCrae and Gross, 2009, p. 337). As discussed earlier, cross-cultural psychology has mostly been concerned with how culture predicts variations in inhibiting or enhancing certain behavioural or physiological manifestations of emotion.

In our metaphor inventory, there is a set of metaphors inviting inferences about emotional regulation (Table 5.11). One group highlights 'enhanced regulation', where anger is described as an enemy to fight in pursuit of self-control, or as a fluid insistently seeking outlet from the emoter's body, while the person tries to keep it inside, preventing it from outpouring. Another metaphor in this group is COLDNESS: contrary to what might seem, expressions like the English *cold anger* or *anger glitters coldly in X's eyes* do not capture a lack of intensity (as if this conceptual metaphor were the opposite of INTENSITY IS HEAT), but rather highlight the idea that the expression of anger is controlled. Taken together, this group of metaphors promotes an understanding of anger as an emotion that is (or needs to be) controlled and regulated, rather than allowed to manifest itself.

In contrast to the 'enhanced regulation' group, other metaphors referring to behavioural regulation highlight the opposite pattern: unrestrained manifestation. Relevant source domains present anger as a fluid that pours, flows or surges out of the emoter's body (COMING OUT), or makes it out in a violent way (EXPLOSION/BURST). In the same group we find EMOTER IS AN ANIMAL, whereby the person experiencing anger is represented as displaying animal behaviour.

Emotional expression (manifestation) is captured by several anger metaphors (or subtypes) highlighting the visibility of the emotion. Again, two groups can be distinguished (see Table 5.11). In the first one, source domains make it explicit that anger is perceptible (visible), as it is metaphorically located in what can be loosely termed as 'outer body parts', that is, parts of the person involved in expressive behaviour, such as the eyes, the face and the voice; similarly, anger can be conceptualized as a SOURCE OF LIGHT, therefore also visible. In a second group of metaphors, anger is less visible or simply not perceptible ('internalized'). In these metaphors, anger is located in 'internal' body parts, such as inside the BODY, HEART, SOUL or CHEST.

Testing for differences in the distribution of metaphorical patterns profiling these types of emotion expression and regulation (Fisher exact) yields results largely congruent with our expectations (Table 5.12). The metaphors highlighting enhanced emotion regulation are more salient in the metaphorical representation of anger in Russian and Spanish as compared to English, while unrestrained regulation patterns are

Table 5.12 Distribution of metaphorical patterns in the metaphors highlighting expression and regulation of anger (overall per language)

			En	Ru	Sp	$p_{en/ru}$	$p_{en/sp}$	$p_{sp/ru}$
Regulation	enhanced	N	252	324	261			
		N_{total} - N	3,643	3,307	2,931	***	*	ns
	unrestrained anger	N	256	161	105			
		N_{total} - N	3,639	3,470	3,087	***	***	ns
Expression	visible	N	166	161	92			
		N_{total} - N	3,729	3,470	3,100	ns	*	**
	'internalized'	N	185	177	198			
		N_{total} - N	3,710	3,454	2,994	ns	***	ns

Notes: N = number of metaphorical patterns (collapsing across words) in the metaphors of the focus;
$p_{x/y}$ = p-value (Fisher exact) in comparing language X and language Y.
*/**/*** indicates $p < 0.05/0.01/0.001$ (corrected), respectively.
En = English, Ru = Russian, Sp=Spanish.

Table 5.13 Summary of comparisons between English vs Russian/Spanish translation equivalents where p-values (Fisher exact) reached the corrected levels of significance

Semantic foci		**Ru and Sp**		**En**	p
Regulation	enhanced	vozmuschenie	>	indignation	***
		ira		anger	*
		obida		resentment	***
	unrestrained anger	jarost'	<	rage	***
		furia		fury	***
		dosada		frustration	*
		frustración			**
		irritación		irritation	*
Expression	visible	jarost'	<	fury	***
		furia			**
		irritación		irritation	**
		rabia		anger	**
	'internalized'	ira	>	anger	*
		irritación		irritation	***
		dosada		frustration	*

Notes: */**/*** indicates $p < 0.05/0.01/0.001$ (corrected), respectively.
En = English, Ru = Russian, Sp = Spanish. > shows the direction of effect.

more prominent in English. A significant difference is also observed between English and Spanish in the number of patterns highlighting the visibility of the emotion. While metaphors profiling visibility are more prominent in English, metaphors profiling a more internalized view of anger are more salient in Spanish. The difference did not however reach significance in the Russian versus English contrast. The same pattern was also observed for many of the canonical translation pairs across languages (see Table 5.13).

Table 5.14 Distribution of metaphorical patterns in the metaphors highlighting somatization of ANGER in English and Russian

		English	Russian	$p_{en/ru}$
Somatization	N	813	924	
	N_{total} −N	3,082	2,707	***

Notes: N = number of metaphorical patterns (collapsing across words) in the metaphors of the focus. */**/*** indicate $p < 0.05/0.01/0.001$ (corrected) (Fisher exact), respectively.

Cross-cultural differences in the saliency of the somatic component of anger

Somatization in the psychological literature refers to the degree to which a connection between the body and the emotions is elaborated in a culture. In our inventory, the somatic link is best captured by four metaphors. The main one is the primary metaphor BODY IS A CONTAINER FOR EMOTION. Two more mappings are intrinsically related to it: ANGER IS A PRESSURIZED FLUID and ANGER IS A HOT FLUID IN THE BODY CONTAINER. Conceptualizing ANGER as a physical ailment (ILLNESS) completes the somatic cluster of metaphors.

The results of statistical analysis (Fisher exact) on the distribution of somatic metaphorical patterns in Russian and English provide a very robust confirmation of our expectation that metaphors emphasizing the somatic/physiological component of ANGER would be more saliently represented in Russian than in English (Table 5.14).

Conclusions

This chapter has reported the results of a large-scale corpus-based investigation of the metaphorical representation of salient ANGER concepts in three languages: English, Russian and Spanish. A new analytic method – the 'metaphorical profile' approach – has been applied to twenty thousand contexts of use of ANGER nouns in three representative language corpora and has yielded a metaphor inventory allowing for a very granular assessment of both the shared and the language-specific in the metaphorical representation of ANGER in the three languages.

Commonalities observed in our data include similarities in the most salient metaphors of the overall ANGER categories in each language, their internal hierarchical organization and the conceptual metaphors underlying this internal organization. Congruency has also been observed in the metaphorical profiles of cross-language translation equivalent terms. Taken together, these findings on languages from three different families contribute to the body of evidence highlighting the cross-cultural aspects of anger.

At the same time, the method also reveals several areas where variation, rather than similarity, surfaces prominently. These areas relate to cross-cultural divergences in appraisal, expression, regulation and the saliency of physiological aspects of anger, that is, components held to be crucial in providing structure to human emotion and its linguistic representation (cf. Fontaine et al., 2007, 2013; Scherer, 2009). Testing the metaphor data with the metaphorical profile approach against a set of hypotheses derived from prior psychological research on variation in these emotion components, we find that our predictions are robustly substantiated in almost all cases. First, negativity in ANGER is more saliently profiled in Russian and Spanish than in English. Second, controlled expression and enhanced regulation are more salient in Russian and Spanish than in English, while the unrestrained manifestation of the emotion is more salient in the latter. Finally, the somatic/physiological component of anger is more prominently represented in Russian than in English.

There are no studies without limitations, and ours is no exception. One of them is that, due to space constraints, only the most telling patterns emerging in the data analyses were reported, and some of the more fine-grained divergences were disregarded (such as, e.g., the – very few – metaphors underlying the ANGER clusters that were specific to one language only). Another limitation is that in the formulation of our hypotheses we had to rely on cross-cultural evidence about the entire anger category (which does not allow us to make more specific predictions about variation in the subtypes of this emotion across cultures). This was motivated by the current lack of psychological research on anger varieties in the cultural groups in question. However, with the very recent emergence of relevant psychological studies (Soriano et al., 2013), this shortcoming is likely to be remedied in our future research.

Notwithstanding these limitations, we hope to have demonstrated that the metaphorical profile approach can be a valuable addition to the current palette of CMT-based methods used in the study of universal versus culture-specific aspects of metaphor. The method has a potential for further applications too. For example, one could focus on the (dis)similarities in the metaphorical pattern distributions to characterize near-synonymous words within a language (like English *fury* and *rage*; cf. Ogarkova and Soriano, 2012), use the metaphorical profiles to identify the closest equivalent of a word in cases of uncertainty (like Spanish *rabia/ira* and Russian *zlost'/ gnev* for the English word *anger*; cf. Soriano et al., 2010) or apply the metaphorical profiles in the characterization of cognate words (like English *frustration* vs Spanish *frustraciyn*; cf. Soriano and Ogarkova, 2012). Finally, a promising area for future research is comparing the insight provided by the metaphorical profile approach with the insight afforded by other types of profiling in corpus-driven cognitive semantics.

Notes

1 This work was supported by grants from the Swiss Network for International Studies (SNIS) and the Swiss Center for Affective Sciences.

2 Following the conventions of Cognitive Linguistics, italics are used for specific terms in a language, and small capitals for concepts and conceptual metaphors.

3 Therefore, anger experiences resulting from insults, mutual ill feeling or offensive visual sights obtain distinct lexical designations in Cree (Watkins, 1938, pp. 284–5).

4 Individualism indexes of these three English-speaking countries are, according to Hofstede (2001), the highest across the cultures studied thus far (89, 90 and 91, respectively). Russia and Spain score much lower on individualism (39 and 51, respectively).

5 The specific procedure was as follows: all extracted KWIC concordance lines were scanned for potential candidates for metaphorical patterns; and for each concordance line we established if there was a contrast between the contextual meaning and the more basic/precise meaning of a lexical unit co-occurring with an emotion lexeme (e.g. in *wave of fury*, '*wave*' is clearly used metaphorically, since fury is not a fluid or even a physical entity). In questionable cases, we relied on dictionaries to identify a historically earlier meaning of a word (e.g. the word 'source' is originally related to 'sources of water', according to the *OED*). Importantly, contexts were used to set apart the same or similar expressions as belonging to the same or different metaphors (e.g. *anger rises* was classified as MORE IS UP, whereas *anger rises within X* was classified as an instance of the 'INCREASE/RISE' entailment in the metaphor ANGER IS A PRESSURIZED FLUID IN THE BODY-CONTAINER). In cases when an expression could be interpreted according to more than one metaphor and when context was not helpful, the highest level of the typology was used (e.g. *anger sweep over X* was classified as FORCE rather than FORCE OF NATURE). Finally, although in most cases each pattern was classified only once, in some cases two classifications were necessary, one for each subpart of the expression. For instance, the expression *anger sparkled in X's eyes* was classified twice: as (1) ANGER IS SOURCE OF LIGHT (*anger sparked*); and as (2) EYES ARE CONTAINERS FOR ANGER (*anger be in X's eyes*; cf. also Stefanowitsch [2006] for a similar observation on the sentence *his eyes were filled with anger*).

6 The *t*-values allow us to identify which variables (i.e. metaphors, in our case) discriminate well between clusters; thus they define the most essential properties of a cluster The *t*-values for any feature for a cluster *c* out of *n* clusters are computed as follows: mean within *c*-mean across all *n* clusters/standard deviation of the mean across all *n* clusters (see Divjak and Gries, 2006, 2008).

7 The actual formula to calculate the productivity index (PI) of a metaphor is given in Oster (2010, p. 749) as: $\frac{\text{N patterns}}{\text{Total N patterns}} * \frac{\text{N types}}{\text{Total N types}}$

8 Generic metaphors include what in the CMT tradition are called EVENT-STRUCTURE metaphorical systems, verbalizing 'notions like states, changes, processes, actions, causes, purposes, and means' (Lakoff, 1993, p. 220).

9 Due to space-related constraints, Table 5.6 includes the findings only on conceptual metaphors, excluding metaphor entailments and values for infrequent metaphors.

10 The *t*-scores we report (even the highest ones) may seem to be generally low, but this is the expected outcome, since we are dealing with same-category emotion nouns. Were the *t*-values higher, we would have doubted whether the words selected for the analyses actually referred to the same emotion category (ANGER).

References

Apresyan, V. and Apresyan, Y. (1993), 'Metafora v semanticheskon predstavlenii emotsij' (Metaphor in the Semantic Representation of Emotions). *Vopsory Yazykoznaniya*, 3: 27–35.

Athanasiadou, A. (1998), 'The Conceptualization of the Domain of FEAR in Modern Greek', in A. Athanasiadou and E. Tabaskowska (eds), *Speaking of Emotions: Conceptualization and Expression*, Berlin and New York: Mouton de Gruyter, pp. 227–52.

Bank of English. <http://www.collinslanguage.com/content-solutions/wordbanks> (accessed 31 December 2012).

Beger, A. and Jäkel, O. (2009), 'ANGER, LOVE and SADNESS Revisited: Differences in Emotion Metaphors between Experts and Laypersons in the Genre Psychology Guides', *metaphorik.de*, 16: 87–108.

British National Corpus. <http://www.natcorp.ox.ac.uk> (accessed 31 December 2012).

Chand, V. (2008), 'Fire and Hot Liquids: Anger in Hindi and English', in F. Boers, J. Darquennes, K. Kerremans and R. Temmerman (eds), *Multilingualism and Applied Comparative Linguistics (Volume II)*, Newcastle upon Tyne: Cambridge Scholars Publishing, pp. 2–24.

Corpus de Referencia del Español Actual. <http://www.corpus.rae.es/creanet.html> (accessed 31 December 2012).

Corpus del Español. <http://www.corpusdelespanol.org> (accessed 31 December 2012).

Ding, Y. (2011), 'Metaphors of SADNESS: Intraconceptual and Interconceptual Variation', unpublished PhD dissertation, The University of Hong Kong.

Divjak, D. and Gries, S. T. (2006), 'Ways of Trying in Russian. Clustering and Comparing Behavioral Profiles', *Corpus Linguistics and Linguistic Theory*, 2(1): 23–60.

—(2008), 'Clusters in the Mind? Converging Evidence from Near-Synonymy in Russian', *The Mental Lexicon*, 3(2): 188–213.

Emanatian, M. (1995), 'Metaphor and the Expression of Emotion: The Value of Cross-Cultural Perspectives', *Metaphor and Symbol*, 10(3): 163–82.

Fontaine, J., Scherer, K. R., Roesch, E. B. and Ellsworth, P. E. (2007), 'The World of Emotions Is Not Two-Dimensional', *Psychological Science*, 18: 1050–7.

Fontaine, J., Scherer, K. R. and Soriano, C. (eds) (2013), *Components of Emotional Meaning: A Sourcebook*, Oxford: Oxford University Press.

Geeraerts, D. and Grondelaers, S. (1995), 'Looking Back at Anger: Cultural Traditions and Metaphorical Patterns', in J. R. Taylor and R. E. MacLaury (eds), *Language and the Cognitive Construal of the World*, Berlin and New York: Mouton de Gruyter, pp. 153–79.

Gevaert, C. (2005), 'The ANGER IS HEAT Question: Detecting Cultural Influence on the Conceptualisation of Anger through Diachronic Corpus Analysis', in N. Delbecque, J. van der Auwera and D. Geeraerts (eds), *Perspectives on Variation*, Berlin and New York: Mouton de Gruyter, pp. 195–200.

Glynn, D. (2002), 'Love and Anger. The Grammatical Structure of Conceptual Metaphors', *Cognitive Approaches to Metaphor*, 36: 541–59.

Helfrich, H. (1999), 'Beyond the Dilemma of Cross-Cultural Psychology: Resolving the Tension Between Etic and Emic Approaches', *Culture and Psychology*, 5(2): 131–53.

Hofstede, G. (2001), *Culture's Consequences, Comparing Values, Behaviors, Institutions, and Organizations across Nations*, Thousand Oaks, CA: Sage Publications.

Hupka, R., Lenton, A. and Hutchison, K. (1999), 'Universal Development of Emotion Categories in Natural Language', *Journal of Personality and Social Psychology*, 77(2): 247–78.

Janda, L. and Solovyev, V. (2009), 'What Constructional Profiles Reveal About Synonymy: A Case Study of Russian Words for SADNESS and HAPPINESS', *Cognitive Linguistics*, 20(2): 367–93.

Kleinman, A. and Kleinman, J. (1985), 'Somatization: The Interconnections in Chinese Society among Culture, Depressive Experiences, and the Meanings of Pain', in A. Kleinman and B. Good (eds), *Culture and Depression: Studies in the Anthropology and Cross-Cultural Psychiatry of Affect and Disorder*, Berkeley: University of California Press, pp. 429–90.

Kövecses, Z. (1998), 'Are There Any Emotion-Specific Metaphors?', in A. Athanasiadou and E. Tabakowska (eds), *Speaking of Emotions: Conceptualization and Expression*, Berlin and New York: Mouton de Gruyter, pp. 127–51.

—(2000a), 'The Concept of Anger: Universal or Culture-Specific?', *Psychopathology*, 33: 159–70.

—(2000b), *Metaphor and Emotion*, Cambridge: Cambridge University Press.

Krupa, V. (1996), 'Nature Metaphors for Emotions in Maori Confronted with Other Languages', *Asian and African Studies*, 5(2): 132–7.

Lakoff, G. (1993), 'The Contemporary Theory of Metaphor', in A. Ortony, (ed.), *Metaphor and Thought*, Cambridge: Cambridge University Press, pp. 202–51.

Lakoff, G. and Johnson, M. (1980), *Metaphors We Live By*, Chicago: University of Chicago Press.

Lakoff, G. and Kövecses, Z. (1987), 'The Cognitive Model of Anger Inherent in American English', in D. Holland and N. Quinn (eds), *Cultural Models in Language and Thought*, Cambridge: Cambridge University Press, pp. 195–221.

Li, J., Wang, L., Fisher, K. (2004), 'The Organization of Chinese Shame Concepts', *Cognition and Emotion*, 18(6): 767–97.

Markus, H. R. and Kitayama, S. (1991), 'Culture and the Self: Implications for Cognition, Emotion and Motivation', *Psychological Review*, 98: 224–53.

Matsuki, K. (1995), 'Metaphors of Anger in Japanese', in J. R. Taylor and R. E. MacLaury (eds), *Language and the Cognitive Construal of the World*, Berlin and New York: Mouton de Gruyter, pp. 137–51.

McCrae, K. and Gross, J. (2009), 'Regulation of Emotion', in D. Sander and K. Scherer (eds), *Oxford Companion to Emotion and the Affective Sciences*, Oxford: Oxford University Press, pp. 337–9.

Mesquita, B. (2001), 'Emotions in Collectivist and Individualist Contexts', *Journal of Personality and Social Psychology*, 80: 68–74.

Nisbett, R. E., Peng, K., Choi, I. and Norenzayan, A. (2001), 'Culture and Systems of Thought: Holistic versus Analytic Cognition', *Psychological Review*, 108: 291–310.

Ogarkova, A. (2007), 'Green-Eyed Monsters: A Corpus-Based Study of the Concepts of ENVY and JEALOUSY in Modern English', *metaphorik.de*, 13: 87–147.

—(2013), 'Folk Emotion Concepts: Lexicalization of Emotional Experiences across Languages and Cultures', in J. Fontaine, K. R. Scherer and C. Soriano (eds), *Components of Emotional Meaning: A Sourcebook*, Oxford: Oxford University Press, pp. 46–62.

Ogarkova, A. and Soriano, C. (2012), 'Conceptual Metaphor in the Study of Emotion: Method and Applications', paper read at the workshop Emotion and Metaphor, Ancient and Modern: Interdisciplinary Perspectives, Geneva (Switzerland), 14 March.

Ogarkova, A., Soriano, C. and Lehr, C. (2012), 'Naming Feeling: Exploring the Equivalence of Emotion Terms in Five European Languages', *Lodz Studies in Language*, 24: 245–76.

Ortony, A. and Turner, T. (1990), 'What's Basic About Basic Emotions?', *Psychological Review*, 97: 315–31.

Oster, U. (2010), 'Using Corpus Methodology for Semantic and Pragmatic Analyses: What Can Corpora Tell Us About the Linguistic Expression of Emotions?', *Cognitive Linguistics*, 21(4): 727–63.

Pavlenko, A. (2002), 'Emotions and the Body in Russian and English', *Pragmatics and Cognition*, 10(1–2): 201–36.

Pragglejaz Group (2007), 'MIP: A Method for Identifying Metaphorically Used Words in Discourse', *Metaphor and Symbol*, 22(1): 1–39.

Radden, G. (1998), 'The Conceptulisation of Emotional Causality by Means of Prepositional Phrases', in A. Athanasiadou and E. Tabaskowska (eds), *Speaking of Emotions: Conceptulisation and Expression*, Berlin and New York: Mouton de Gruyter, pp. 273–94.

Rosch, E. (1978), 'Principles of Categorization', in E. Rosch and B. Lloyd (eds), *Cognition and Categorization*, Hillsdale, NJ: Lawrence Erlbaum Associates, pp. 27–48.

Russell, J. A. (2003), 'Core Affect and the Psychological Construction of Emotion', *Psychological Review*, 110(1): 145–72.

Russian National Corpus. <http://www.ruscorpora.ru> (accessed 31 December 2012).

Scherer, K. R. (2009), 'The Dynamic Architecture of Emotion: Evidence for the Component Process Model', *Cognition and Emotion*, 23(7): 1307–51.

Shaver, P. R., Murdaya, U. and Frailey, R. C. (2001), 'Structure of the Indonesian Emotion Lexicon', *Asian Journal of Social Psychology*, 4: 201–24.

Shaver, P. R., Schwartz, J., Kirson, D. and O'Connor, C. (1987), 'Emotion Knowledge: Further Exploration of a Prototype Approach', *Journal of Personality and Social Psychology*, 52: 1061–86.

Shiroma, P. R. and Alarcon, R. D. (2011), 'Time for Healing: Somatization among Chronically Mentally Ill Immigrants', *Journal of Cultural Diversity*, 18(1). 3–7.

Solomon, R. C. (2006), *Not Passion's Slave*, Oxford: Oxford University Press.

Soriano, C. (2005), 'The Conceptualization of Anger in English and Spanish: A Cognitive Approach', unpublished PhD dissertation, University of Murcia.

—(2013), 'Conceptual Metaphors and the GRID Approach in the Study of Anger in English and Spanish', in J. Fontaine, K. R. Scherer and C. Soriano (eds), *Components of Emotional Meaning: A Sourcebook*, Oxford: Oxford University Press, pp. 410–24.

Soriano, C., Fontaine, J., Ogarkova, A., Mejia, C., Volkova, Y., Ionova, S. and Shakhovskyy, V. (2013), 'Semantic Types of Anger in Spanish and Russian', in J. Fontaine, K. R. Scherer and C. Soriano (eds), *Components of Emotional Meaning: A Sourcebook*, Oxford: Oxford University Press, pp. 339–52.

Soriano, C. and Ogarkova, A. (2012), 'Frustration in Europe: Cultural Specificity in the Meaning of Emotion Cognates', paper read at 35th LAUD Symposium, Koblenz-Landau, 26–29 March.

—(Submitted). 'Metaphorical Profile Analysis in the Study of Anger: A New Method and a New Model.'

Soriano, C., Ogarkova, A. and Lehr, C. (2010), 'Types of Anger and Their Metaphors. MPA in English, German, Spanish and Russian', paper read at the 8th Researching and Applying Metaphor Conference (RaAM), Amsterdam, 30 June–3 July.

Stefanowitsch, A. (2004), 'HAPPINESS in English and German: A Metaphorical-Pattern Analysis', in M. Achard and S. Kemmer (eds), *Language, Culture, and Mind*, Stanford: University of Stanford, pp. 137–49.

—(2006), 'Words and Their Metaphors. A Corpus-Based Approach', in A. Stefanowitsch and S. Gries (eds), *Corpus-Based Approaches to Metaphor and Metonymy*, Berlin and New York: Mouton de Gruyter, pp. 61–105.

Taylor, J. R. and Mbense, T. G. (1998), 'Red Dogs and Rotten Mealies: How Zulus Talk about Anger', in A. Athanasiadou and E. Tabakowska (eds), *Speaking of Emotions: Conceptualisation and Expression*, Berlin and New York: Mouton de Gruyter, pp. 191–226.

Tower, R. K., Kelly, C. and Richards, A. (1997), 'Individualism, Collectivism and Reward Allocation: A Cross-Cultural Study in Russia and Britain', *Journal of Social Psychology*, 36: 331–45.

Triandis, H. C. (2001), 'Individualism-Collectivism and Personality'. *Journal of Personality*, 69(6): 907–24.

Triandis, H. C. and Gelfand, M. J. (1998), 'Converging Measurement of Horizontal and Vertical Individualism and Collectivism', *Journal of Personality and Social Psychology*, 74: 118–28.

Voronov, M. and Singer, J. A. (2002), 'The Myth of Individualism-Collectivism: A Critical Review', *The Journal of Social Psychology*, 142(4): 461–80.

Watkins, E. A. (1938), *A Dictionary of the Cree Language*, Toronto: Church of England in Canada.

Wierzbicka, A. (1992), *Semantics, Cognition and Culture: Universal Human Concepts in Culture-Specific Configurations*, Oxford: Oxford University Press.

Yu, N. (1995), 'Metaphorical Expressions of Anger and Happiness in English and Chinese', *Metaphor and Symbolic Activity*, 10(2): 59–92.

—(1998), *The Contemporary Theory of Metaphor in Chinese: A Perspective from Chinese*, Amsterdam: John Benjamins.

6

Conceptual Metaphor in Intercultural Communication between Speakers of Aboriginal English and Australian English

Farzad Sharifian[1]

Introduction

Miscommunication between speakers of Australian Aboriginal English and Australian English has disadvantaged the former in a variety of contexts ranging from the school and hospital to the courtroom (e.g. Christie and Harris, 1985; Eades, 1996, 2000; Kearins, 1985; Lowell and Devlin, 1998; Malcolm, 1979, 1982; Mobbs, 1986; Sharifian, 2001; Sharifian et al., 2004). For example, Aboriginal English is not recognized by many educators as a legitimate variety of English, but is merely treated as an incorrect form of the language. Lack of recognition of Aboriginal English and its conceptual system by the educational institutions often lets intercultural miscommunication between Aboriginal students and non-Aboriginal educators and students go unnoticed. The discomfort this causes for the students leads to a sizeable number dropping out from school.

Cass et al. (2002) also report significant miscommunication between Aboriginal patients and their medical, nursing and allied professional carers, which is seriously detrimental to the provision of health services to Aboriginal people. They report linguistic and cultural distance as one of the main sources of this observed miscommunication. In the area of legal justice, Eades's (2007) analysis has revealed a number of cases of miscommunication, with serious damaging legal consequences for Aboriginal speakers, between Aboriginal and non-Aboriginal people in the courts. This miscommunication systematically occurs due to differences between the two varieties of English, which vary in terms of their phonological, grammatical, pragmatic and discourse features. Eades (2007, p. 320) maintains that '[g]iven that the language of the law is general Australian English, and that many non-Aboriginal Australians are unaware of differences between general Australian English and Aboriginal English, Aboriginal English speakers are clearly linguistically disadvantaged in legal contexts'. Research has revealed that even everyday words such as 'home' and 'family' are likely to evoke contrasting cultural meanings among Aboriginal and non-Aboriginal Australians (e.g. Sharifian, 2005).

This chapter reveals how the differences between Aboriginal English and Australian English can be significantly accounted for using the framework of Cultural Linguistics, in particular the notion of *conceptual metaphor*. Presenting examples from Aboriginal English the chapter demonstrates that metaphor in Aboriginal English can be viewed on a continuum ranging from fundamental metaphors that reflect Aboriginal worldview to cases where the metaphor appears to be just a figurative use of language. In other words, at one end of the continuum, the conceptual metaphor involved provides a cognitive framework, a frame of thought, and at the other end, it has only a rhetorical function. As a preamble to the analysis of the examples of metaphor in Aboriginal English, the following section presents an overview of the theoretical framework adopted in this study and a discussion of research on metaphor.

Cultural Linguistics and metaphor research

Cultural Linguistics is a sub-branch of Linguistics with a multidisciplinary origin that explores the relationship among language, culture and conceptualization (Palmer, 1996; Sharifian and Palmer, 2007; Sharifian, 2011, 2013, forthcoming). It shares the view with cognitive linguistics that meaning is conceptualization but places emphasis on the cultural construction of conceptualization. Cultural Linguistics employs analytical tools such as 'cultural schema', 'cultural category' and 'cultural-conceptual' metaphor to explore features of language that have a cultural basis. I refer to these notions collectively as *cultural conceptualizations* (Sharifian, 2003, 2008, 2011).

The meanings of many lexical items of human languages lend themselves best to cognitive schemas that are abstracted from cultural experiences. Also, many lexical items serve as labels for categories that are culturally established. For example, we categorize events, based on their function, associated behaviour and material culture, as 'wedding', 'funeral', 'house warming' and so on. These event categories are usually defined culturally and have prototypes that may differ from one culture to another. But we also have knowledge about various aspects of these events, such as knowledge of the expected procedures, people's roles and norms about sub-events. This type of knowledge is always culturally constructed and is captured in cognitive schemas that speakers draw on when engaged in or thinking about these events.

An important class of conceptualization, which is central to both cognitive linguistics and Cultural Linguistics, is conceptual metaphor. The seminal work on conceptual metaphor within cognitive linguistics by Lakoff and Johnson (1980) characterized metaphor as fundamental to human thought and action, rather than simply a figure of speech. Lakoff and Johnson argue that our 'ordinary conceptual system, in terms of which we both think and act, is fundamentally metaphorical in nature' (p. 545). They also argue that since our conceptual system structures how we perceive the world, 'the way we think, what we experience, and what we do every day is very much a matter of metaphor' (p. 545).

If language is closely linked to our conceptual system, it serves as a laboratory for exploring our conceptualizations including conceptual metaphors. One of the examples that Lakoff and Johnson (1980, p. 456) give is the conceptual metaphor of TIME IS MONEY, reflected in expressions such as 'You're wasting my time', 'You need to budget your time' and 'Do you have much time left?' In recent years, many studies have shown how a close analysis of language use can highlight underlying conceptual metaphors (e.g. Cameron and Low, 1999; Cameron and Maslen, 2010; Yu, 2009a,b). The theoretical framework of conceptual metaphor has been productively used in several areas, including the analysis of political discourse (e.g. Musolff, 2004, 2010).

Conceptual metaphor is also central to Cultural Linguistics, in that it focuses on exploring the cultural basis of conceptual metaphor, and its important implications for the cognitive nature of conceptual metaphor (e.g. Kovecses, 2005; Sharifian et al., 2008; Yu, 2009a,b; see also Quinn, 1991, for a similar interest in cognitive anthropology). As Yu (2003, p. 14) maintains, 'the relation between metaphor, body, and culture is extremely intricate, with all of them mingled together, and each of them penetrating the others, giving rise to a colourful spectrum of cognition'. Chapters in Sharifian et al. (2008) explore cultural traditions that have given rise to conceptual metaphors of internal body organs, such as that of THE HEART AS THE SEAT OF EMOTIONS, showing that the links between particular organs and their associated emotions are not universal. In Indonesian, for instance, it is *hati* (the liver) that is associated with love (Siahaan, 2008). Siahaan traces back such conceptualizations to the ritual of animal sacrifice, especially the interpretation of the liver organ, known as 'liver divination', which was practised in ancient Indonesia. Ning Yu (2009b) explores the origin of the conceptualization of *xin* (heart) in ancient Chinese philosophy and traditional Chinese medicine. According to the Chinese conceptualization, the heart is traditionally believed to be the central faculty of cognition as well as being the physiological centre of the human being, and even, in a cosmic view, the 'mirror of the universe'. In other words, the heart is seen as governing the body, including the brain. Yu reveals how this conceptualization is still widely manifested in the Chinese language today.

The approach of Cultural Linguistics has also been applied to explore the conceptual basis of Aboriginal English (e.g. Malcolm and Rochecouste, 2000; Malcolm and Sharifian, 2005; Sharifian, 2006). In this chapter, I focus on the exploration of conceptual metaphor in Aboriginal English and discuss how unfamiliarity with culturally constructed metaphor in Aboriginal English often leads to miscommunication between speakers of Aboriginal English and speakers of non-Aboriginal English. But first, a description of Aboriginal English is in order.

Aboriginal English

'Aboriginal English' collectively refers to the indigenized varieties of English spoken by Aboriginal people in Australia (e.g. Arthur, 1996; Eades, 1991, 1995; Harkins, 1990, 2000; Kaldor and Malcolm, 1991; Malcolm, 1994a,b). Although Aboriginal people come from a variety of cultural-linguistic backgrounds, with a fair level of generalization it is possible to refer collectively to the varieties of English that they speak as 'Aboriginal English'. This is apparent, in particular, in the similarities in the conceptual systems and the worldviews that characterize most varieties of English spoken by Aboriginal people. These varieties came into existence as a result of various contact-induced linguistic processes such as pidginization, depidginization, creolization and decreolization based on the interaction between English and Aboriginal languages. However, varieties of Aboriginal English did not develop solely due to the need for a lingua franca between Aboriginal people and European settlers. Aboriginal people who were displaced by Europeans from their original settlement areas, and who collectively spoke more than 250 different languages, needed a lingua franca to communicate with each other. Thus, Aboriginal English is not a Western variety, but as Eades (1991, p. 57) notes, it 'is a distinctive dialect of English which reflects, maintains and continually creates Aboriginal culture and identity'. Malcolm (2001, p. 217) also observes that 'AbE [Aboriginal English] is a symbol of cultural maintenance; it is the adopted code of a surviving culture'.

In terms of syntax, Aboriginal English is more variable than Australian English (Malcolm, 2001, 2004). It has been noted that less structured varieties of Aboriginal English share many features with creoles and substrate languages (Dixon, 1980; Harkins, 1990). Aboriginal English has certain distinctive pragmatic norms which reflect Aboriginal cultural systems. Eades (e.g. 1982, 1988, 1992, 1993, 1994, 1995, 1996, 2000) has observed that Aboriginal speakers rely on rather indirect strategies for seeking information whereas Anglo-Australians usually try to elicit information in a direct and repeated manner. Eades has also observed that silence achieves certain functions for Aboriginal speakers, which are unfamiliar to non-Aboriginal speakers, who can easily interpret silence as non-compliance. Such cultural differences in communication style have had serious implications for legal cases involving allegations of murder and of deprivation of liberty by police officers (Eades, 1995, 1996, 2000).

Recent research on semantic aspects of Aboriginal English has adopted a cultural-conceptual approach that largely draws on Cultural Linguistics. It has, for example, been observed that even everyday words such as 'family', 'home' and 'sorry' evoke cultural schemas and categories among Aboriginal English speakers that generally characterize Aboriginal cultural experiences (Malcolm and Sharifian, 2002; Sharifian, 2005). The word 'family', for instance, is associated with categories in Aboriginal English that move far beyond what is described as the 'nuclear' family in Anglo-Australian culture. A person who comes into frequent contact with an Aboriginal person may be referred to using a kinship term such as 'brother' or 'cousin' or 'cousin brother' (Malcolm and Sharifian, 2007, p. 381). The word 'mum' may also be used to refer to people who are referred to as 'aunt' in Anglo-Australian culture. Such usage of kin terms does not stop at the level of categorization but usually evokes schemas associated with certain rights and obligations between those involved. The word 'home' in Aboriginal English evokes categories that are usually based far more on family relationships than the possession of a building by the nuclear family. For instance, Aboriginal English speakers may refer to their grandparents' place as 'home'. Unfamiliarity with the schemas that inform Aboriginal English discourse has often led to miscommunication that has disadvantaged Aboriginal speakers (e.g. Sharifian, 2001; Sharifian et al., 2004; Sharifian et al., 2005).

Metaphor in Aboriginal English

Aboriginal conceptualizations of the land

In this section, I use examples from Aboriginal English to show how conceptual metaphor may be viewed along a continuum in terms of its cognitive and linguistic status/processing. At one end of the continuum what appears to be rhetorical from the perspective of an outsider to Aboriginal English is actually a culturally constructed conceptualization originating from the Aboriginal worldview. Thus, to the speaker, such conceptualizations are real beliefs about the world and life and as such are understood by speakers as literal, although from the perspective of an outsider to the culture they are likely to be viewed as cases of conceptual metaphor. That is, from the *etic* perspective, such conceptualizations appear as conceptual metaphor, while from the *emic* perspective, they are part of the speaker's real worldview, with no element of figure of speech. This class of conceptualizations, which may be termed *fundamental metaphors*, includes religious metaphors (e.g. Feyaerts, 2003). A more neutral, and therefore more appropriate, term to use in such cases is the umbrella term of Cultural Linguistics: *cultural conceptualization* (Sharifian, 2011).

As an example of fundamental metaphors, in Aboriginal English a speaker may state that 'This land is me'. This seemingly rhetorical statement, particularly from a non-Aboriginal perspective, in fact dwells in the Aboriginal conceptualization of ANCESTOR BEINGS ARE PART OF THE LAND and I AM PART OF ANCESTOR BEINGS, with the resulting conceptualization of I AM PART OF THE LAND. According to the worldview of the Dreamtime, Ancestor Beings returned to the land in the form of stones, trees and the like after the Creation. Therefore they are now considered to be part of the land, and since according to the same worldview, an Aboriginal person is an extension of his/her Ancestor Beings, the land itself is conceptualized as embodying the person. The following excerpt from an Aboriginal English speaker further elaborates on Aboriginal conceptualizations of the land:

(1) You see my people see land ownership as being totally different to the English way of ownership because we, ours used to be really the land owns us and it still *is* that to us. You know the land ah, grows all of us up and it really does, no human is older than the land itself it just isn't and no living marsupial is as old as the land itself. Everything that's been and gone with life in the flesh has died but the land is still here. (Rob Randall[2] a Yankunytjatjara Elder, 2012)

As reflected earlier, the Aboriginal conceptualization of the relationship between people and the land is that of 'the land owns us' and 'the land grows us up'. The general underlying conceptualization here is that of LAND AS PROGENITOR, whereas the dominant understanding from the perspective of Anglo-Australian is rather 'land is a possession that can be bought and sold'. Another closely related Aboriginal conceptualization of the land is that of LAND AS A HUMAN BEING, which is reflected in the following excerpt from an Aboriginal Elder:

(2) If you look at the land and you watch the land talk to you boy you know you won't starve, you won't go thirsty, you know it's there to show you. It's talking to you all the time, every time a blossom blooms, every time different coloration and that come on your plants and your trees and that you look at it and you start to understand it and you say 'now what's it doing that for' 'why is it goin' like that' and then you watch it next time it comes around and then and then the penny drops you know then 'oh so that's what that's happened' there with that see so it's things like this that people have got to start to understand about, um about our people and their lifestyle. (Max 'Duramunmun' Harrison, 2009)[3]

It can be seen that in this example the speaker characterizes the land as being able to talk to people and care for them and provide for them. The land does this, for example, by giving people clues using signals through natural events, such as blooming blossoms and colour changes in plants. This kind of characterization of the land is consistent with the conceptualization of land as close kin, in particular as a mother or father.

In the Aboriginal worldview, land also enjoys a sacred position and is strongly associated with Aboriginal spirituality, a topic that has long been a matter of significant debate and conflict between Aboriginal and non-Aboriginal speakers. This is best reflected in the following excerpt from the same interview by the aforementioned Elder:

(3) Um if we said that that place was sacred over there you know across Uluru. If I sat down I was tellin' a lot of politicians or someone you can't develop over there because that place is sacred over there and the first thing that they would do, then they would go and they would look to see what was sacred about it or they would try and bring the sacredness down, and you know they'd say 'well so what's sacred about it?' You know but they can't understand the energy or the ceremonies that went into the land and the singing that went into the land, into the rocks ah into the trees ah they cannot understand that and ah and so they've got to look to find some to identify something there. They're trying to look for that sacredness thing, you can't see sacredness. (Max 'Duramunmun' Harrison, 2009, ibid.)

This excerpt clearly reflects miscommunication between Aboriginal and non-Aboriginal speakers regarding 'the sacredness of the land'. The sacredness that is referred to in this excerpt is associated with many aspects of the environment, such as rocks, hills, lakes, trees and the like, for Aboriginal people. This spirituality is rooted in the worldview of Aboriginal people, according to which, as mentioned before, Ancestor Beings during the Dreamtime created the land, the people and the animals and at the end of their journey themselves turned into topographical features (Charlesworth et al., 1990). Thus the underlying cultural conceptualization here is that Ancestor Spirits are part of the land, which is why the land is so sacred to Aboriginal people.

Aboriginal conceptualizations of rain

The spirituality that characterizes Aboriginal English, and is often the source of miscommunication between Aboriginal and non-Aboriginal speakers, is not limited to the domain of land, but influences many other aspects of the speaker's language. Words such as 'sing', 'smoke', 'medicine', 'rain' and so on may be used to refer to Aboriginal spiritual experiences that are part of their cultural conceptualizations and are largely unfamiliar to non-Aboriginal speakers (Sharifian, 2010). The following is an excerpt from a conversation between the author and an Aboriginal English speaker[4] where the word 'rain' is used to refer to an Aboriginal conceptualization:

(4) C: same like when it's death or funeral times when it's burial, might not, might be good, and then this cloud comes and it's the rain it's called the midjal, it rain, it's a sad rain, it's crying rain, . . . the old fallas crying for umm not crying for the falla who's gone cause they're with them, they're crying for the fallas that're there, they're cryin' sad for watchin' all the people mob cryin', you know, and it's a soft rain, a different rain.

It can be seen that the speaker describes the rain as 'the old fallas crying' for survivors of the person who is deceased. Here 'the old fallas' refers to the spirits of the ancestors and, as reflected in the text, the deceased person is now believed to be with the ancestors. According to the speaker, the spirits of her ancestors are crying because they are sad, watching people mourning and crying for the deceased. It is to be noted that although from the outsider perspective conceptualization of ANCESTOR SPIRITS' TEARS AS RAIN appears metaphoric, for the speaker it is an indisputable reality that is part of her worldview. Another use of the word 'rain' by the same speaker to refer to an Aboriginal conceptualization is as follows:

(5) that, that rain, the rain 'ere, the angry rain, das when some, you done somethin' or someone's done somethin', that did bad an it's like it's not rainin' and it comes and it's like bangin', loud, sort of lashin', makes the trees go shshsht, you know, hitti' out that sort of rain an' it can come out like that but then you find out after someone doin' somethin', and you go th'as what it was . . .

Here the speaker identifies a particular type of rain as 'angry rain' and states that it falls when someone has done something wrong, described as 'someone doin' something'. When asked to elaborate on this expression the speaker continued as follows:

(6) someone, if it's not me, someone done something shouldna, something, something, could be went out somewhere where they should've not went, might have went out to [name of a place] might've went to [name of a place], and coming back an then next minute it's starts raining but it's a wind an it's got the wind with it, that's Warra rain that is, tha's Warra baad rain you know, that's bad thing, someone savage stirred up them all them fallas now.

The underlying cultural conceptualization here is THE ANCESTOR SPIRITS' ANGER AS RAIN. This anger is explained in the excerpt here as the result of breaking a cultural taboo, such as someone visiting a forbidden place, for example, the 'country' or the sacred place of another cultural group, without their permission. Again, such conceptualizations would appear to be rhetorical to non-Aboriginal speakers, but they are intended literally by the speaker and form part of the Aboriginal worldview. From a technical perspective, the expressions discussed so far involve conceptual mapping from the domains of land and rain to the domains of ancestors and ancestors' emotions. However, these mappings are part of the Aboriginal worldview and spirituality, which are unfamiliar to many non-Aboriginal speakers, leading to miscommunication with Aboriginal speakers.

Aboriginal conceptualizations of medicine

A set of Aboriginal conceptualizations that reveal mapping from a Western domain to an Aboriginal domain is that of HEALING AS MEDICINE. The word 'medicine' can be used in Aboriginal English to mean 'spiritual power' (Arthur, 1996, p. 46). The following is an example of the use of the 'medicine' in this sense in Aboriginal English:

(7) That when . . . my mum was real crook and she . . ., she said, 'I woke up an it was still in my mouth . . . the taste of all the medicine cause they come an' give me some medicine last night an' she always tells us that you can't move . . . an' you wanna sing out an say just . . . sorta try an' relax. That happened to me lotta times I was about twelve'.

In this recount the speaker remembers that once her mother was ill and she told them the next morning that 'they' went to her and gave her some 'medicine' she could still taste. She also describes the feeling that results from the medicine as wanting to shout and then forcing oneself to relax. Without having the requisite schema, the audience of the recount given earlier would be likely to think that 'they' refers to medical professionals who visited the mother after hours and gave her syrup or a tablet. However, further discussion with the speaker made it clear that her mother was referring to ancestor beings using their healing power to treat her illness. Again, unfamiliarity with cultural schemas that underlie the use of instances of discourse such as the one given here often causes miscommunication between Aboriginal and non-Aboriginal speakers.

Associated with this conceptual metaphor is the use of 'doctor' or 'doctor man' or 'medicine man' to refer to 'a spiritually powerful person whose powers include healing' (Arthur, 1996, p. 25). Elkin (1977, p. xx) observes that medicine men are 'magical practitioners, for they cure some sicknesses by magical rituals and spells. In many parts they are sorcerers as well; they know how to, and may, insert evil magic, extract "human fat", or cause the soul to leave the victim's body, bringing about sickness and death'. The following excerpt reveals how the use of the word 'doctor' can lead to miscommunication between an Aboriginal English speaker and a non-Aboriginal English one.

(8) Aboriginal English speaker: There's no doctor man 'round 'ere anymore.
Non-Aboriginal English speaker: Not even a clinic or something?

It is to be noted here that while the domain of healing for Aboriginal speakers is associated with their worldview, the mapping from the domain of 'medicine' to 'healing' appears to be less of an unalienable tenet of the speaker's worldview than the connections of the domain of kinship and the domain of land. In other words, the speaker is likely to be aware of the culturally relative nature of such usage, as they would be familiar with the Western domain and the Aboriginal domain.

Nature metaphor and creative metaphor in Aboriginal English

Moving along the continuum, there are expressions in Aboriginal English that reflect mappings based on Aboriginal conceptualizations of certain aspects of nature, such as that of the MOON AS A LIVING BEING, reflected in expressions such as 'when the moon jumps up'. At the most rhetorical end of the spectrum Aboriginal English includes expressions that reveal creative conceptual mappings that are understood as metaphorical by the speaker, such as using 'riding the white horse' to refer to kneading dough when making damper.

Another example of this kind of metaphor is the use of the expression 'foot Falcon' to mean 'travelling on foot, especially long distances'. The following is an example of the use of this expression:

(9) Aboriginal English speaker: We footfalcon to Carnarvon.
Non-Aboriginalspeaker: Do you have a falcon?
AboriginalEnglishspeaker: (laughing) You got one too.
Non-Aboriginalspeaker: me? (puzzled)
AboriginalEnglishspeaker: *Yeah.*

The use of the word 'Falcon', to refer to the make of a car, here implies a long distance trip. As such distances are usually travelled by car, especially by non-Aboriginal people, it also ironically reflects the fact that the speaker(s) cannot afford any other kind of Falcon. This sort of playful expression can, as this interaction shows, also lead to miscommunication between Aboriginal and non-Aboriginal speakers.

Concluding remarks

Analysing a number of examples, this chapter shows how unfamiliarity with Aboriginal English, in particular its conceptual system, has led to miscommunication between speakers of Aboriginal English and other non-Aboriginal Australians. This continues to disadvantage Aboriginal English speakers in various contexts in which they have to communicate with non-Aboriginal people, from the classroom to the courtroom. It is hoped that the analysis of data from Aboriginal English from the perspective of Cultural Linguistics will provide awareness and recognition of the conceptual basis of Aboriginal English, leading to a reduction in the disadvantage that Aboriginal English speakers are likely to experience in various contexts.

We now return to the observation made at the beginning of this chapter – that metaphor can be viewed along a continuum, with fundamental metaphors that reflect Aboriginal worldview at one end to cases where the metaphor appears to be a figure of speech at the other. In summary, conceptualizations such as ANCESTOR SPIRITS AS BEING PART OF THE LAND and ANCESTOR SPIRITS' EMOTIONS AS RAIN do not appear metaphoric from the emic perspective, but rather from the worldview of the speakers. As mentioned before, in such cases the conceptualization provides a cognitive frame for making sense and organizing their cultural experiences. Thus, the function of the observed conceptualization is schematic rather than metaphoric. It provides the speaker with a cultural schema that can constitute the speaker's world. There are also metaphors in Aboriginal English that reflect cross-cultural mapping from Western domains of experience, such as that of medicine, to Aboriginal cultural domains, such as that of healing. It is likely that in such cases the speaker here is more conscious of the mapping across the two domains, since they have access to both in the normal course of their life. At the other end of the continuum, there are expressions in Aboriginal English that reflect creative conceptual mappings that are rather playfully constructed.

In general, the observations made in this chapter suggest that explorations of the cultural basis of conceptual metaphor have significant implications for conceptual metaphor theory. For example, such explorations reveal that there are several dimensions to conceptual metaphors. They include the degree to which what appears to be metaphorical/rhetorical is based on cultural conceptualizations that constitute the speaker's worldview, the degree to which a conceptual mapping is the result of cross-cultural mapping (HEALING AS MEDICINE) and the degree to which speakers are conscious of the cross-domain mapping involved in an expression. Explorations of these questions using data from different languages and language varieties can contribute to a deeper understanding of the interplay among culture, conceptualization and human cognitive processing.

Notes

1 The author received financial support from Australian Research Council twice throughout the conduct of the research that forms part of this chapter (ARC DP and Australian Postdoctoral Fellowship [project number DP0343282], and ARC DP [project number DP0877310]).

2 <http://www.youtube.com/watch?v=w0sWIVR1hXw&feature=relmfu>

3 <http://www.youtube.com/watch?v=06UpQQQ7cBM>

4 This excerpt and the next three formed part of the data collected for Sharifian (2010). The data were collected in the form of naturalistic conversations between the author and an Aboriginal English speaker.

References

Arthur, J. (1996), *Aboriginal English: A Cultural Study*, Melbourne: Oxford University Press.

Cameron, L. and Low, G. (eds) (1999), *Researching and Applying Metaphor*, Cambridge: Cambridge University Press.

Cameron, L. and Maslen, R. (eds) (2010), *Metaphor Analysis: Research Practice in Applied Linguistics, Social Sciences and the Humanities*, London: Equinox.
Cass, A., Lowell, A., Christie, M., Snelling, P. L., Flack, M., Marrnganyin, B. and Brown, A. (2002), 'Sharing the True Stories: Improving Communication between Aboriginal Patients and Healthcare Workers', *The Medical Journal of Australia*, 176(10): 466–70.
Charlesworth, M., Kimber, R. and Wallace, N. (1990), *Ancestor Spirits: Aspects of Australian Aboriginal Life and Spirituality*, Geelong: Deakin University Press.
Christie, M. and Harris, S. (1985), 'Communication Breakdown in the Aboriginal Classroom', in J. B. Pride (ed.), *Cross-Cultural Encounters: Communication and Miscommunication*, Melbourne: River Seine, pp. 81–90.
Dixon, R. M. W. (1980), *The Languages of Australia*, Cambridge: Cambridge University Press.
Eades, D. (1982), 'You Gotta Know How to Talk . . .: Ethnography of Information Seeking in South-East Queensland Aboriginal Society', *Australian Journal of Linguistics*, 2: 61–82.
—(1988), 'They Don't Speak an Aboriginal Language, or Do They?', in I. Keen (ed.), *Being Black: Aboriginal Cultures in 'Settled' Australia*, Canberra: Aboriginal Studies Press, pp. 97–115.
—(1991), 'Aboriginal English: an Introduction', *Vox*, 5: 55–61.
—(1992), *Aboriginal English and the Law: Communicating with Aboriginal English Speaking Clients. A Handbook for Legal Practitioners*, Brisbane: Queensland Law Society.
—(1993), 'The Case for Condren: Aboriginal English, Pragmatics and the Law', *Journal of Pragmatics*, 20: 141–62.
—(1994), 'A Case of Communicative Clash: Aboriginal English and the Legal System', in J. Gibbons (ed.), *Language and the Law*, London: Longman, pp. 234–64.
—(1995), 'Cross-Examination of Aboriginal Children: The Pinkenba Case', *Aboriginal Law Bulletin*, 3(75): 10–11.
—(1996), 'Legal Recognition of Cultural Differences in Communication: The Case of Robyn Kina', *Language and Communication*, 16: 215–27.
—(2000), 'I Don't Think it's an Answer to the Question: Silencing Aboriginal Witnesses in Court', *Language in Society*, 29(2): 161–96.
—(2007), 'Aboriginal English in the Criminal Justice System', in G. Leitner and I. G. Malcolm (eds), *The Habitat of Australia's Aboriginal Languages: Past, Present, and Future*, Berlin and New York: Mouton De Gruyter, pp. 299–326.
Elkin, A. P. (1977), *Aboriginal Men of High Degree* (2nd edn), St Lucia: University of Queensland Press.
Feyaerts, K. (ed.) (2003), 'The Bible through Metaphor and Translation: A Cognitive Semantic Perspective', *Religion and Discourse, Vol. 15*, Bern: Peter Lang.
Harkins, J. (1990), 'Shame and Shyness in the Aboriginal Classroom: A Case for Practical Semantics', *Australian Journal of Linguistics*, 10: 293–306.
—(2000), 'Structure and Meaning in Australian Aboriginal English', *Asian Englishes*, 3(2): 60–81.
Kaldor, S. and Malcolm, I. G. (1991), 'Aboriginal English – an Overview', in S. Romaine (ed.), *Language in Australia*, Cambridge: Cambridge University Press, pp. 67–83.
Kearins, J. (1985), 'Cross-Cultural Misunderstandings in Education: Communication and Miscommunication', in J. B. Pride (ed.), *Cross Cultural Encounters*, Melbourne: River Seine, pp. 65–79.
Kovecses, Z. (2005), *Metaphor in Culture: Universality and Variation*, Cambridge: Cambridge University Press.

Lakoff, G. and Johnson, M. (1980), *Metaphors We Live By*, Chicago: University of Chicago Press.
Lowell, A. and Devlin, B. (1998), 'Miscommunication between Aboriginal Students and Their Non-Aboriginal Teachers in a Bilingual School', *Language, Culture and Curriculum*, 11(3): 367–89.
Malcolm, I. G. (1979), 'The West Australian Aboriginal Child and Classroom Interaction', *Journal of Pragmatics*, 3: 305–20.
—(1982), 'Communicative Dysfunction in Aboriginal Classrooms', in J. Sherwood (ed.), *Aboriginal Education: Issues and Innovations*, Creative Research: Perth, pp. 153–72.
—(1994a), 'Aboriginal English Inside and Outside the Classroom', *Australian Review of Applied Linguistics*, 17(2): 147–80.
—(1994b), 'Discourse and Discourse Strategies in Australian Aboriginal English', *World Englishes*, 13(3): 289–306.
—(2001), 'Aboriginal English: Adopted Code of a Surviving Culture', in D. Blair and P. Collins (eds), *English in Australia*, Amsterdam: John Benjamins, pp. 201–22.
—(2004), 'Australian Creoles and Aboriginal English: Morphology and Syntax', in B. Kortmann, K. Burridge, R. Mesthrie, E. W. Schneider and C. Upton (eds), *A Handbook of Varieties of English, Volume 2: Morphology and Syntax*, Berlin: Mouton de Gruyter, pp. 657–81.
Malcolm, I. G. and Rochecouste, J. (2000), 'Event and Story Schemas in Australian Aboriginal English Discourse', *English World-Wide*, 21(2): 261–89.
Malcolm, I. G. and Sharifian, F. (2002), 'Aspects of Aboriginal English Oral Discourse: An Application of Cultural Schema Theory', *Discourse Studies*, 4(2): 169–81.
—(2005), 'Something Old, Something New, Something Borrowed, Something Blue: Australian Aboriginal Students' Schematic Repertoire', *Journal of Multilingual and Multicultural Development*, 26(6): 512–32.
—(2007), 'Multiword Units in Aboriginal English: Australian Cultural Expression in an Adopted Language', in P. Skandera (ed.), *Phraseology and Culture in English*, Berlin: Mouton de Gruyter, pp. 375–98.
Mobbs, R. (1986), 'But I Do Care! Communication Difficulties Affecting the Quality of Care Delivered to Aborigines', *Medical Journal of Australia*, 144(Special Supplement): 53–5.
Musolff, A. (2004), *Metaphor and Political Discourse. Analogical Reasoning in Debates about Europe*, Basingstoke: Palgrave-Macmillan.
—(2010), *Metaphor, Nation and the Holocaust: The Concept of the Body Politic*, New York: Routledge.
Palmer, G. B. (1996), *Toward a Theory of Cultural Linguistics*, Austin: University of Texas Press.
Quinn, N. (1991), 'The Cultural Basis of Metaphor', in J. W. Fernandez (ed.), *Beyond Metaphor: The Theory of Tropes in Anthropology*, Stanford: Stanford University Press, pp. 56-93.
Sharifian, F. (2001), 'Schema-Based Processing in Australian Speakers of Aboriginal English', *Language and Intercultural Communication*, 1(2): 120–34.
—(2003), 'On Cultural Conceptualisations', *Journal of Cognition and Culture*, 3(3): 187–207.
—(2005), 'Cultural Conceptualisations in English Words: A Study of Aboriginal Children in Perth', *Language and Education*, 19(1): 74–88.
—(2006), 'A Cultural-Conceptual Approach and World Englishes: The Case of Aboriginal English', *World Englishes*, 25(1): 11–22.

—(2008), 'Distributed, Emergent Cultural Cognition, Conceptualisation, and Language', in R. M. Frank, R. Dirven, T. Ziemke and E. Bernandez (eds), *Body, Language, and Mind (Vol. 2): Sociocultural Situatedness*, Berlin and New York: Mouton de Gruyter, pp. 109–36.

—(2010), 'Cultural Conceptualizations in Intercultural Communication: A Study of Aboriginal and Non-Aboriginal Australians', *Journal of Pragmatics*, 42: 3367–76.

—(2011), *Cultural Conceptualisations and Language: Theoretical Framework and Applications*, Amsterdam and Philadelphia: John Benjamins.

—(2013), 'Cultural Linguistics and Intercultural Communication', in F. Sharifian and M. Jamarani (eds), *Language and Intercultural Communication in the New Era*, New York: Routledge/Taylor and Francis, pp. 60–79.

—(Forthcoming), 'Cultural Linguistics', in M. Yamaguchi, D. Tay and B. Blount (eds), *Towards an Integration of Language, Culture and Cognition: Language in Cognitive, Historical, and Sociocultural Contexts*, Basingstoke: Palgrave MacMillan.

Sharifian, F., Dirven, R., Yu, N. and Niemeier, S. (eds) (2008), *Culture, Body, and Language: Conceptualizations of Internal Body Organs across Cultures and Languages*, Berlin and New York: Mouton De Gruyter.

Sharifian, F., Malcolm, I. G., Rochecouste, J., Königsberg, P. and Collard, G. (2005), 'They Were in a Cave: Schemas in the Recall of Aboriginal English Texts', *TESOL in Context*, 15(1): 8–16.

Sharifian, F. and Palmer, G .B. (eds) (2007), *Applied Cultural Linguistics: Implications for Second Language Learning and Intercultural Communication*, Amsterdam and Philadelphia: John Benjamins.

Sharifian, F., Rochecouste, J. and Malcolm, I. G. (2004), '"It was all a bit confusing . . ." Comprehending Aboriginal English Texts', *Language, Culture, and Curriculum*, 17(3): 203–28.

Siahaan, P. (2008), 'Did He Break Your *Heart* or Your *Liver*? A Contrastive Study on Metaphorical Concepts from the Source Domain Organ in English and in Indonesian', in F. Sharifian and R. Dirven (eds), *Culture, Body, and Language: Conceptualizations of Internal Body Organs across Cultures and Languages (Applications of Cognitive Linguistics)*, Berlin and New York: Mouton De Gruyter, pp. 45–74.

Yu, N. (2003), 'Metaphor, Body, and Culture: The Chinese Understanding of *Gallbladder* and *Courage*', *Metaphor and Symbol*, 18(1): 13–31.

—(2009a), *From Body to Meaning in Culture: Papers on Cognitive Semantic Studies of Chinese*, Amsterdam and Philadelphia: John Benjamins.

—(2009b), *The Chinese HEART in a Cognitive Perspective: Culture, Body, and Language*, Berlin and New York: Mouton de Gruyter.

7

Cultural Influence on the Use of DOG Concepts in English and Kabyle Proverbs[1]

Sadia Belkhir

Introduction

Metaphor is one of the cognitive and linguistic devices that carry cultural knowledge and beliefs. By means of metaphor, speakers communicate their views and attitudes towards the world around them. What makes this possible is the fact that metaphor has the feature of being laden with subjective elements that mirror speakers' feelings towards things, actions, events or other people. Animal metaphor is a good example of this, expressing people's views of other people. It has been claimed that the use of animal metaphors in language is overwhelmingly negative and goes against speakers' positive attitudes towards animals (Deignan, 2003; Kövecses, 2002; MacArthur, 2001). The present chapter proposes to investigate the cultural influences on the use of 'dog'/'*aqjun*' in English and Kabyle proverbs with the aim of exploring the way dog behaviour is used to represent human behaviour and the kind of events and situations they are involved in. For this objective, the *Great Chain of Being* theory (Kövecses, 2002; Lakoff and Turner, 1989; Lovejoy, 1936) together with the description of cultural representations of dogs will serve in conducting this study.

Background: the *Great Chain of Being*

The notion of the *Great Chain of Being*, attributed to Lovejoy (1936), implies that the world's beings are not equal but are hierarchically ordered on a vertical scale with God at the top, inanimate things at the bottom and humans and animals in between (Bunnin and Yu, 2004, p. 289). Lovejoy called this the principle of *gradation*, claiming that this notion dates back to Plato's and Aristotle's philosophies of the natural world that Neoplatonists further developed. In addition to *gradation*, Lovejoy (1936) introduced two other components underlying the *Great Chain of Being*: *plenitude* and *continuity*. He says, '[I]n its internal structure the universe is a "plenum", and the law of continuity, the assumption that "nature makes no leaps", can with absolute confidence be applied in all the sciences, from geometry to biology and psychology' (p. 181).

It is claimed that the *Great Chain of Being* concept is of Jewish-Christian origin (Kövecses, 2002; Lakoff and Turner, 1989; Taylor, 1984). This idea has not remained constant but has been subjected to modifications in different periods. For instance, in medieval Europe, the *Great Chain of Being* was adapted in such a way as to include a hierarchy of human beings 'from the king, princes, and various ranks of nobles down through vassals, peasants, and perhaps even slaves, all occupying particular slots in vertical relation to one another' (Marks, 2008, p. 68), reflecting how their social relations were categorized. Marks argues that '[t]he Great Chain of Being . . . represented an imposition of medieval European political relations upon the natural world' (p. 68). In a similar vein, Lakoff and Turner (1989, p. 210) point out that 'the existence of these global and microcosmic hierarchies in the cultural model of the great Chain, and its conscious elaborations in the West, has had profound social and political consequences'. A notorious example of these consequences during the twentieth century was Hitler's use of the *Great Chain of Being* in creating metaphors to legitimate his idea of 'exterminatory' racism (Musolff, 2008, p. 7).

It is clear that the idea of the *Great Chain of Being* has greatly influenced Western thought, leading to the emergence of particular attitudes not only towards different groups of human beings but also towards non-human creatures (animals and plants). Taylor (1986, p. 129) asserts that '[m]ost people in our Western civilization are brought up within a belief-system according to which we humans possess a kind of value and dignity not present in "lower" forms of life. In virtue of our humanity we are held to be nobler beings than animals and plants'. Lakoff and Turner (1989, p. 208) further maintain that the *Great Chain of Being* has to do with dominance: 'In this cultural model, higher forms of being dominate lower forms of being by virtue of their higher natures'. In their view, dominance characterizes both human-animal and human-human relationships.

Like Lakoff and Turner (1989), Kövecses (2002) sustains the possible universality of the *Great Chain of Being*. 'This folk theory of the relationship of things in the world, in the Jewish-Christian tradition, goes back to the Bible. But the folk theory can be found in many cultures and it may well be universal' (p. 127). If this is so, we may expect to find similarities in the way people of different cultures consider the natural world and the categorization of their own social relations. The fact that human beings impose their own social categorization on that of animals manifests itself in language, especially in figurative language that equates people and animals. In these instances, reference to human beings' features and behaviours via animals is made to denote some metaphoric meanings. Kövecses explains this phenomenon in the following terms: 'The only way these meanings can have emerged is that humans attributed human characteristics to animals and then reapplied these characteristics to humans. That is animals were personified first, and then the "human-based animal characteristics" were used to understand human behaviour' (p. 125).

The *Great Chain of Being* theory inspired Lakoff and Turner's (1989) analysis of the GREAT CHAIN metaphor in order to understand the meaning of proverbs through the comprehension of human features and behaviour, and vice-versa, via analogy with animals and objects. They claim that '[t]he GREAT CHAIN metaphor . . . allows us to comprehend general human character traits in terms of well-understood non-human attributes; and conversely it allows us to comprehend less well-understood aspects of the nature of animals and objects in terms of better-understood human characteristics' (p. 172). What makes the GREAT CHAIN metaphor appropriate for the interpretation of proverbs in Lakoff and Turner's view is that it has four components working together. First, the Maxim of Quantity ensures that enough information, and not more, is supplied to allow comprehension. Second, the GREAT CHAIN organizes entities on a vertical scale. Third, the NATURE OF THINGS shows the relationship between the characteristics of the ranked entities with their behaviours in the GREAT CHAIN OF BEING. Fourth, the GENERIC IS SPECIFIC metaphor takes generic-level structure from specific-level schemas. In this way, it allows the understanding of an unlimited number of situations metaphorically with reference to only one given situation described in a proverb.

Apart from the GREAT CHAIN metaphor, this study also draws on Kövecses (2002) notion of the *main meaning focus* of a metaphor. He defines this as a 'major theme' that characterizes the source domain and is mapped onto the target domain. It is fixed and widely accepted by the individuals of the same speech group (p. 110). The main meaning focus of the conceptual metaphor HUMAN BEHAVIOUR IS ANIMAL BEHAVIOUR is *objectionability* or *undesirability*. Most animal-related metaphors, according to Kövecses, 'capture the negative characteristics of human beings' (p. 125).

Research procedure

A description and contrastive analysis of the main meaning foci denoted in the proverbs is the research procedure adopted in the present investigation. This method permits the exploration of similarities and differences in the use of 'dog'/'*aqjun*' in the two languages. Once the analysis of the main meaning foci is achieved, the results obtained are analysed with reference to the *Great Chain of Being* theory and the cultural representations of dogs.

The corpus consisted of thirty-one English and sixteen Kabyle proverbs, yielding a total of forty-seven proverbs. The English proverbs were taken from *The Oxford Dictionary of English Proverbs* (Wilson, 1970), Fergusson's *The Penguin Dictionary of Proverbs* (2000) and Manser's *The Facts on File Dictionary of Proverbs* (2007). The Kabyle proverbs were extracted from Nacib's *Proverbes et Dictons Kabyles* (2009) and At Mansur's *Dictionnaire de Proverbes Kabyles* (2010). The selected proverbs involve the HUMAN BEHAVIOUR IS DOG BEHAVIOUR metaphor. All the phrases selected for consideration satisfied the requirement of being considered a proverb, rather than an idiom. A proverb is a complete sentence that is often metaphorical and used to convey some wisdom or accepted truth.

Dogs in British and Kabyle cultures

Dogs are domestic mammals belonging to the canine race. They live all over the world and are the closest of all domestic animals to humans, fulfilling multiple roles (as working animals, pets, guards etc.). It is impossible to deny the great amiability of dogs and their permanent eagerness to please their owners to gain their esteem. Nevertheless, in English, the word 'dog' is often used metaphorically with negative connotations. For example, Deignan (2003) reports that a study conducted by MacArthur (2001) on Spanish and English native speakers' attitude towards animals and their linguistic animal metaphors shows that, although English and Spanish speakers have a positive view of dogs, their metaphoric use of the word 'dog' is negative (Deignan, 2003, p. 258). In Kabyle, the use of the word '*aqjun*' (dog) is considered impolite and it is mainly employed for insulting (Dallet, 1982, p. 657; Genevois, 1963, p. 58). Therefore, each time Kabyle speakers mention the word '*aqjun*', they immediately apologize for doing so by using the word '*Ḥaca*' (apologies). When used metaphorically as an insult, the word '*aqjun*' means a man who does not have respect for himself.

The main difference between the way that dogs are regarded in English- and Kabyle-speaking communities is that while the British keep dogs as pets, the Kabyle essentially use the 'Atlas dog' or 'Kabyle sheep dog' for guarding flocks, their homes and belongings. The Kabyle dog is kept outside the home and is rarely allowed to get in. This is because it is used for guarding other domestic animals and possessions and is considered a dirty animal. However, the Kabyle view the dog as being very patient and enduring. This attitude is apparent in the following saying: '*aqjun yefka-yas Ṛebbi ṣṣber, yeskad kan swallen*' (Dallet, 1982, p. 657) (Allah has given patience to the dog; he is content with asking for something with his eyes).

Descriptive account of the proverbs' main meaning foci

In this section, the proverbs' main meaning foci are examined. This analysis is conducted on the basis of the proverbs' documentation in the aforementioned dictionaries.

Main meaning foci in English proverbs

Twenty-two of the thirty-one English proverbs examined convey a main meaning focus of 'undesirability' and nine convey that of 'desirability'.

Undesirability

Six of the proverbs use the figure of the dog to comment on the cause and outcomes of arguments and disputes.

(1) In every country, dogs bite.
(2) Two dogs strive for a bone, and a third runs away with it.

(3) Quarrelsome dogs get dirty coats.
(4) Quarrelling dogs come halting home.
(5) Two dogs and a bone never agree.
(6) Many dogs may easily worry one hare.

A further six use the dog to refer to people's propensity to complain or to threaten.

(7) Barking dogs seldom bite.
(8) Dogs bark as they are bred.
(9) Dogs bark and the caravan goes on.
(10) The dog that hunts foulest, hits at most faults.
(11) The dog bites the stone, not him that throws it.
(12) The dog that is idle barks at his fleas, but he that is hunting feels them not.

Example (7) uses the dog to represent falsity, or insincerity in behaviour, and this extends to notions of disloyalty or untrustworthiness in other proverbs, as the following examples show.

(13) Dogs wag their tails not so much in love to you as to your bread.
(14) Better to have a dog fawn on you than bite you.
(15) The dog that fetches will carry.
(16) The dog that licks ashes trust not with meal.
(17) Dumb dogs are dangerous.
(18) Every dog is a lion at home.
(19) When a dog is drowning, everyone offers him drink.

Other negatively evaluated attributes of humans, such as selfishness or ingratitude, are also described in terms of dog behaviour.

(20) He that keeps another man's dog shall have nothing left him but the line.
(21) While the dog gnaws bone, companions would be none.
(22) The dog returns to his vomit.

Desirability

Among the proverbs that can be used to highlight positive aspects of human behaviour (loyalty, steadfastness, application), we find the following:

(23) Dog does not eat dog.
(24) If you would wish the dog to follow you, feed him.
(25) The foremost dog catches the hare.
(26) A good dog deserves a good bone.
(27) It's a poor dog that deserves not a crust.
(28) A dog is man's best friend.

Interestingly, it is sometimes when the dog is approaching the end of its life, or seen as inactive (even dead), that something positive may be taken from the proverb:

(29) An old dog barks not in vain.
(30) Dead dogs bite not.
(31) Let sleeping dogs lie.

Main meaning foci in Kabyle proverbs

The examination of the meaning of the sixteen Kabyle proverbs has allowed me to find thirteen proverbs involving a main meaning focus of undesirability and three of desirability. These examples are followed by a fuller gloss than the English proverbs (the meaning and use of which can be ascertained in the works referred to in the section on research procedure).

Undesirability

(32) Aqjun isseglafen ur iteṭṭara.
the-dog barking not bite not
(A barking dog does not bite).

This proverb conveys the same meaning as English proverb (7), referring to threats that may not be carried out. Similar also to the English proverbs are those Kabyle ones which draw parallels between dogs and conflict among humans:

(33) Amennuɣ gizem yibbwas, amennuɣ bwgdi kullas.
the-quarrel of-the-lion one-day the-quarrel of-the-dog everyday
(The lion quarrels once, the dog quarrels every day).

It is better not to quarrel so much with people. Quarrelling everyday is incorrect and characterizes dogs but not lions. Similarly, this behaviour characterizes wicked people and not good ones.

(34) Addred aqjun, dmedd aεkwaz.
Mention dog take a-stick
(When you mention the dog, take a stick).

Aggressive behaviour yields defensive reactions from others.

(35) Laεb n weqjun d tikarrac, wwin n wemcic d tixebbac.
Playing of the-dog it-is bites that of the-cat it-is scratches
(The dog's playing is biting, that of the cat is scratching).

What is supposedly 'playing' for some is in fact harmful behaviour for others.

(36) Ţnaγen am yiḍan di tesraft.
Quarrel-they like the-dogs in a-pit
(They quarrel like dogs in a pit).

It is better not to be so aggressive. Quarrelling in a pit may cause harm to each dog. This goes for people's excessive aggressive behaviour that can be harmful.

The other proverbs in this group highlight various undesirable aspects of behaviour or attributes, such as arrogance, lack of authority or impudence:

(37) Isseglaf wqjun 99 tikwal γef qarrus, tis miyya ibab-is.
he-barks the-dog 99 times on head-his the hundredth to master-his
(The dog barks 99 times for himself and the hundredth time for his master).

It is not exemplary to be selfish. The dog barks more to protect itself than its master. This shows the dog's selfishness. This behaviour is similar to that of someone who serves his own interests before those of others.

(38) Tekkseγ iselfan i wegdi, ihebber dgi.
I-remove fleas from the dog he-bites in-me
(While I remove the dog's fleas, he bites me).

It is not correct to be ungrateful. The dog bites someone who removes its fleas. This is an act of ingratitude.

(39) Muqqer wugdi ur tiwi taεrict.
is-grand the-dog not contain the-garret
(The dog is so grand that the garret does not contain him).

Being grand and arrogant is ridiculous.

(40) Fkas iwegdi aclim, ad yečč neγ ad yeqqim.
give-him to dog bran will he-eat or will he-let
(Give to the dog bran, he eats it or leaves it).

It is disrespectful to be so exacting when there is shortage in food and/or means. A dog that refuses to eat the bran that is given to him and wants to eat something else behaves unpleasantly because it is impolite to be exacting when there is a lack of food. This goes for human beings as well.

(41) Aqjun ikelben d imawlan at iḥekmen.
Dog being-mad it-is masters will control-him
(A mad dog must be controlled by his masters).

Parents should control their insolent children. A dog that is mad must be taken in hand, as it may cause harm to people. This behaviour is similar to children's insolence that is disagreeable and thus must be controlled by parents.

(42) Balak a kɛeğben leḥnak, llan ula s aqjun ḥaca-k.
Don't-be you-seduced cheeks there-are even in dog apologies-you
(Don't be seduced by the cheeks, even the dog, apologies, has the same).

Someone's deceptive appearance should be distrusted. Having big cheeks is deceptive and misleading. This should be distrusted in the same way as should people's deceptive appearance.

(43) Mi ɣaben yezmawen, ad sraɛrɛen yiḍan.
When disappear-they the-lions will howl-they dogs
(When lions disappear, dogs howl).

Indiscipline spreads when authority is absent. Dogs' disagreeable howling occurs in the absence of lions. This is similar to undisciplined people who behave badly in the absence of authority.

(44) Sxeṣren aɣ zzhu yiḍan.
Spoilt-they us joy the-dogs
(Dogs spoilt our joy).

Impudence is unacceptable.

Desirability

(45) Iqwjan-neɣ ur seglafen-ara fellas.
dogs our not bark-they not on-him
(Our dogs do not bark at him).

Attitude towards familiar persons is obviously favourable. Not barking at a familiar person is desirable behaviour. It is similar to the favourable attitude that a person has towards someone familiar.

(46) Yerbaḥ weqjun ɛalqen-as taqlaṭ.
he-succeeded the-dog they-put-him a collar
(The dog succeeded, they put a collar on him).

Even an underestimated person can succeed. Succeeding is desirable as it is rewarded. Here the dog's succeeding is as good as that of an underestimated person.

(47) D laɛmer bwqjun.
It-is life of-dog
(It's a dog's life).

Unbreakable endurance and resistance are good qualities. Living a long life as a sign of good health is desirable. Similarly, someone who has unbreakable endurance and resistance is favourable.

So far, I have investigated the main meaning foci conveyed in the proverbs. The findings indicate a predominance of the negatively slanted proverbs over the positively slanted ones. This goes for both English and Kabyle proverbs.

Discussion of the findings

As was previously stated, the discussion of the aforementioned results relies on the theoretical framework selected for the present study, that is, the GREAT CHAIN metaphor and cultural views of dogs. The points that I have selected for discussion concern the similarities and differences in the characterization of dogs in English and Kabyle proverbs: discussion of the convergence in the characterization of dogs and the socio-cultural specificities influencing the use of dogs to represent human actions and behaviour, as well as the events and situations they are involved in.

Convergence in the characterization of dogs

The earlier given account of the main meaning foci conveyed in the proverbs reveals similarities in the characterization of dogs. Some dog characteristics and behaviours are found to be common to the proverbs in both English and Kabyle; for example, BARKING, QUARRELLING and BITING. An explanation that can be given to this fact is that barking, quarrelling and biting are kinds of behaviours shared by all dogs irrespective of breed and geographical area. Therefore, both English and Kabyle people use these dog characterizations to refer to human behaviour regardless of their socio-cultural environment (Belkhir, 2012, p. 223). Another shared feature relates to the predominance of negatively slanted proverbs over positively slanted ones in both languages. Twenty-two English proverbs convey the main meaning focus of undesirability and nine the main meaning focus of desirability. Thirteen Kabyle proverbs are found to convey the main meaning focus of undesirability and three the focus of desirability. The theory of the GREAT CHAIN metaphor offers an explanation to this phenomenon by describing the application of human behaviour categorization on that of dogs and vice-versa. This is achieved through a cross-domain mapping of dog behaviour and human behaviour.

Figure 7.1 shows how the categorization of the behaviour of higher-order beings, that is, human beings, is applied to that of dogs, which are lower-order beings, as claimed by Marks (2008), Lakoff and Turner (1989) and Kövecses (2002). The latter contends that, in the system of the GREAT CHAIN metaphor, animal metaphoric meaning is formed by

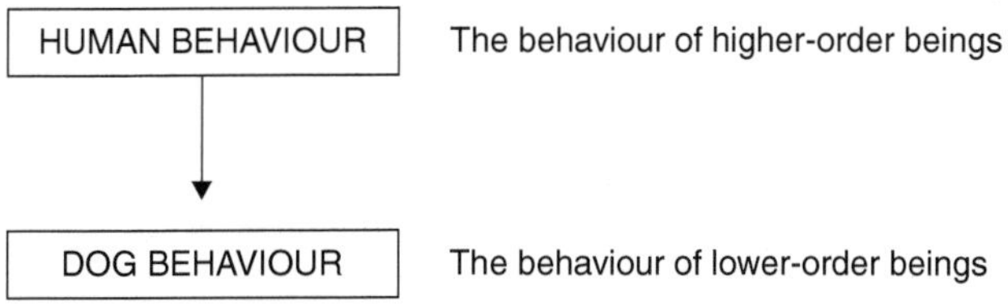

Figure 7.1 Application of human behaviour categorization on dogs.

applying human features and behaviour to animals, and then applying them back again to humans in order to refer to them and their behaviour (Kövecses, 2002, p. 125). Dogs are known to have behaviours that bother people, such as barking all the time, biting, quarrelling and so on. Hence, these undesirable behaviours are used figuratively to represent undesirable human behaviour.

Following this reasoning, the overwhelming number of negatively slanted dog proverbs does not relate to dogs' actual behaviour but to humans' conduct in society and their social relationships characterized by inequality and injustice (the rich vs the poor, the politically dominant group vs the oppressed one etc.). This creates conflict and contention between people and leads to the rise of negative feelings like anger and hatred. People's categorization of their social relationships is applied to dogs and manifests itself through the overwhelming negative use of dogs in proverbs. For instance, the English proverb (5) and the Kabyle proverb (33) reflect contention between people. Other proverbs reflect dispute, such as proverbs (3) and (5). Aggressiveness that is caused by disagreement between people is reflected in Kabyle proverbs (34) and (36).

If the hierarchy principle of the GREAT CHAIN metaphor is applied for the purpose of clarifying the question of what makes people apply their negative attitudes towards other people on dogs in proverbs, this fact can be explained in terms of dominance. In other words, humans consider themselves superior beings and give themselves the right to have power and dominance over other creatures, as maintained by Lakoff and Turner (1989) and Taylor (1986). Dogs are classified at a lower level on the GREAT CHAIN OF BEING scale, and this makes them less important than humans. This leads humans to have a low-value view of dogs and refer to them metaphorically to conceptualize undesirable human behaviour in terms of dog behaviour.

It is interesting to observe that in addition to the ranking of humans above dogs in the proverbs, as illustrated in Figure 7.1, we can also notice the ranking of lions above dogs and their respective behaviours. This ranking is mapped onto human beings and their behaviours and is noticeable in examples (18), (33) and (43) where LION is presented as superior to DOG and lion behaviour as being better than dog behaviour.

Figure 7.2 shows the application of the behaviour of higher-order beings on the ranking of lower-order beings and their behaviour. As was previously observed, Marks (2008, p. 68) asserts that the way people categorize their own social relationships influences their way of arranging the natural world around them, which leads them to organize animals into a realm like that of human beings. This is what explains the categorization of the lion as the noble king of all beasts. Important questions arise here.

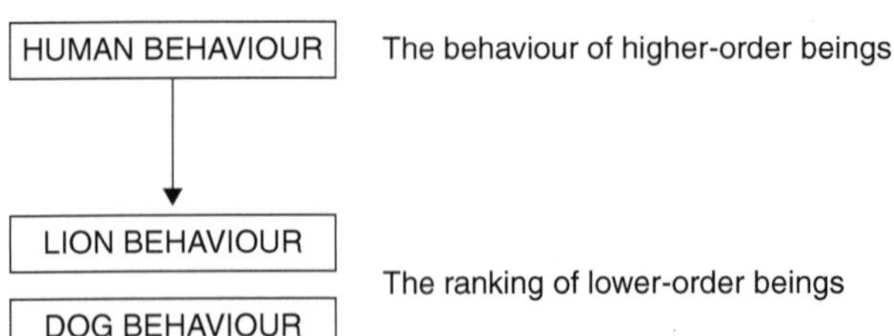

Figure 7.2 Application of human behaviour categorization on animal behaviour ranking.

Why is the lion ranked above the dog, and lion behaviour considered better than dog behaviour in some proverbs? Is this a universal or cultural phenomenon?

In order to find an answer to these questions, it is worth looking at the way the lion is viewed in English and Kabyle cultures and compare this with the already mentioned cultural representations of dogs. Generally, the lion is viewed as a noble animal that inspires fear and respect, unlike the dog. This view is common to English and Kabyle cultures and is reflected in the two Kabyle proverbs (33) and (43) and the English proverb (18). In British culture, the lion represents 'the national emblem of Great Britain' (*Random House Webster's Unabridged Dictionary*, 2001, p. 1119). According to the *Longman Dictionary of the English Language and Culture* (2005, p. 811), 'Lions are usually considered to be strong, brave, and frightening, and the lion is sometimes called "the king of the JUNGLE". In the UK, the lion is often used on flags and signs to represent the country'. Although the lion is not an animal living in the United Kingdom, it is given the important position of king because the country is a monarchy. Moreover, the British Rugby Union team that plays in international matches bears the name 'the British Lions' (p. 164). When used metaphorically, the word 'lion' means 'a famous and important person' (p. 811) or 'a man of great strength and courage' (*Random House Webster's Unabridged Dictionary*, 2001, p. 1119). Kabyle people know the lion because it lived in Kabylia but disappeared at the beginning of the twentieth century (Nacib, 2009, p. 94). According to Nacib, the proverb has immortalized the lion's qualities (nobleness, courage, power and loyalty) in the Kabyle collective memory. In the Kabyle culture, the lion is an animal that everyone fears and respects as shown by the expression '*izem bu tissas*' (redoubtable lion that inspires fear and respect) (Dallet, 1982, p. 946). The word '*izem*' (lion) refers metaphorically to a courageous and brave man. Some Kabyle men and boys are named '*aγiles*', a synonym of '*izem*'. In addition, when Kabyle speakers use the word '*izem*', they do not apologize for doing so like they do when they mention the dog. Hence, both English and Kabyle people perceive lions as superior to dogs and lion behaviour as being better than dog behaviour because of cultural influences.

The ranking of lions above dogs in both English and Kabyle cultures is a valuable fact that should not be discarded. It has been shown that the concept LION is superior to DOG in some proverbs. This reveals that the excess of derogatory dog proverbs is not a simple question of HUMAN as superior vis-à-vis ANIMAL, as claimed by Lakoff and Turner (1989) and Taylor (1986). As was demonstrated earlier, people rank the lion above the dog because of the socio-cultural beliefs and attitudes they have towards these animals. That is, they feel need and friendship for the servile and faithful dog, but feel respect and fear for the courageous and brave lion. These cultural representations influence their conceptualization of lion behaviour as being better than dog behaviour.

A further point that is also worth discussing is the existence of positively slanted dog proverbs in both English and Kabyle. This similarity proves that the use of dogs to describe human beings' conduct is not only influenced by the socio-cultural relationships existing between people that determine the attitudes that people have towards other people belonging to their own social group, as claimed by Marks (2008), but also by the cultural relationship between people and their dogs. In sum, both human-human relationships and human-dog relationships influence the characterization of dogs in the proverbs. In fact, both English and Kabyle possess proverbs conveying desirable main meaning focus and representing dogs positively. This sustains the aforementioned claim. For instance, English proverb (28) reflects the close relationship that links English people to their dog which leads them to consider this domestic animal as their best friend. Kabyle proverb (45) shows the trust that Kabyle people put in their dog for not barking at familiar persons while guarding their homes and belongings.

Therefore, it should be taken into account that, in both the English and Kabyle cultures, people have positive attitudes towards dogs, as they find them very useful. The English like their dogs and regard them as members of the family. Kabyle people view dogs as patient animals and find them very valuable in protecting and guarding their livestock, homes and possessions. Such positive attitudes justify the presence of dog proverbs conveying positive meaning. The ubiquity of positive attitudes towards dogs in both English and Kabyle cultures and the significant occurrence of positively slanted proverbs show that the hierarchy principle of the GREAT CHAIN OF BEING does not suffice as an explanation of why most dog proverbs are derogatory and that an explanation in terms of socio-cultural influences is necessary. Therefore, one should not discard the occurrence of such proverbs even though they are few in number because of the significant information they bear about socio-cultural beliefs and attitudes that influence conceptualization.

Culture-specificity in the use of dogs

Although the descriptive account of the main meaning foci conveyed in the proverbs shows the presence of similarities, like the predominance of negatively slanted proverbs over the positively slanted ones in both languages and the use of common dog characteristics and behaviours to represent human behaviour, the characterization of dogs also displays differences.

Significant instances indicating culture-specific influence on the metaphoric use of the DOG concept in proverbs to refer to humans and their conduct support the claim that the GREAT CHAIN OF BEING metaphor model is only an effective analytical tool if it takes into account socio-cultural specificities. An example that can be provided is the dog behaviour of HUNTING, which is characteristic for English proverbs (see examples [6], [10] and [25]) but not for Kabyle ones. It is part of the British culture for dogs, like greyhounds, to be used to hunt hares and participate in competitions in which the dog that is foremost and catches the hare is the winner. This cultural tradition is British, but in no way Kabyle. British dogs are involved in a culture-specific situations and events in which Kabyle dogs are not. This leads to a variation in the use of dogs in English and Kabyle proverbs because of the difference in the roles assigned to dogs in the two socio-cultural environments. Therefore, British dog behaviours involve HUNTING FOULEST, WORRYING A HARE and BEING FOREMOST while Kabyle dogs' behaviours do not (Belkhir, 2012, p. 223).

Another example reveals the influence of people's cultural perceptions on the use of dogs and indicates cultural dissimilarity in the figurative use of dogs. Kabyle people perceive dogs as patient and enduring animals;, they conceptualize HUMAN ENDURANCE in terms of DOG'S LONG LIFE in proverb (47). This is completely different from the way the British conceptualize a dog's life (Belkhir, 2012, p. 223). In fact, the English idiomatic expression 'a dog's life' meaning 'an unhappy existence full of problems or unfair treatment' (*Oxford Dictionary of Idioms*, 1999, p. 102) proves to be a convincing argument that backs up the culture-specificity of dog use in the proverbs of the two languages.

It has already been observed that the experience of dogs in English and Kabyle cultures is somewhat different. Dogs have played multiple roles in human societies, and currently in the United Kingdom they are thought of as the paradigm pet, or 'man's best friend'. For the Kabyle people, however, dogs are not pets, but rather working animals used to guard flocks, homes and belongings. Unlike in the United Kingdom, they are seldom allowed inside the house, so the relationship is not as close as it is in England. These socio-cultural dissimilarities are reflected in the way that dogs are depicted in the proverbs.

Interesting cases that support this assertion can be mentioned. The characterization of the dog as a selfish animal is found in both English and Kabyle. This is noticeable in proverbs (21) and (37). However, the actions and situations in which the dog is involved are peculiar to each language's proverbs. This difference originates from the different relationships speakers of English and Kabyle have with dogs. In the Kabyle proverb (37), the role of the dog as a working animal used as a guard in Kabyle society influences the characterization of the dog as barking so much to protect itself but too little to protect its master when accomplishing its job of watchdog. This is not the case in the English proverb (21) where GUARDING is not used but GNAWING BONE is, which is completely distinct dog behaviour.

Furthermore, in some proverbs in both languages, the dog is characterized as an ungrateful animal. But, here again, the actions and situations involved differ under the influence of the socio-cultural specificity of human-dog relationship. This is observable in proverbs (20) and (38). In the former example, the dog is depicted as being ungrateful when leaving a foreign master who has treated it well. In this English proverb, the master-dog relationship is clearly reflected because the dog leaves the present owner but shows loyalty to its old master. In Kabyle proverb (38), the dog's ingratitude is described via different behaviour; that is, the dog bites someone who removes its fleas.

All in all, although the *Great Chain of Being* is an idea that is not exclusively relevant to the Jewish-Christian tradition or to Western culture, but also to the North-African non-Jewish-Christian Kabyle culture, and thus may be universal, as suggested by Kövecses (2002) and Lakoff and Turner (1989), it does not, on its own, suffice to account comprehensively for the use of dogs in proverbs. Consequently, it needs to be supplemented with complementary socio-cultural information in order to be effective.

Conclusion

This study was exploratory in nature. It aimed at investigating the use of dogs in English and Kabyle proverbs involving the HUMAN BEHAVIOUR IS DOG BEHAVIOUR metaphor.

The main findings reached after the examination of the proverbs' main meaning foci revealed the existence of some convergence in the characterization of dogs but also distinct and peculiar ways of using dogs to represent human behaviour due to cultural specificity.

One of the similarities that were found was the overwhelmingly negative use of dogs in both English and Kabyle proverbs. It has been shown that this observable fact cannot be explained by means of the GREAT CHAIN OF BEING metaphor theory alone. The explanation suggested within the framework of this theory was that humans ranked themselves above animals in the scale of beings and had dominance over dogs that are given low value in metaphoric proverbs. However, this explanation overlooked the influence of people's favourable attitudes towards dogs on their positive use of these animals in some proverbs.

This study, it should be stressed, has explored the use of dogs in the proverbs of two languages only, and this has limited the scope of the research. In addition, the results reached were bound to the corpus including proverbs involving the HUMAN BEHAVIOUR IS DOG BEHAVIOUR conceptual metaphor and which have been extracted from selected books and dictionaries. Therefore, these findings relate solely to the present study and cannot be generalized. Nevertheless, it is hoped that this modest piece of research has contributed to the widening of knowledge about the subject matter and has provided ideas for future research.

Note

1 I am deeply grateful to Andreas Musolff for his precious advice and encouragement. I am also very grateful to David Appleyard for his valuable assistance in the interpretation of the English proverbs.

References

At Mansur, R. (2010), *Dictionnaire de Proverbes Kabyles*, Tizi-Ouzou: Editions Achab.

Belkhir, S. (2012), 'Variation in Source and Target Domain Mappings in English and Kabyle Dog Proverbs', in S. Kleinke, Z. Kövecses, A. Musolff and V. Szelid (eds), *Cognition and Culture – The Role of Metaphor and Metonymy*, Budapest: Eötvös University Press, pp. 213–27.

Bunnin, N. and Yu, J. (2004), *The Blackwell Dictionary of Western Philosophy*, Oxford: Blackwell Publishing.

Dallet, J.-M. (1982), *Dictionnaire Kabyle-Français*, Paris: Selaf.

Deignan, A. (2003), 'Metaphorical Expressions and Culture: An Indirect Link', *Metaphor and Symbol*, 18(4): 255–71.

Fergusson, R. (2000), *The Penguin Dictionary of Proverbs* (2nd edn), Aylesbury: Market House Books.

Genevois, H. (1963), *350 Enigmes Kabyles*, Fort National: Contribution à l'Etude Ethnographique du Maghreb.

Kövecses, Z. (2002), *Metaphor: A Practical Introduction*, Cambridge: Cambridge University Press.

Lakoff, G. and Turner, M. (1989), *More Than Cool Reason: A Field Guide to Poetic Metaphor*, Chicago: University of Chicago Press.

Longman Dictionary of the English Language and Culture (2005), Harlow: Pearson Education.

Lovejoy, A. O. (1936), *The Great Chain of Being*, Cambridge, MA: Harvard University Press.

MacArthur, F. (2001), 'Making Semantically Opaque Metaphors Transparent in FL Instruction: Descriptive Versus Explanatory Adequacy of the Concept of Attribute Saliency', paper presented at the Fourth Seminar on Researching and Applying Metaphor, University of Tunis, Tunisia.

Manser, M. H. (2007), *The Facts on File Dictionary of Proverbs* (2nd edn), New York: Facts on File.

Marks, J. (2008), 'Great Chain of Being', in J. Hartwell Moore (ed.), *Encyclopedia of Race and Racism*, Farmington Hills, MI: Gale Group, pp. 68–73.

Musolff, A. (2008), 'What Can Critical Metaphor Analysis Add to the Understanding of Racist Ideology? Recent Studies of Hitler's Anti-Semitic Metaphors', *Critical Approaches to Discourse Analysis across Disciplines*, 2(2): 1–10. <http://cadaad.net/files/journal/CADAAD2-2-Musolff-2008-Critical_Metaphor_Analysis.pdf> (accessed 11 September 2012).

Nacib, Y. (2009), *Proverbes et Dictons Kabyles* (2nd edn), Alger: Enag.

Oxford Dictionary of Idioms (1999), Oxford: Oxford University Press.

Random House Webster's Unabridged Dictionary (2nd edn) (2001), New-York: Random House.

Taylor, P. W. (1984), 'Are Humans Superior to Animals and Plants?', *Environmental Ethics*, 6(2): 149–60. <http://www.umweltethik.at/download.php?id=406> (accessed 9 September 2012).

—(1986), *Respect for Nature: A Theory of Environmental Ethics*, Princeton: Princeton University Press. <http://books.google.fr/booksid=SzXwxu_PydUC&printsec=frontcover&num=100&hl=fr#v=onepage&q&f=false> (accessed 12 September 2012).

Wilson, F. P. (1970), *Oxford Dictionary of English Proverbs* (3rd edn), Oxford: Oxford University Press.

Part Three

Metaphor, Globalization and Intercultural Communication

8

English Idioms Borrowed and Reshaped: The Emergence of a Hybrid Metaphor in Spanish[1]

José L. Oncins-Martínez

Introduction

Crystal (2011, p. 70) remarks that 'loan words are the invisible exports of a world where people talk to each other'. However, judging from the growing field of what is usually termed 'Anglicism studies', the role of English as an international vehicle of communication seems to have created an unprecedented imbalance in intercultural dialogue, with most of the talking done by speakers of English. Their verbal formulation of ideas may be adopted wholesale by their non-English-speaking interlocutors, sometimes in the form of the literal translation of idioms and metaphors that originate in culture-specific conceptualizations (see Fiedler, 2011, 2012; Martí-Solano, 2012; Oncins-Martínez, 2007, 2012; or Rozumko, 2012). The speakers of the language that borrows such idioms are often regarded as somewhat passive participants in the increasing Anglicization of their language, which is lamented by authorities such as the language academies that oversee and attempt to preserve the purity of national languages such as Spanish or French (Grijelmo, 2001; Marías, 2001; see Paffey, 2012, for the Spanish Academy's attitudes towards Anglicisms).

As the works of Görlach (2001), Fischer and Pułaczewska (2008) or Furiassi et al. (2012) confirm, English words and expressions of all kinds are constantly used by speakers of other European languages, mainly as lexical loanwords and loan translations or calques (see also Piirainen, 2012, pp. 515–17). Among the latter, idiomatic expressions are particularly interesting because of what they reveal about the interplay between culture and cognition. The role of culture as a major force in the shaping of metaphor has been demonstrated by scholars of different schools (e.g. Deignan, 2003; Boers, 2003; Sharifian, 2011; Musolff, 2007; Kövecses, 2005, 2009). Thus, a borrowed metaphor is also a borrowed cultural item.

Through the close analysis of one example of an idiom that has emerged from the contact between the English 'the ball is in someone's court' and the Spanish *la pelota está en el tejado* (lit. 'the ball is on the roof'), this chapter aims to show how the recipient language and culture interact in shaping the form and sense of a calqued metaphor. The non-linear interactions described here result in a hybrid idiom that defies any explication in terms of its conceptual coherence, as Martín Baró (2012) has pointed out. Nevertheless, the resulting 'hybrid' metaphor that has emerged is used unproblematically in everyday communication among speakers of Spanish and indeed has made its way into the lexicon. I suggest that this metaphor illustrates how the 'pressure of coherence' (Kövecses, 2005, 2009), in this case cultural coherence, overrides cognitive coherence.

Detailed case study: *estar la pelota en el tejado de alguien*

The newly coined Spanish expression *estar la pelota en el tejado de alguien* sheds exceptionally clear light on the roles of the source and target cultures interacting in every language-contact situation. Put succinctly, the idiom is a rapidly expanding hybrid that has been recently coined in Spanish as the result of the combination of a long-established Spanish idiom *estar la pelota en el tejado* ('to be the ball on the roof'), which in turn is losing ground due to the influence of its English 'cousin', and the calqued idiom *la pelota está en el campo de alguien*, which started to circulate in the 1970s as a loan translation of a well-known English idiom from tennis: 'the ball is in someone's court'. What is really interesting in this case, especially from the point of view of the interplay between cognition and culture, is that even though both idioms draw on similar ball-game metaphors, the resulting hybrid combines elements of the two source domains in such a way that a cognitive explanation of it proves quite complicated. In spite of this, the hybrid works. Indeed, the expression *estar la pelota en el tejado de alguien* has become widespread in Spanish; people use it and understand it when others use it, and it has even found a place in general and idiom dictionaries.

The shades and changes of meaning that concur in the genesis and vicissitudes of this hybrid idiom illustrate exceptionally clearly the potential of a language-speaking community to create a novel way of talking about events and situations on the basis of its own culture-specific conceptualizations. In order to trace its origin, development and rapid expansion it is necessary to explain in detail the three idioms that have participated in this contact situation, namely, the long-established Spanish expression with *pelota* and *tejado* – which is in gradual decline today, the English idiom from tennis and the Spanish calque deriving from the latter.

Data and methodology

Texts containing the four different idioms under scrutiny were sampled from Mark Davies's Corpus of Historical American English (COHA) and Corpus of Contemporary American English (COCA) and from the Spanish Royal Academy's *Corpus Diacrónico del Español* (CORDE) and *Corpus de Referencia del Español Actual* (CREA), all of them freely available through their respective websites.[2] The historical corpora (COHA [1810–2009] and CORDE [c. 950–1974]) were used to date the first occurrences of the expressions in the two languages and, more generally, to trace their development. On the other hand, the contemporary corpora (COCA [2010–present] and CREA [1975–2004]) allow us not only to explore the behaviour of each idiom in its natural context of use but also to see how and when new coinages appear. In order to complement this material (especially when the results were too scarce), two other sources were used: Google and the archives of two widely circulated, long-established Spanish newspapers, *ABC* and *La Vanguardia*.[3] Finally, general and phraseological dictionaries were also used to check whether more idioms were recorded and also to see to what extent their meanings coincided, or differed, in the two languages.

As regards the method for identifying and collecting the idioms, the search engines provided by the interfaces of the websites of the aforementioned sources were used. A search was made for all the instances of the collocations of the head words (e.g. 'ball' and 'court', or *pelota* and *tejado*) within a six-word window. They were then filtered to eliminate false hits (i.e. literal usages) and to separate the occurrences of the *pelota* + *tejado* idiom from those of *pelota* + *tejado de*.

A Spanish GAME metaphor: *la pelota está en el tejado*

Ever since the nineteenth century the expression *la pelota está en el tejado* has been used in Spanish to denote a stalemate situation in which a matter is still to be solved or when a business outcome is still uncertain (first recorded in the eleventh edition of the *Diccionario de la Real Academia* of 1869; henceforth DRAE). The *Collins Spanish Dictionary*, for instance, includes this expression in its entry for '*pelota*' – 'la pelota sigue en el tejado (fig)' – which is translated as 'the situation is still unresolved'. The expression has its origin in an old popular game, *juego de pelota* (lit. ball game), which was initially played on the streets and squares. Later on the game evolved into several outdoor and indoor ball games, among them the well-known and typically Spanish *frontón*, the name given both to the wall against which the ball is thrown by the players in alternative turns and to the hall in which the game is played. That balls could frequently end up on the roofs of the houses surrounding the area of play – hence the idiom – is made clear in this passage from Lope de Vega's *La Dorotea* (1632), which includes them among the various abandoned items that roof menders had to remove periodically:

> Los trastejadores, que desde el tejado ajeno van echando a la calle cuanto hallan: allá va una pelota, allá va una bola, allá unas calzas Viejas. (Lope de Vega, *La Dorotea* IV.i)
>
> (The roof menders who, from others' roofs, remove and throw back on the street anything they find: there goes a ball, there goes a pellet, there an old pair of breeches.)

The metaphor underlying the idiom could be cast as A STALEMATE SITUATION IS A GAME WITH A BALL STUCK ON THE ROOF. The scenario that serves as the source domain is that of a ball game like the one described, in which the ball accidentally gets stuck on the roof and, consequently, the game comes to a halt, at least momentarily. Indeed,

Table 8.1 Occurrences of the idiom *la pelota está en el tejado*

1	depende de quién gane. Aún está la	**pelota en el tejado**. Al fin y al cabo, lo que	1982
2	. ¿Y qué? – De momento, aún está la	**pelota en el tejado**. Lo del lunes, seguro. -No	1985
3	hasta pronto, pero de momento la	**pelota está en el tejado**. Sin embargo, lo segu	1986
4	sión está pues sin definir, con la	**pelota en el tejado**, pero evidentemente la pre	1987
5	s hombre muerto . . . -Ni hablar. La	**pelota está todavía en el tejado** y puede caer	1988
6	as, rezad, rezad mucho, porque la	**pelota está en el tejado**". Nosotros no entendí	1996
7	o mandato del PSOE -y aún está la	**pelota en el tejado** – se puede ver con claridad	1996
8	ados no lleva a ninguna parte. La	**pelota sigue en el tejado**.	2001
9	n. Para los demás ejercicios, la	**pelota está en el tejado**. 'Ésta era una forma d	2001

Source: CREA.

even though the possibilities that the ball may fall back down or that the participants may climb up to rescue it are coherent with the mini-narrative of this specific ball-game scenario (Musolff, 2007, p. 74), these optional elements are very rarely instantiated. The expression is almost invariably used to refer to a situation of impasse in which it is not in the hands of the participants to change or to alter the course of action or to go on with whatever activity they may plan or wish to engage in.

Practically all the occurrences of the idiom found in the corpora instantiate this scenario, highlighting the participants' lack of agency. After searching for *pelota* and *tejado* in the two corpora, four occurrences of the idiom were found in the CORDE (two in 1879 and one each in 1893 and 1931) and nine in the CREA. In this latter corpus, the first five hits were found occurring at the beginning of the period within a reduced span of six years (1982–6) whereas the other four appeared scattered throughout the rest of the span – a clear sign of the decline in the use of the expression pointed out before. Table 8.1 shows the nine hits from the CREA.

As can be seen, all the occurrences instantiate the metaphor of the stalemate situation, which is marked by the presence of temporal adverbials such as *aún*, *de momento* or *todavía* ('still', 'for the time being', 'yet'). The target situation is normally one in which the participants cannot act to change the course of events so the only thing they can do is to wait. Occurrences 1 and 6, for instance, refer to a war situation with the participants waiting for the end of a war in which they play the passive role of victims. Occurrence 2 shows a group of comedians hoping to have a contract signed, and occurrence 3 has an exile telling his relatives about the uncertainty of a future with a possible return to his homeland as long as the political situation remains unchanged. Occurrence 5, however, instantiates one of the other two possible (if rare) moments of the mini-narrative pointed out before, the one in which the ball may fall back on the playing ground. It is contained within example (1) presented here, where it can be seen in its context. The speaker explicitly mentions the entailment that derives from that scenario (note the interplay of metaphors from two different game scenarios, chess and a ball game).

(1) Porque Conde y Abelló están moviendo muy bien sus peones. Yo creo que Letona es hombre muerto . . .

- Ni hablar. **La pelota está** todavía **en el tejado** y puede caer de uno u otro lado. Lo que ocurra mañana en Londres puede ser decisivo.
- Yo creo que Letona ha perdido ya la partida.

(Because Conde and Abelló are moving their pawns well. I think Letona is a dead man . . .
- No way. **The ball is** still **on the roof**, and it may fall down on either side. What happens tomorrow in London may be decisive.
- I think Letona has already lost the game).

Agency is still absent, as it is not up to the participants themselves but to an external agent or force ('what happens tomorrow in London) that the situation referred to in the target domain may change.

Finally, as regards the other possibility that one of the participants could climb up to the roof to recover the ball so that the game may continue, neither the CORDE nor the CREA yielded any instantiations of it. However, among the collection of some fifty occurrences obtained through Google's search engine, I found one example in the novel *Los Conspiradores*, by F. Hernando (1885):

(2) Al cabo de tres días Tomás se despidió de sus amigos: Caballeros, les dijo, **la pelota está en el tejado** y hay que recogerla para volver á jugar: esto es, el Rey aun no está en el trono y hemos de trabajar hasta ponerle en él.
(After three days, Tomás said goodbye to his friends: Gentlemen, he said, **the ball is on the roof**, and it must be picked up/recovered to play again: that is to say, the king is not in the throne yet and we must work to put him there.)

The instantiations in examples (1) and (2) are so unusual that they would be probably perceived by most readers as literary creations. In fact, they could be used as examples of 'elaboration', one of the four modes of metaphorical creativity in literary language (Lakoff and Turner, 1989, pp. 67ff). In any case, they do not illustrate the conventional meaning of the idiom but an 'active' variant of it.

Even though the historical corpus (CORDE) contains just four occurrences of this idiom, its long-established presence and continuity throughout the twentieth century can also be corroborated in the archives of any Spanish newspaper, where dozens of occurrences can easily be found. Besides, this source of data offers the added value of the drawings and cartoons with which some news reports are illustrated. A search for the idiom in the archives of the *ABC* produced two hits from 1897 with their corresponding satirical drawings. In one of them (Figure 8.1), two contending politicians are portrayed as *pelotaris* (*pelota* players) gazing at the ball on the roof. The illustration captures the moment of impasse before the election, as the text below it (3) explains.

(3) Y el momento actual no puede ser más interesante. **La pelota está en el tejado.**
(And the present moment could not be more interesting. **The ball is on the roof.**)

Figure 8.1 *La pelota está en el tejado.*
Source: Mecachis (Eduardo Sáenz Hermua), *Portfolio de la semana. El gran partido,* Blanco y Negro, núm. 346, 18 de diciembre de 1897. Tinta, grafito y *gouache* sobre cartulina, 351 x 318 mm. Museo ABC, Madrid.

These early occurrences confirm the entrenchment and highly conventional nature of this idiom. Its continued currency in present-day Spanish is attested by the fact that general and idiom dictionaries of Spanish, such as DRAE, Moliner (2008) or Seco et al. (2004), record the expression.

An English GAME metaphor: 'the ball is in someone's court'

It is not surprising to find that this idiom originated in the English language, because England is the cradle of a large number of ball games. Among these, football and tennis are perhaps the most popular, as is shown by the fact that these are the two games explicitly mentioned in the OED's entry for the 'phrases and phraseological combinations' with 'ball' as a headword. The quotation for 'the ball is in one's (or another's) court' in the OED is dated 1963, although the idiom had been circulating in the language long before. The COHA records much earlier uses, such as the following:

(4) **The ball is in their court**, and we are pressuring them as much as possible in order to obtain a decision as soon as possible. (1875)

In (5), also obtained through COHA, the tennis origin of the expression is made explicit by the user:

(5) As we say in tennis, '**the ball is in your court**'. Your government is interested in your problems and in helping you solve them. (1968)

The conceptual mapping that motivates this idiomatic expression can be cast as NEGOTIATING IS A GAME OF TENNIS. In this tennis scenario, it is up to the player in whose court the ball is to play it so that the game can continue. Table 8.2 contains occurrences from COCA that illustrate some of the aspects of the metaphor that are most typically instantiated in English.

As can be seen, this idiom invariably mentions the metaphorical player(s) whose action is expected in the different target domains, expressed through different possessive constructions, for example, occurrence 3 'in your court', occurrence 5 'in the court of the several factions' or occurrence 1 'in the court of folks in Congress'. The action is sometimes specified in the text after the court phrase, either within the same clause, for example, occurrence 2 '. . . to begin to improve'; occurrence 5 ' . . . to agree', or in a different one, as in occurrence 3 'to make a definitive move'; occurrence 4 'They need to'. In occurrences 6 and 7, the interactive nature of the scenario is made more explicit by the juxtaposition of the players in whose court the ball is found ('Japan' and 'the Government') and those in the other 'court' (the 'we' of the sentences immediately following them). In these examples, the presence of a number of players (we) is not altogether incoherent with a tennis scenario, where games can be played in singles or doubles.

As the condition of the ball being in another's court marks a new moment in the time frame of the situation with respect to a previous one, it is not surprising that 'now' appears so frequently to indicate the temporality of the situation. In a search for the string 'the ball is' with a window of nine collocates to the right and to the left, the first content word that appears is, not surprisingly, 'court' (eighty-two hits), and not too far behind is 'now', with thirty-nine hits. Of these, eighteen appear to the right (almost all of them immediately after 'is') and twenty-one to the left (generally before 'the'). Here are two typical examples:

(6) spokesman says **the ball is now in the Security Council's court**. One council diplomat

(7) officials say that **now the ball is in the Palestinian court** and they have to now crack

Table 8.2 Occurrences of 'the ball is in . . . court'

1	gt, really,	**the ball is in the court** of folks in Congress, whether Congress really wants to
2	w onwards,	**the ball is in the court** of the Nigerian government to begin to improve the
3	dicates that	**the ball is in your court** and the moment's come to make a definitive move
4	right now.	**The ball is in their court**. They need to help define how taxes are going
5	up officials,	**the ball is in the court** of the several factions of kanaka maoli to agree
6	sition is clear.	**The ball is in the court** of Japan now. We've made our position very clear
7	at the rally.'	**The ball is now in the Government's court**. We are ready and willing to
8	Summing up,	**the ball is in whose court**? Mr. FAHRENKOPF: Well, right now, you have

Source: COCA.

Perhaps the most salient feature that this tennis metaphor highlights is the dynamic nature of the interaction, which takes place in alternative turns. For even though the idiom actually describes the static moment between the metaphorical turns, the most obvious entailment, hence the one most frequently instantiated, is that one of the participants has a move to make (e.g. [7]). And this is basically what distinguishes the English tennis idiom from the Spanish one with *pelota* and *tejado*. While the former always involves some kind of action from either of the two sides, the latter emphasizes the moment of impasse of the target situation, as was shown in the previous section.

In principle, the comprehension of the 'ball . . . court' English idiom, due to its transparency, should not pose any problems for speakers of languages other than English where the expression does not exist. Furthermore, even users unfamiliar with tennis can process its meaning without much effort by drawing on knowledge of any other ball game played on a pitch divided into two halves, like football or basketball. This explains why even though Spanish never had an equivalent version of this idiom, it has easily adopted it in the last three decades or so, as the next section shows.

The calqued Spanish metaphor: *estar la pelota en el campo de alguien*

The literal translation of 'the ball is in another's court' has recently occurred in Spanish, where a search for the collocation *pelota* ('ball') + *campo* ('court') within a six-word window yields plenty of examples of this calque. As regards the specific source domains that the English and Spanish idioms draw on, it is important to note at the outset that in their respective languages 'ball' and *pelota* are neutral as to the kind of round object used in competitive sports, that is, both apply to tennis, football and so on. In contrast, 'court' and *campo* are not. Whereas English 'court' normally refers to the surface where tennis is played and is never used for football, in Spanish, *campo* applies to the area of play in many different ball games, like football, basketball, tennis and so on.[4] Interestingly, in Spanish the default case is football, as can be seen in the description offered by the DRAE:

> **campo** 7. Mitad del terreno de juego que, en ciertos deportes, como el fútbol, corresponde defender a cada uno de los dos equipos.
>
> (campo 7. Half of the field which, in certain games, like football, has to be defended by each of the two teams)

Thus, while there is no doubt that in English tennis is the source domain that the metaphor draws on, the literal translation of the idiom into Spanish, where 'court' is rendered as *campo*, may evoke other scenarios, as some of the examples will show.

Although both tennis and football have been played in Spain since the late nineteenth century, their phraseology, or at least this particular idiom, has taken quite a long time to become a part of the lexicon of the language. A search for the aforementioned collocation *pelota* + *campo* in the CORDE (where the data end in 1974) yields no results for the figurative expression, and it is only in the CREA that the idiom begins to emerge. Its first occurrence is dated in 1985:

(8) El líder del PASOK apoyó la decisión de su padre de dimitir y precipitar así la crisis, con lo que no sólo detiene el tiro, sino que devuelve la **pelota** al **campo** contrario. (*El País*, 1985)
(The leader of the PASOK supported his father's decision to resign and thus trigger the crisis, consequently he is not only stopping the shot, but returning the **ball** to the other's **court/half.**)

The fact that no results are found in the CORDE or that the earliest one from the CREA is dated 1985 does not necessarily mean that other cases had not occurred earlier – like other corpora, CORDE and CREA do not record every instance of language use. Indeed, a search for the same string in the archives of *La Vanguardia* or *ABC* provides a few. The first occurrence of a figurative usage of this expression occurs in 1973, and curiously enough it is the translation of an exchange between two Ministers of Foreign Affairs: A. Gromyko, from the Soviet Union, and G. E. Thorn, from Luxembourg, in the context of the talks between the EEC and COMECON in Brussels:

(9) En la carrera por alcanzar Bruselas tendría que olvidarse de la frase de Gromyko a su colega Luxemburgués de Asuntos Exteriores, Thorn, cuando le dijo: '**La pelota está en vuestro campo**: os toca jugar'. (*ABC*, 1973)
(In the race to reach Brussels one should forget Gromyko's phrase to his colleague from Luxembourg's Foreign Affairs, Thorn, when he told him: '**The ball is in your court/half**. It's your turn to play.')

The possibility that the source domain may be other than tennis is well illustrated by example (10), as the ball is being played with the hands:

(10) En el fondo la pelota está en nuestras manos [. . .] De manera que aquí la pelota la tenemos que jugar nosotros. (*ABC*, 1974)
(Basically the ball is in our hands [. . .] Hence here we have to play the ball.)

As occurs with the English original idiom, the presence of temporal adverbials like *ahora* ('now') signals the transitional moment of the game/negotiation:

(11) Según ha podido saber este corresponsal, la última versión – a diferencia de anteriores borradores – ha dejado en suspenso el estatuto de Sarajevo [. . .] a la espera de reacciones. Ahora, **la pelota está en el campo de los contendientes.** (*La Vanguardia*, 1994)
(As this correspondent has been able to find out, the latest versions – unlike earlier drafts – has put the statute of Sarajevo on the back burner [. . .] awaiting reactions. Now, **the ball is in the contenders' court/half.**)

Observing the process of consolidation of this idiom in Spanish, it can be seen that whereas until the 1970s occurrences of it were rare, from then on they increased enormously (at least until the mid-1990s, where the calque entered into competition with the hybrid discussed later). This increase is especially obvious in a period of the history of Europe when Spain started to negotiate entry to the EEC, and was finally accepted as a full EEC member. This correlation between real-life events and the preference for certain metaphors seems to me to be of special import for cognitive linguistics (cf. Boers, 1999). It is also worthy of note that the entrenchment of this metaphor has been considerable although, if not because, its Spanish-speaking users see a football rather than a tennis match beneath the surface of its linguistic realization. This is undoubtedly the case with the next example (12), in which L. Sanz, the president of the Real Madrid Football Club, quite conveniently draws on the expression in the context of the negotiations to renew Raúl's contract, perhaps under the 'pressure of coherence' (Kövecses, 2005, 2009):

(12) Sanz parecía firme, inamovible: '**La pelota está en su campo**. Son ellos los que tienen que decidir – Raúl y su representante. No quiero salirme de la trayectoria que me he marcado, porque si lo hacemos, no habría servido de nada'. (*El Mundo*,1996)
(Sanz appeared firm, unmoveable: '**The ball is in his court/half**. It's they who have to decide –Raul and his agent. I don't want to leave the route I've traced for myself, because if we do, everything would have been worthless'.)

As Kövecses (2009, p. 18) explains, the speaker's choice of metaphor can be influenced by various factors, such as the physical environment, social context, cultural context and the communicative situation in which metaphor is used. This last factor is obviously what motivates the metaphor chosen in (12). However, the 'appropriation' of the original tennis metaphor in this example does not affect its function which, in essence, is still NEGOTIATING IS PLAYING A GAME.

Once the expression *la pelota está en el campo de alguien* was consolidated, the aforementioned phenomenon of idiomatic hybridization took place. This calque had to coexist with the well-established Spanish idiom described earlier, *la pelota está en el tejado*, with which it shares the game domain of experience and one of its elements – the ball – but not the meaning. This coexistence has eventually given rise to the new idiomatic expression *la pelota está en el tejado de X* ('the ball is on X's roof/the roof of X'), in a sort of 'blend' that seems to challenge some of the cognitive constraints imposed by the two different scenarios that are fused, but which, nevertheless, seems to be gaining ground at the expense of the calque just discussed and, to a lesser extent, of the Spanish STALEMATE idiom described earlier.

The emergence of the hybrid: *la pelota está en el tejado de alguien* ('the ball is on someone's roof')

The historical corpus CORDE does not contain any occurrences of this idiom, but plenty can be found in CREA, which testifies to its novelty. In order to explore this idiomatic expression and see in what ways it may have been affected by its 'cousin' borrowed earlier on (*pelota* + *campo*), a search was carried out again for the collocation *pelota* + *tejado* within a six-word window. Quite surprisingly, the results showed that out of the thirty-six hits that the search yielded, only nine corresponded to the original

Spanish idiomatic expression (occurrences 1–9 in Table 8.1). The rest had *tejado* qualified, through either a prepositional phrase with *de* ('of') + noun (*de Bruselas, de ellos, del socialismo*) or a possessive adjective (*su/tu tejado*) very much like 'court' in the English idiom (cf. occurrences 1–8 in Table 8.2). The adverbial *ahora* ('now') also appears in most of them, indicating that the action is to be completed or carried on by the other side. Table 8.3 gives ten examples taken at random.

So it seems that out of the cohabitation of the newly coined calque and the old Spanish one a new idiom has been born, namely, '*estar la pelota en el tejado de alguien*', which would result in a nonsensical expression if translated into English, at least idiomatically speaking: 'the ball is on someone's roof'. Indeed, the new idiom (where 'the roof' replaces 'the court' as the place where the ball lies) strangely draws on the two different ball-game scenarios simultaneously, which makes a conceptual explanation of it rather complicated, as pointed out by Martín Baró (2012, p. 22). His summary of the problem deserves full quotation:

> Ya se usaba la combinación de pelota y tejado en el *modismo estar la pelota en el tejado*, con el significado de estar pendiente de resolución un asunto o negocio, lo cual se entiende porque, si una pelota se encaja en un tejado, no se sabe de qué lado puede caer o si caerá. Pero al añadir a tejado un posesivo, la metáfora no resulta muy feliz. La locución inglesa *The ball is in your court*, 'La pelota está en tu campo', tiene un pase. Pero ¿cuántas veces nos hemos subido al tejado de nuestra casa a recoger una pelota que había caído en él?
>
> (The combination of the words 'ball' and 'roof' has since long existed [in Spanish] in the idiom 'the ball is on the roof', meaning that one is waiting for some matter or business to be decided; this is understandable because if a ball gets caught on a roof, it is uncertain on which side it will fall, if it falls. But when we add a possessive adjective to 'roof', the metaphor becomes rather infelicitous. The English phrase 'the ball is in your court' may be fine. But how many times have we climbed onto our own roof to recover a ball which has landed on it?)

One cannot but agree with Martín Baró that the metaphor is not a felicitous one. In this mixed scenario, a strange blend of tennis (or football) and *frontón* with two roofs, going on with the game proves to be somewhat more complicated than in the tennis

Table 8.3 Occurrences of the idiom *la pelota está en el tejado de . . .*

1	r la noche que la	**pelota está en el tejado de** IU. Así que, fundame	1994
2	ón económica. La	**pelota está ahora en el tejado del** Gobierno. Ta	1994
3	diciendo que 'la	**pelota está en el tejado de** ellos', PSOE e IU-C	1994
4	español envía la	**pelota al tejado del** Gobierno, que hace años que	1994
5	n del sector. La	**pelota está ahora en el tejado de** la Entitat Met	1994
6	o encuentro'. La	**pelota está ahora en el tejado de** Clemente. Inc	1994
7	ahora coloque la	**pelota en el tejado de** la Comunidad que va a gob	1995
8	candidatura. La	**pelota está en el tejado de** la Federación Intern	1995
9	fecha límite. La	**pelota está ahora en el tejado de** Moreiras, a qu	1995
10	del PP vasco, 'la	**pelota está ahora en el tejado del** socialismo va	1995

Source: CREA.

scenario of the English idiom. As Martín Baró says, we do not normally go up to the roof to recover the ball; nor, I would add, are there normally any roofs around tennis courts, where the ball may accidentally land (and even if there were, and a ball should get stuck there, the event would not be considered a part of the game; and players would be unlikely to bother trying to recover the ball anyway). But what makes the idiom almost impossible to explain is the presence of the two roofs. Indeed, *tu tejado* ('your roof') entails the existence of another one. Are we to assume that there is a roof at each end of the court? The scenario bears little resemblance to any real-life ball game.

Infelicitous though the metaphor may be, the expression seems to work, and those who use it manage to convey their ideas. Only this can explain its repeated use. As regards its meaning, a closer look at occurrences 1–10 in Table 8.3 shows that the hybrid basically conceptualizes the same idea as the 'ball . . . court' idiom and its Spanish calque. Moreover, it also conveys the dynamism of these two idioms, with the *ahora* ('now') inviting the other side to make a move. An illustrative example will suffice to show this:

(13) La Comunidad de Madrid presenta oficialmente la candidatura. La pelota está en el tejado de la Federación Internacional (IAAF), que el día 21 tomará la decisión. (*El Mundo*, 1995)
(The [Autonomous] Community of Madrid is officially presenting its candidacy. The ball is on the roof of the International Federation (IAAF), who will take a decision on the 21st.)

In spite of the cognitive challenge that the expression poses, summarized in Martín Baró's ironic complaint, it seems to have become quite successful, for not only has it gained currency in the last two or three decades but it has done so at the expense of the calque, which has been declining since the hybrid started to circulate. That the hybrid should be replacing the calque should come as no surprise, given the semantic and pragmatic similarities that exist between the two idioms, that is, the hybrid presents itself as an alternative for the calque. What is really surprising is that users may choose to apply this idiom with all the problems its processing seem to pose, instead of the more transparent, hence easier, calque. But the fact is that speakers have already made their choice. As was said before, the dictionaries of Seco et al. (2004) and Moliner (2008) gloss it along with the Spanish one; but neither records the calque.

The situation is further complicated as some corpus occurrences of this hybrid display a great amount of creativity, like this one from the *ABC*, in which the author uses both expressions, that is, the one with *tejado* ('roof') and the one with *terreno* ('court/half'), side by side:

(14) La búsqueda de un final a estas negociaciones comerciales que caminan hacia su tercer año de retraso, y no por culpa española. Ahora **la pelota está en el tejado** comunitario o, más bien, **en el terreno** del Comité 113 de la C.E.E. (*ABC*, 1975)
(The search for an end to these negotiations which are on their way to the third year of delay, and not because of Spain. Now **the ball is on the** community **roof**, or rather, **in the** Committee's **court/half**.)

A still greater display of creativity is to be found in this combination from the newspaper *El País*, where a 'hot potato', instead of a 'ball', is passed on and finally ends up on the roof:

(15) Ahora la patata caliente se encuentra de nuevo **en el tejado** de la Eurocámara. (*El País*, 2004)
(Now the hot potato is again **on the roof** of the European Parliament.)

'*Patata caliente*' ('hot potato') is another calque borrowed from English quite recently. But the way in which the metaphor is instantiated in Spanish is slightly different. While figurative 'hot potatoes' in English are normally dropped, in Spanish they behave more like 'bucks', as they are not dropped but passed on to others, who are given the difficult task of handling or dealing with them. In principle, there seems to be no connection whatsoever between a ball and a hot potato metaphorically speaking. However, since the size and shape of a potato makes it coherent with a game scenario and both can be used to conceptualize a problem, users again find no difficulty in making sense out of the combination.

One further instance of this kind of creative use that shows that mixing metaphors (see Gibbs and Lonergan, 2009; Kimmel, 2010) is not infrequent in Spanish is also provided by the CREA. This time the roof metaphor is combined with another game metaphor, *mover ficha*, from any of a variety of board games (chess, draughts, checkers).

(16) Pedro Pacheco, quiso resaltar ayer que 'la pelota está ahora en el tejado de Bruselas', que es 'quien debe mover ficha' y despejar 'de una vez' qué acepta de lo notificado por el Estado. (CREA, 1999)
(Pedro Pacheco wanted to stress yesterday that 'the ball is now on Brussels' roof', which 'should make its move' and clarify 'once and for all' that it accepts what has been notified by the State.)

The imagistic incompatibility in the Spanish hybrid metaphor recalls Kimmel's discussion of 'mixed metaphors in a single clause'. As Kimmel (2010, p. 112) points out, clashes such as this are counteracted by 'shallow processing' of the idiom (Gibbs, 1999; Vega, 2007). The majority of users most likely only engage in shallow processing of this idiom; those who dare to go into deep processing, like Martín Baró earlier, can only conclude that the metaphor mix is infelicitous.

Conclusions

This chapter has examined how a hybrid metaphor, *estar en el tejado de alguien/algo* ('to be on someone/something's roof'), has emerged in Peninsular Spanish in the last twenty years, as a result of the contact between the autochthonous idiom *estar en el tejado* ('be a stalemate') and the loan translation *estar en el campo de alguien* ('to be in someone's court/half'). As has been seen, the three idioms co-exist in Spanish nowadays. However, the hybrid has gained ground at the expense of both the Spanish idiom and the calque from English. The reason why this is happening is more difficult to explain. Each idiom is used to describe a different situation – stalemate as opposed to invited action – so they are not competing. Perhaps, due to the repeated exposure to the new hybrid, speakers now simply prefer it to the older one, which is being relegated to a lower position.

The hybrid metaphor that has emerged from this situation of contact challenges the notion that a coherent metaphorical scenario and/or conceptual mapping will motivate any particular instance of metaphorical language use. The fact that the hybrid metaphor implies the presence of one or two roofs as pertinent to the ball game being played defies any rational explanation, as roofs, if not absent, are largely irrelevant to games such as tennis or football. Players do not scramble to retrieve balls from surrounding roofs in order to keep the game/negotiation going. The addition of the 'roof' to the game scenario is a curious and somewhat uncomfortable inclusion, at least as far as its cognitive underpinning is concerned. Nevertheless, as has been seen, speakers of Spanish feel quite comfortable using this expression to describe negotiations or any other kind of interactive activity more generally. Of course, speakers of Spanish, if asked a posteriori how they imagine the scene depicted by the idiom, might come up with some plausible explanation, just as a researcher might appeal to the notion of conceptual integration or blending theory (Fauconnier and Turner, 2002) to explicate why the resulting metaphor might prove cognitively digestible, rather than simply absurd. However, a more parsimonious explanation might well be found in a discourse-oriented view of metaphorical language, particularly as it relates to the cultural context in which it is produced. Such a discourse-oriented view of this hybrid would draw attention to the fact that there exists a strong mutual attraction between *pelota* and *tejado*. This is evident in the strength of the collocation between the two words in Spanish, which instantiates a deeply entrenched scenario in the culture of Spanish speakers. Use of *tejado* would thus be 'primed' by use of *pelota* (Hoey, 2005, p. 9) or, to put it in terms of dynamical systems theory (Gibbs and Cameron, 2008; Cameron et al., 2009), *pelota* acts as an attractor for *tejado*, and the resulting hybrid metaphor emerges from this.

Kövecses (2009) points out that metaphorical creativity may arise from the 'pressure of coherence', which refers to the way that speakers tend to try to be coherent with various aspects of a particular communicative situation when using metaphors. The search for cultural coherence, which includes finding a fit with the language that both expresses and constitutes part of speakers' cultural conceptualizations would, in this view, prevail over cognitive coherence in a case such as this, allowing speakers not only to produce this anomalous metaphor but also to combine it with others with which it shares a vague 'family resemblance' (*mover ficha* or *patata caliente*).

The examination of a single case, such as has been carried out in this study, makes it impossible to draw any firm conclusions about what exactly contributes to the creation of a hybrid such as this. However, it is unlikely to be a singular or rare case, and hybrid metaphors of this type are likely to be present in other languages which have been open to the influence of idioms and conventional metaphors from other languages, including English. Further research into this phenomenon would be needed in order for a more detailed and nuanced view of the emergence of such metaphors in discourse to be provided and to identify more exactly the cognitive and cultural forces at work in shaping these unusual, cognitively challenging metaphors.

Notes

1 I would like to thank Michael Kimmel, Ramón López-Ortega and Fiona MacArthur for their helpful suggestions and insightful comments on earlier drafts of this chapter.
2 Corpus of Historical American English (COHA). <http://corpus.byu.edu/coha/>; Corpus of Contemporary American English (COCA). <http://www.americancorpus.org>; *Corpus Diacrónico del Español* (CORDE). <http://corpus.rae.es/cordenet.html>; *Corpus de Referencia del Español Actual* (CREA). <http://www.corpus.rae.es/creanet.html>.
3 These resources are especially useful for the period 2005–present, for the data in the CREA end in 2004.
4 In this context, *terreno* (field), *parte* (part) or *lado* (side) are synonyms for *campo*, which are sometimes used in variants of this idiom.

References

Boers, F. (1999), 'When a Bodily Source Domain Becomes Prominent. The Joy of Counting Metaphors in the Socio-Economic Domain', in R. W. Gibbs and G. J. Steen (eds), *Metaphor in Cognitive Linguistics*, Amsterdam and Philadelphia: John Benjamins, pp. 47–56.

—(2003), 'Applied Linguistics Perspectives on Cross-Cultural Variation in Conceptual Metaphor', *Metaphor and Symbol*, 18: 231–8.

Cameron, L., Maslen, R., Todd, Z., Maule, J., Stratton, P. and Stanley, N. (2009), 'The Discourse Dynamics Approach to Metaphor and Metaphor-Led Discourse Analysis', *Metaphor and Symbol*, 24: 63–89.

Crystal, D. (2011), 'The Consequences of Global English', in P. Powell-Davies (ed.), *Word for Word: The Social, Economic and Political Impact of Spanish and English*, Madrid: Instituto Cervantes, British Council España and Santillana, pp. 67–72.

Deignan, A. (2003), 'Metaphorical Expressions and Culture: An Indirect Link', *Metaphor and Symbol*, 18: 255–71.

Fauconnier, G. and Turner, M. (2002), *The Way We Think: Conceptual Blending and the Mind's Hidden Complexities*, New York: Basic Books.

Fiedler, S. (2011), 'The Sky is the Limit – The Influence of English on German Phraseology', in J. Szerszunowicz, B. Nowowiejski, K. Yagi and T. Kanzaki (eds), *Focal Issues of Phraseological Studies Vol. I*. Bialystok: University of Bialystok Publishing House, pp. 247–68.

—(2012), 'Der Elefant im Raum. . .: The influence of English on German phraseology', in C. Furiassi, V. Pulcini and F. Rodríguez González (eds), *The Anglicization of European Lexis*, Amsterdam and Philadelphia: John Benjamins, pp. 239–59.

Fischer, R. and Pułaczewska, H. (eds) (2008), *Anglicisms in Europe: Linguistic Diversity in a Global Context*, Newcastle upon Tyne: Cambridge Scholars Publishing.
Furiassi, C., Pulcini, V. and Rodríguez González, F. (eds) (2012), *The Anglicization of European Lexis*, Amsterdam and Philadelphia: John Benjamins.
Gibbs, R. W. (1999), 'Researching Metaphor', in L. Cameron and G. Low (eds), *Researching and Applying Metaphor*, Cambridge: Cambridge University Press, pp. 29–47.
Gibbs, R. W. and Cameron, L. (2008), 'The Social-Cognitive Dynamics of Metaphor Performance', *Cognitive Systems Research*, 1–2: 64–75.
Gibbs, R. W. and Lonergan, J. E. (2009), 'Studying Metaphor in Discourse: Some Lessons, Challenges, and New Data', in A. Musolff and J. Zinken (eds), *Metaphor and Discourse*, Basingstoke: Palgrave Macmillan, pp. 51–61.
Görlach, M. (2001), *A Dictionary of European Anglicisms: A Usage Dictionary of Anglicisms in Sixteen European Languages*, Oxford: Oxford University Press.
Grijelmo, A. (2001), *Defensa Apasionada de la Lengua Española*, Madrid: Punto de Lectura.
Hoey, M. (2005), *Lexical Priming: A New Theory of Words and Language*, London: Routledge.
Kimmel, M. (2010), 'Why We Mix Metaphors (and Mix Them Well): Discourse Coherence, Conceptual Metaphor, and Beyond', *Journal of Pragmatics*, 42(1): 97–116.
Kövecses, Z. (2005), *Metaphor in Culture: Universality and Variation*, Cambridge: Cambridge University Press.
—(2009), 'Metaphor, Culture and Discourse: The Pressure of Coherence', in A. Musolff and J. Zinken (eds), *Metaphor and Discourse*, Basingstoke: Palgrave Macmillan, pp. 11–24.
Lakoff, G. and Turner, M. (1989), *More Than Cool Reason: A Field Guide to Poetic Metaphor*, Chicago: University of Chicago Press.
Marías, J. (2001), 'Fastidiosos y Muy Embarazados', *El Semanal*, 29 April, p. 12.
Martí-Solano, R. (2012), 'Multi-word Loan Translations and Semantic Borrowing', in C. Furiassi, V. Pulcini and F. Rodríguez González (eds), *The Anglicization of European Lexis*, Amsterdam and Philadelphia: John Benjamins, pp. 199–216.
Martín Baró, A. (2012), *Cómo hablamos y escribimos*, Segovia: Asociación Cultural Isla del Náufrago.
Moliner, M. (2008), *Diccionario de Uso del Español* (3rd edn), Gredos: Madrid.
Musolff, A. (2007), 'Popular Science Concepts and Their Use in Creative Metaphors in Media Discourse', *metaphorik.de*, 13: 67–85.
Oncins-Martínez, J. L. (2007), 'Using Corpora for Exploring and Assessing the Influence of English on Contemporary Spanish', in M. Davies, P. Rayson, S. Hunston and P. Danielsson (eds), *Proceedings of the 2007 Corpus Linguistics Conference*. <http://www.birmingham.ac.uk/research/activity/corpus/index.aspx> (accessed 11 March 2013).
—(2012), 'Newly-Coined Anglicisms in Contemporary Spanish', in C. Furiassi, V. Pulcini and F. Rodríguez González (eds), *The Anglicization of European Lexis*, Amsterdam and Philadelphia: John Benjamins, pp. 217–38.
Paffey, D. (2012), *Language, Ideologies and the Globalization of 'Standard' Spanish*, London: Bloomsbury.
Piirainen, E. (2012), *Widespread Idioms in Europe and Beyond. Toward a Lexicon of Common Figurative Units*, Peter Lang: New York.

Rozumko, A. (2012), 'English Influence on Polish Proverbial Language', in C. Furiassi, V. Pulcini and F. Rodríguez González (eds), *The Anglicization of European Lexis*, Amsterdam and Philadelphia: John Benjamins, pp. 261–80.
Seco, M., Andrés, O. and Ramos, G. (2004), *Diccionario Fraseológico Documentado del Español Actual*, Madrid: Aguilar.
Sharifian, F. (2011), *Cultural Conceptualisations and Language*, Amsterdam and Philadelphia: John Benjamins.
Vega, R. (2007), *Creativity and Convention. The Pragmatics of Everyday Figurative Speech*, Amsterdam and Philadelphia: John Benjamins.

9

'Economic Conquistadors Conquer New Worlds': Metaphor Scenarios in English-Language Newspaper Headlines on Spanish Foreign Direct Investment

Jasper Vandenberghe, Patrick Goethals and Geert Jacobs

Introduction

The starting point of this chapter is the observation that, as a result of Spain's economic expansion at the end of the twentieth century, the international media used a number of frequently reproduced metaphorical structures referring to Spain's rich history of violent confrontations dating from its colonial past, with the term 'new conquistadors' as the most famous example. Even today, these images remain active in the minds of a majority of English-language media audiences as a result of a series of discursive traditions, spread since the sixteenth century, through which Spain's military expansionism, colonial atrocities and religious fanaticism were repeatedly denounced (López de Abiada, 2007).

In the 1990s, the Spanish investments in Latin America received considerable attention from the international business media. Noya (2004) identifies three striking features that contributed to the visibility of these Spanish business actions: their geographical, temporal and sectoral concentration. In the 1990s, Spanish investors set their sights almost exclusively on the American continent. Moreover, they made their (massive) investments almost completely in the period of a single decade at the end of the twentieth century (contrary, e.g., to US investors, who had been active in Latin America throughout the Cold War era). Finally, the Spanish companies mainly ventured into the Latin-American utility sector which was increasingly being privatized. These sectors have an immediate impact on local consumers, and the Spanish interventions more than once offended local nationalist sentiments (Noya, 2004, p. 48). In addition, several events around the globe in the 1990s commemorated Spain's colonial past. In 1991, the first Ibero-American Summit was held in Guadalajara, Mexico. The 1992 Olympics in Barcelona and the World's Fair in Seville coincided with the commemorations of the 500th anniversary of Columbus's voyage to the New World, and in 1998, several initiatives commemorated the end of Spain's colonial regime in 1898, when Spain lost the last of its remaining overseas colonies. This focus on Spain and its relations with (Latin)America paved the way for international business media professionals to draw historical analogies that compared the Spanish actions to salient events dating from Spain's colonial past.

In this study, we investigate how Spanish foreign direct investment (FDI) was depicted in English-language newspaper headlines over a period of twenty years (1990–2010). This case study further investigates the use of socio-culturally informed metaphorical projections in media discourse (Nerlich, 2005; Nerlich et al., 2002; Zinken et al., 2008). The analysis reveals how the newspapers in the corpus often used Spain's colonial past as a metaphorical frame of reference for Spain's international business activity.

In the following, we first briefly review the literature on metaphorical constructions in newspaper headlines, and pay special attention to the concepts of *discourse metaphor* and *metaphor scenario*. Then we decompose one emblematic discourse metaphor ('economic conquistadors') to illustrate how discourse metaphors and metaphor scenarios work together in discursive metaphorical framing. After describing our corpus we present the metaphorical constructions and scenarios we identified in the newspaper headlines. In the discussion, we first explore why these specific scenarios cropped up in their respective contexts. Then we further examine the link between these scenarios and the intercultural preservation of national stereotypes. Finally we briefly touch upon the paradox between national frames of reference and globalization.

Review of the literature

For the purpose of this chapter, the focus of attention is on the headlines and leads of newspapers. Recent developments in the field suggest that headlines should be considered 'a discourse type in [their] own right' (White and Herrera, 2009, p. 135). Headlines of newspaper articles are interesting features because of their general, two-fold function of summarizing the content of the article and attracting the attention of the readers (White, 1998, p. 45). Vivid (discourse) metaphors are often used to fulfil these functions because of their compactness and expressiveness (Feyaerts and Brône, 2005; Greco, 2009). Moreover, Zinken (2003) found that in newspaper articles, vivid metaphors mainly occur in headlines, leads, first and last sections of texts and in the texts underneath pictures. White (1998, p. 44) showed that headlines are often very highly culturally bound.

This study draws on two recent developments in the research field of metaphorical language use: *discourse metaphors* and *metaphor scenarios*. First, we focus on the connection between metaphor and collective socio-cultural experience. For this study, we draw on the concept of discourse metaphor (Nerlich, 2005; Zinken et al., 2008) to study the use of socio-culturally informed ornamental metaphorical projections in newspaper headlines and leads. Second, the chapter also builds on the concept of metaphor scenarios (Musolff, 2006) because socio-culturally informed scenarios can provide powerful narrative and discursive framing devices for media professionals.

The influential work of Lakoff and Johnson (1980) has proved to be useful for the analysis of established, conventional metaphors such as LIFE IS A JOURNEY, ANGER IS HEAT, LIGHT IS GOODNESS. This classical framework has a strong experientialist basis because it posits that, universally, our way of understanding the world grows out of bodily experience. At a later stage, this focus was adapted to include not only individual body experience, but also collective socio-cultural experience (Johnson, 1992; Lakoff, 1987). Still, Zinken (2003, p. 507) argues that the socio-cultural situatedness of metaphors has hardly been modelled by cognitive linguists.

Several studies have recently paid greater attention to the connection between metaphor and culture (Deignan, 2003; Kövecses, 2005; Nerlich et al., 2002) which resulted in the creation of a new concept: discourse metaphor (Nerlich, 2005; Zinken et al., 2008). This specific type of metaphor is defined as 'a relatively stable metaphorical projection that functions as a key framing device within a particular discourse over a certain period of time' (Zinken et al., 2008, p. 363). Moreover, discourse metaphors 'highlight salient aspects of a socially, culturally, or politically relevant topic' and the 'source concepts [. . .] occupy an important place in cultural imagination' (Nerlich, 2005, p. 72).

The cultural motivation of these metaphors can be described as a kind of intertextuality (Zinken, 2003) because the link between source and target domain is based on discursive rather than conceptual mappings. These metaphors 'seem to be discursively embedded in a relatively stable reservoir of cultural myths and social representations available in social memory – e.g. memories of past wars' (Zinken et al., 2008, p. 367). The study by Nerlich et al. (2002) on the socio-cultural conceptualizations of foot and mouth disease in the United Kingdom in 2001 showed that images of plague-filled medieval villages were used frequently by journalists of the *Guardian Unlimited* to construct their news stories on this topic. Zinken et al. (2008, p. 368) suggest that new topics and events are often discussed in terms of cultural and mythical commonplaces, with a source domain which is much older than the target domain, especially in times of social upheaval.

The source concepts used in discursive metaphorical framing can be organized into mini-narratives through metaphor scenarios. Musolff (2006) defines a metaphor scenario as

> a set of assumptions made by competent members of a discourse community about 'typical' aspects of a source-situation, for example, its participants and their roles, the 'dramatic' storylines and outcomes, and conventional evaluations of whether they count as successful or unsuccessful, normal or abnormal, permissible or illegitimate, etc. (p. 28)

Moreover, these scenarios 'enable the speakers to not only apply source to target concepts but to draw on them to build narrative frames for the conceptualization and assessment of socio-political issues' (p. 36).

In their study of the discourses around carbon offsetting during a period of increased media attention to climate change, Nerlich and Koteyko (2010) identified two metaphor scenarios based on the widely shared socio-cultural conceptualization of the Wild

West: a 'gold rush' scenario and a 'cowboy' scenario. Moreover, their research indicates that journalists used these scenarios in two different ways. On the one hand, they were used to highlight the romantic aspects of the Wild West by activating assumptions about the rough and outdoor life, adventure or braveness. On the other hand, they were also found to be used to 'caution against the "permissiveness" that the Wild West can connote and the dangers posed by greed and exploitation' (Nerlich and Koteyko, 2010, p. 49) by activating assumptions about treachery, brutality and lawlessness.

Economic conquistadors in a Spanish conquest scenario

In the following, we show how the theoretical concepts related to discursive metaphorical framing can be applied to the socio-culturally grounded metaphors in our corpus. Consider the popular, metaphorical projection in the following headline taken from our corpus, in which 'conquistadors' stands for the Spanish investors:

(1) Economic conquistadors conquer new worlds (*New Zealand Herald*, 14 June 2006)

This metaphorical source-target projection fits the definition of discourse metaphor perfectly. First, there can be no doubt about the lasting impact of the discovery of the Americas and the subsequent conquest and colonization of the continent by the Spaniards in the sixteenth century. As such, the metaphorical projection can certainly be seen as a salient image with an important place in the socio-cultural imagination of the English-speaking world. Moreover, in the case of the Spanish investments abroad, the term also highlights a salient socio-cultural topic. Mergers and acquisitions are likely to have a major impact on a number of different implicated parties, especially in cross-border mergers and acquisitions, where the acquiring company potentially faces a clash of both corporate and national cultures. Thus, in this case, the term can also be used to refer to a time of social upheaval. Finally, the source concept of the Spanish conquistador is much older than the target concept of the Spanish investor.

Discourse metaphors are important narrative and discursive framing devices for media professionals (Koteyko et al., 2008) because they activate narratively linked metaphor scenarios which 'seem to provide a stable stock of metaphors, stories, and images that exhibit high conceptual entrenchment and international appeal, and which are very familiar and easy to access and understand' (Nerlich and Koteyko, 2010, p. 43). Media professionals often construct creative, witty headlines on the basis of these scenarios. In example (1), the firm basis of the headline is to be found in the description of this business activity by means of the metaphor structure (INTERNATIONAL) BUSINESS IS COLONIZATION in the verb 'to conquer'. A crucial feature of this structure is 'the domination of a territory with its corresponding implications' (White and Herrera, 2003, pp. 303–4). These characteristics of the metaphor structure are consistent with the dictionary entry of the verb as 'to acquire by force of arms' and 'to acquire by fighting, win in war, to make a warlike conquest of, to subjugate' (OED Online). However, this headline presents a more complex picture because the verb also relates to the agent (economic conquistadors) and the object of the action (new worlds). This headline efficiently activates a socio-culturally grounded scenario with a rich conceptual structure: the history of the original conquistadors who conquered the New World in the sixteenth century. As such, these Spanish business manoeuvres are introduced into the frame of a warlike international conflict which links the investors' actions in the present to the actions of the Spanish conquistadors in the past.[1]

As a result of the linking of the two concepts (Spanish investors are like Spanish conquistadors), the reader is encouraged to dive into the reservoir of salient Spanish historical events available in collective socio-cultural memory. Thus, the reader might project onto the Spanish investors some of the stereotypical qualities commonly associated with the Spanish conquistadors because, as Musolff (2006, pp. 35–6) argues, metaphor scenarios 'carry with them normative assumptions concerning the intentions, states of minds, and emotions of the scenario participants, and concerning the chances of success and social acceptability of the "scenes" they are "enacting"'.

Spain's sudden rise to superpower status in the sixteenth and seventeenth centuries provoked a centuries-long rivalry with its economic and religious enemies. The anti-Spanish feelings which circulated in other nations (particularly in Northern Europe) formed the basis for a negative reading of Spain's colonial history. Spain became a 'typological emblem of religious and political intolerance, tyranny, misrule, conspiracy, cruelty, barbarity, bloodthirstiness, backwardness, slothfulness, and degeneracy' (DeGuzmán, 2005, p. 5). Although, according to López de Abiada (2007), there never existed a concerted international anti-Spanish propaganda campaign, there undoubtedly circulated various discursive traditions which tapped into these negative stereotypes. This tradition is called the Black Legend, a term coined by the Spanish sociologist and historian Julián Juderías at the beginning of the twentieth century. In his book *La leyenda negra y la verdad histórica* (The Black Legend and historical truth; 1914), he spoke out against what he considered the malicious, unfair and biased representation of Spain and the Spaniards as cruel fanatics at the hands of foreign writers. Our interest in the Black Legend lies in the narrative potential of these discursive traditions as the source domain for the metaphor scenarios and discourse metaphors identified in our corpus. Influenced by these age-old discursive traditions, the scenario of the Spanish conquest activates a set of normative assumptions about the participants and the courses of action (Musolff, 2006). Are these 'economic conquistadors', in their attempts to take over companies in these so-called new worlds, going to behave the same way as their predecessors did when they conquered the New World five hundred years ago?

The English-language newspaper headlines

The corpus was created by conducting a search for the English-language newspapers on the Lexis Nexis electronic database for the time period from 1 January 1990 to 1 January 2010, using the keywords 'Spanish companies' and 'Latin America'. The data selection was further refined with a secondary manual search (Schafraad et al., 2006). Articles were deemed relevant for this study if the central topic was an overview of Spanish FDI and if the wave of investments in Latin America was mentioned. In order

Table 9.1 English-language newspapers

Financial Times	46	*Guardian Unlimited*	1
The New York Times	7	*New Straits Times* (Malaysia)	1
The International Herald Tribune	6	*The Calgary Herald* (Alberta)	1
The Miami Herald	6	*The Express*	1
The Times	4	*The New Zealand Herald*	1
The Herald (Glasgow)	2	*The Observer*	1
The Washington Post	2	*The Sunday Telegraph*	1

to decide this, titles, keyword-concordances and sometimes the body of the text were closely read. This reduced the initial selection of 665 items to a total of 80 articles. The articles were published in fourteen different English-language newspapers, from all over the world. More than half of the articles were published by the *Financial Times* (46). *The New York Times* came in second, but with considerably fewer articles (7). Seven newspapers were represented in this corpus with only one article on this topic (Table 9.1).

The timeline in Figure 9.1 spans the twenty-year period and represents the number of selected articles published each year. Three peaks can be observed: 1998 (the year in which Spanish companies made a number of eye-catching investments in Latin America); 2001–2 (the peak of the financial crisis in Latin America, with major implications for the Spanish companies); and 2005–7 (the period in which Spanish companies ventured into areas other than Latin America, especially Great Britain).

Discourse metaphors and metaphor scenarios in the data

Typical of business media discourse, and of news stories on mergers and acquisitions in particular, is the use of CONTEST or CONFLICT metaphors (Eubanks, 2000; Greco, 2009; Koller, 2005). These are also found in 75 per cent of the headlines in our corpus. This high hierarchical metaphor structure (Greco, 2009, p. 204) includes BUSINESS IS WAR, as in headlines (2) and (3), and BUSINESS IS A GAME/SPORT, as in headline (4) (the bold in all these headlines is ours).

(2) **War of words** over Argentine airline – Aerolineas Argentinas carrier expected to file for protection against creditors amid **battle with Spain** (*Financial Times*, 16 July 2001)
(3) **Counterattack** in cyberspace (*Financial Times*, 8 March 2000)
(4) Spain **comes into play** in the World **arena** of power (*The Times*, 19 October 2000)

However, in twenty-one headlines in our corpus (25 per cent), this CONFLICT metaphorical framework seems to be used as the basis to introduce an encyclopaedic and socio-culturally informed metaphor scenario which is further enriched by the use of ornamental metaphorical projections, or discourse metaphors. These discourse metaphors and metaphor scenarios seem to be tapping into the historical commonplace of Spain as a conquering nation.

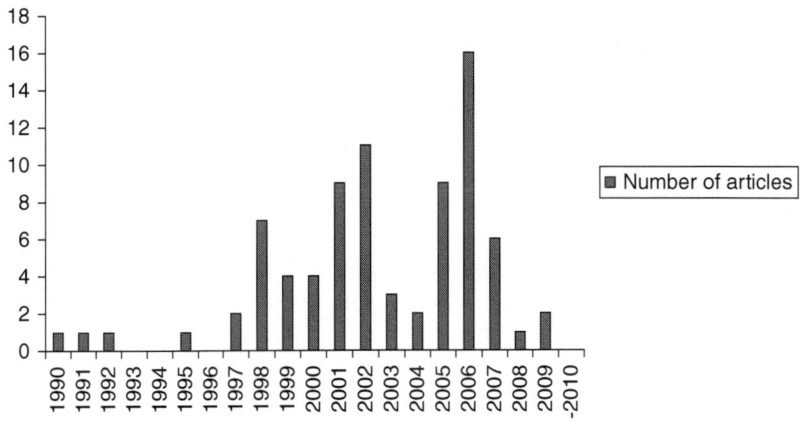

Figure 9.1 Timeline 1990–2010.

The analysis of this corpus reveals that English-language media professionals predominantly tapped into two specific historical events: the discovery of the New World and the so-called Spanish Armada. Moreover, it is also striking to find a high concentration of these specific metaphor scenarios in the first and third peaks of news coverage on the Spanish investors (see Figure 9.1): 1997–2000 (Spanish investments in Latin America), and 2006 (Spanish acquisitions in Great Britain). For the second peak, which contains the news coverage on the financial crisis in Latin America and its impact on the Spanish companies, no clear pattern of metaphor scenarios and discourse metaphors could be identified. In theory, it is possible to draw historical comparisons between the financial crisis and historical moments when Spain was losing influence. For instance, the decay of the Spanish colonial empire began soon after Spain had reached the peak of its colonial power. The decline of Spain as a world power came with a long period of socio-economic difficulties, called '*la decadencia española*'. However, the English-language headline writers in our corpus did not use this period as a source domain for metaphor scenarios or discourse metaphors, probably because these analogies are less readily available in the collective socio-cultural memory of their audiences. In headline (5), the headline writer does refer to the 'New World' in the context of the financial crisis, but this difficult situation for the Spanish companies is contrasted to Spain's golden sixteenth century. At that time, the Spanish conquerors brought back gold and other riches from the New World, whereas 'this time', the Spanish companies are losing money because of the crises in the New World:

(5) This time, *New World* costs Spain (*International Herald Tribune*, 13 December 2005)

In our corpus, the narrative frame of the conquest and subsequent colonization of the New World is often used in the context of the wave of Spanish investments in Latin America at the end of the 1990s (eight out of seventeen headlines in our corpus). This business event generated a lot of interest from the international business media. The

English-language media included in our corpus refer to the discovery of the Americas after Christopher Columbus had undertaken his famous voyage to the west (8) and the subsequent colonization of the continent, by using both the English words 'conqueror' (6) and 'explorers' (7), and the Spanish-derived 'conquistador' (9) and (10) to refer to the Spanish investors. Moreover, the Spanish business manoeuvres are stereotypically described as 'a new onslaught on the region' (6) and as 'invading Latin America in search of its corporate treasures' (10).

(6) Return of the **conqueror** – Nearly a century after the end of **Spain's empire in Latin America**, its companies are leading **a new onslaught on the region** (*Financial Times*, 5 March 1997)
(7) The new **Spanish explorers** – Many companies are discreetly turning themselves into pocket-sized multinationals, as David White explains (*Financial Times*, 19 January 1998)
(8) **Voyage to the west** (*Financial Times*, 19 January 1998)
(9) **Conquistadores** once more – Until recent **expansion into Latin America**, Spanish 'multinationals' were no such thing (*Financial Times*, 19 October 1998)
(10) Return of the **conquistador** – This time round **the Spaniards are invading Latin America** in search of its corporate **treasures**, and the tensions are growing (*Financial Times*, 29 June 1999)

It must be added, however, that the English-language media professionals also use the scenario of the Spanish explorations when Spanish companies started to diversify their investments into other parts of the world. It looks like the English-language headline writers consider this historical event to be so deeply entrenched in their audience's general knowledge of Spain that they frequently use this scenario to describe the actions of Spanish companies across the globe.

(11) With capital in hand, Spain revisits **its empire** (*New York Times*, 29 June 2003)
(12) **Economic conquistadors conquer new worlds** (*New Zealand Herald*, 14 June 2006)

At their peak where the Spaniards started to venture into other parts of the world (2005–2006), the English-language newspapers in our corpus are particularly interested in the upsurge of Spanish investments in Great Britain in 2006. In this phase, the headline writers make a different, but equally interesting historical analogy (five out of sixteen headlines). This time, the English-language media professionals tap into one of the most notable historical confrontations between Spain and Great Britain: the Spanish Armada. Most of the references to the Armada are found in articles published on the topic of Spanish investments in Great Britain in 2006 (five out of six headlines in our corpus).

(13) The **corporate Armada** is on its way to Britain – Douglas Hamilton looks at the confident wave of Spanish firms **looking for new areas to conquer** (*The Herald* [Glasgow], 3 April 2006)

(14) **Armada of acquisitions** heralds **new reign of Spain** (*The Herald* [Glasgow], 15 November 2006)
(15) The new £30bn **Spanish Armada** – It used to be a laidback country of sun and fun. But here we reveal how Spain, once the weakest economy in Europe, has now become one of its strongest – by buying UK firms and relying on expat ingenuity (*Express* [UK], 18 December 2006)

The Spanish Armada refers to the Spanish fleet that sailed against England in 1588, attempting to overthrow Elizabeth I, stop her from intervening in the Spanish Netherlands and to protect Spanish sea communications with its overseas colonies from English privateers. Influenced by anti-Spanish discursive traditions, non-Spaniards at the time referred with heavy irony to the 'Invincible Armada'. The fleet proved anything but invincible as it was defeated by the English. This ironic reading is also found in headline (16), where the headline writer adds 'at last', suggesting that even though the Spanish attempt to get a foothold in Great Britain failed in the sixteenth century, they finally made it at the beginning of the twenty-first century.

(16) **Spain's ship** comes in **at last** (*The Times*, 8 June 2006)

This headline mainly works as an attention-getter, and to be sure that the readers understand the historical reference, the journalist begins the article by explaining the headline. Moreover, s/he does not shy away from enriching the scenario with more colourful elements such as 'to plunder' and 'jewels':

(17) However, unlike the Spanish fleet that was defeated after Sir Francis Drake famously finished a game of bowls in 1588, the latest Spanish attempt **to plunder** one of the richest **jewels** in British business looks as if it is going to be successful (*The Times*, 8 June 2006)

In the corpus, there is another headline based on a similar metaphor scenario. Headline (18) builds on a historic, popular phrase which is likely to resonate in the minds of the *New York Times*'s North American readership:

(18) Forget **the Maine**. Spain is back (*New York Times*, 15 February 1998)

In this article on Spanish investments in the United States, the journalist from the *New York Times* uses a salient historical event in the history of Spanish-American relationships as an attention grabber. The USS Maine was a US battleship which had been sent to Cuba to protect US interests during the Cuban revolt against Spain. On 15 February 1898, the battleship was blown up and destroyed, killing nearly three-quarters of the crew. Even though until today the cause of the explosion remains unclear, American public opinion quickly blamed Spain (Schmidt, 2005, pp. 29–30). This led to an emotional outburst around the country, which was popularized in the phrase 'Remember the Maine. To hell with Spain!' The sinking of the Maine was one of the events which eventually led to the Spanish-American War. It must be noted, however, that this reference is much more specific, and thus much more difficult to decipher, than the much better known narrative frame of *the conquistador*. On the other hand, it is also possible that this historic event was 'in the news' at the time because of the hundredth anniversary of the Spanish-American War. To be sure, the journalist explains this historical allusion in the very first lines of the article.

(19) THE explosion of the battleship Maine in Havana harbor 100 years ago today set the stage for Spain's retreat from the last remnants of its empire in the New World, and for the emergence of the United States as a global power. Yet as the American Century draws to a close, a resurgent Spain is once again flexing its muscles in Latin America and pushing aside any lingering memories of 'El Desastre,' as the Spanish-American War is often called there. (*New York Times*, 15 February 1998)

Discussion

This analysis reveals that the English-language newspapers, at times, set up attention-grabbing metaphor scenarios based on Spain's rich history of belligerent confrontations dating from its colonial past. In this discussion, we want to focus on three interrelated aspects of this socio-culturally grounded intercultural narrative framing. First, we discuss why these specific intercultural scenarios cropped up in their respective discursive contexts. Second, we explore the link between these scenarios and national stereotyping, discuss the potential dangers of these narrative frames for international relations and show how these scenarios and metaphors can be used differently, depending on which side of the coin the media professional wishes to highlight. Finally, we will briefly touch upon the paradox between national frames of reference and globalization.

First, we try to reveal why these metaphor scenarios cropped up in their respective discursive contexts. Vivid metaphors are a well-known stylistic resource to pull potential readers into reading the body of the article. They are also used to reduce complexity of news events. Situations that are difficult to grasp can be made more accessible by comparing them to a similar situation. The functions of metaphors as attention-getters and complexity-reducers contribute to the 'highly expressive, vivid, and inventive style' of print media discourse (Koller, 2004, p. 3). Moreover, discourse metaphors, especially the hyperbolical comparisons to historical events identified in this corpus, add extra drama to news stories. One way of adding drama to news stories is to build them on a socio-culturally grounded scenario. In media accounts of mergers and acquisitions, setting up narrative frames of winners and losers has been identified as a common journalistic practice as media professionals instinctively search for interesting angles to construct good and appealing stories (Hellgren et al., 2002; Vaara and Tienari, 2002). Moreover, in the case of cross-border mergers and acquisitions, journalists often set up national frames of reference in which these investments are played out at the national or supranational level. Consider the lead from headline (10): 'the Spaniards are invading Latin America', in which 'the Spaniards' metonymically stands for the Spanish investors and 'Latin America' for the companies they are acquiring. These (supra)national references and the warfare metaphorical construction 'to invade' mutually shape and reinforce the emotive framing of these investments as a confrontation between these two geopolitical regions. This scenario brings in the highly emotive factor of territorialism, and the reaction against a territorial threat. In this example, the headline writer indeed refers to the 'growing tensions' between the powerful nation and the targeted region.

Unsurprisingly, the English-language headline writers in our corpus cast Spain in the role of the powerful agent in these scenarios and seem to be tempted to exploit these creatively by comparing these contemporary events to events from Spain's colonial past. Indeed, as the examples in our corpus show, the media professionals seem to tap into different historical events depending on the context of the contemporary news story: the conquest and colonization for Spanish investments in Latin America (1997–2000), the Spanish Armada for Spanish investments in Great Britain (2006) and, if only once in this corpus, the USS Maine for Spanish investments in the United States. In order to explain why these historical analogies are used in these specific news stories, it is also necessary to consider the discursive context in which these news stories were developed. In the 1990s, Spanish-American relations were repeatedly in the news, with the commemorations of Columbus's voyage in 1992, and the hundredth anniversary of the end of the Spanish-American War in 1998. This paved the way for the English-language media professionals to draw historical analogies that compared the Spanish actions to salient events dating from Spain's colonial past.

The creation and intercultural exploitation of the scenarios identified in this study may also be explained by the existence of international 'news waves'. Fishman (1980) showed how news coverage of crimes was framed as *crimes against the elderly* on a small scale initially, and how this representation was then picked up by other news media. He called this journalistic phenomenon a 'news wave'. It looks like that is what happened to the conquest scenario as well. In the article published on 15 February 1998 in the *New York Times* (headline 18), the journalist writes that 'one Colombian magazine calls [the investments] "the second Spanish conquest."'[2]

Interestingly, both the conquest (1997–9) and the Armada metaphors (2006) become highly recognizable and repetitive in their respective coverage peaks. In fact, they even seem to have become commonplaces. In that same *New York Times* article (15 February 1998), the journalist chooses to build his article around a different historical analogy by referring to the USS Maine (headline 18). However, in the body of the article, the journalist refers to the 'Spanish conquest' as well. In the following example (20), the journalist points out that the fact that the British press exploits the image of the Spanish Armada does not come as a surprise, because the comparison between the historic and the contemporary encounter is a predictable one to make.

(20) UK economy grows used to the Spanish acquisitions – When Spanish construction group Ferrovial emerged last week as a potential bidder for BAA, the UK airport operator, the British press **predictably** labelled it part of a **corporate Spanish Armada raiding British assets** (*Financial Times*, 14 February 2006)

Media professionals often make use of collective memory and narratives to make sense of the present, and use explicit historical analogies to help interpret present events

(Edy, 1999; Le, 2006; Zelizer, 2008). The three historical events identified in this corpus are certainly part of the collective memory of the media audiences for whom the news stories were intended. Both the Armada and the USS Maine scenarios are likely to resonate in the minds of these audiences because they are an important part of British and US culture, respectively. In the case of the Latin American conquest and colonization scenario, there is no link which immediately connects Spain and Latin America to Great Britain or the United States. Still, the historical reference to the Spanish *conquistadores* seems to resonate as well. This suggests that the scenario of the Spanish conquest and colonization made it into the collective memory of a global community (Houchin-Winfield et al., 2002).

Second, it is important to explore the link between these metaphor scenarios and discourse metaphors, and the intercultural preservation of national stereotypes. In most of these news articles, the constant factor is the representation of Spain as the powerful agent. Moreover, some of these headlines clearly indicate a certain fear of things to come (or at least a certain reticence towards the future actions of the Spanish investors on the part of the journalists), whether it be in Latin America, Great Britain or the United States. The historical comparisons encourage the reader to activate scenarios that are richly loaded with encyclopaedic and socio-cultural information. In this context, it means activating the rich, albeit stereotypical, historical context of Spain's territorialism in the past, and, consequently, transposing upon the Spanish investors the stereotypical image of the aggressive Spanish explorers, conquerors, colonizers and exploiters. In headline (6), the Spaniards are described as 'leading a new onslaught', that is, 'a fierce or destructive attack' (OED) on Latin America. In (10), the headline writer describes them as 'invading Latin America' and explicitly refers to the growing tensions between the Spanish investors and their Latin-American targets. In (14), the reference to the Spanish Armada can be interpreted as to instil fear in the British people, because this image 'traditionally haunted Britain' (Valdeón García, 2007, p. 74). In the example with the USS Maine (18), the transition of the second part of the phrase from 'to hell with Spain!' to 'Spain is back!' denotes a certain fear about what the Spaniards are going to do to the American economy.

Of course, media professionals mainly build on these scenarios for rhetorical and stylistic reasons. However, it is important to note that journalistic uses of historical analogies also have important consequences for representations of national identities, which in turn may have an impact on intercultural relations (Le, 2006). Metaphor scenarios and discourse metaphors can indeed be seen as 'important tools for carrying a set of historical memories and commonplaces from one generation to the other' (Hellsten, 2009, p. 197). As a result, the cultural prejudices and preconceptions that are firmly rooted in these scenarios are also transferred (Hellsten, 2009). Edy (1999, p. 78) also notes that there are dangers associated with the journalistic use of historical analogies because they 'can be constructed so that the outcome of certain courses of action in response to the current problem appear predictable.' Indeed, the very use of the historic analogy, and its perceived usefulness in media discourse as a predictor of the future, seems to rely on a broader cultural commonplace, namely, that history repeats itself.

Interestingly, and perhaps surprisingly because of the influence of the discursive traditions aiming at discrediting Spain, the data in our corpus show that Spain's economic internationalization was also framed in a more positive way. At times, Spanish investors are also admired and lauded for their audacity. In (7), the headline writer uses the much more positively charged term of the 'explorers', and in the lead, the companies are described rather positively as 'discreetly turning themselves into pocket-sized multinationals'. In the lead of headline (15), the writer compares the 'former' Spain to the 'new' Spain by highlighting its successful conversion into one of Europe's strongest economies, 'by buying UK firms and relying on expat ingenuity'. There is also another article (21) with a perhaps more subtle historical allusion in 'building empires', in which the boldness (or economic courage and fearlessness) of Spanish investors is admired:

(21) New **boldness** that make Spanish business **stand out** – Spainish (sic) groups are **building empires** beyond national borders with the aim of diversification (*Financial Times*, 14 June 2005)

This shows how these scenarios can be interpreted differently. Consider, for example, the frequently used discourse metaphor of the 'new conquistadors'. The interpretation differs when different qualities of the Spanish investors are highlighted because these trigger different socio-cultural elements stored in long-term memory. Depending on which aspects best fit the broader scenario set up by the media professional for a particular news story, the Spanish investors can either be framed as *forceful aggressors* or as *audacious pioneers*.

It can be noted that the scenarios of the conquest, the Armada and the USS Maine, and the behaviour associated with them, are consistent with the common journalistic practice of constructing good and appealing stories (Hellgren et al., 2002; Vaara and Tienari, 2002). Expanding companies are often compared to soldiers and armies in business media discourse; they are audacious, adventurous, daring and determined when entering new markets, but also bloodthirsty, greedy and aggressive when taking over companies. In our corpus, the negative interpretation of these metaphor scenarios focuses on the greedy, bloodthirsty and aggressive nature of the Spaniards, whereas the positive interpretation focuses more on the bravery of the Spaniards, and the heroic qualities of the Spanish explorers who audaciously ventured into unknown territories. However, there is another important intercultural side to this coin. It does not really matter whether the interpretation is positive or negative. The story is always about European villains or heroes. The indigenous population (or the Latin American companies) are merely the object of the action. As Stern (1992, p. 23) observes: 'Their role is to accept or rebel against that which is done to them.'

Third, setting up national frames of reference combined with national stereotyping seems to be a highly conventionalized pattern in intercultural media representations of cross-border mergers and acquisitions (Kuronen et al., 2005; Riad and Vaara, 2011; Tienari et al., 2003). In this case, the historical events associated with the Spanish investors come to stand metaphorically and metonymically for the whole Spanish identity. Indeed, it is telling how, probably under the influence of the age-old discursive traditions aimed at discrediting Spain, the stereotypical image of the aggressive Spaniards still remains active in the collective socio-cultural memory of the English-speaking world. Nevertheless, in spite of the so-called globalization (or transnationalization) of the economy, it is becoming increasingly difficult to maintain the claim that companies, especially multinationals, are firmly rooted in their homelands (Desai, 2009).

Processes of organizational globalization are generally characterized by two underlying counterforces (Naisbitt [1994] calls this the global paradox). In theory, globalization transcends national boundaries, but this 'blurring of national boundaries is continually counterbalanced by social and cultural forces that sustain them' (Ailon-Souday and Kunda, 2003, p. 1073). Indeed, these national frames of reference seem to be extremely effective in reducing the complexities of contemporary global business realities, and references to national identity and national stereotypes prove to be a highly useful resource to maintain this framework of international confrontation (Riad and Vaara, 2011). Thus, it seems unlikely that media professionals will give up this convenient frame to guide their understanding of global business any time soon.

Conclusion

In this study, we considered a specific case which clearly demonstrates the rhetorical and intercultural potential of discourse metaphors and metaphor scenarios in media discourse commenting on an intercultural (business) event: Spanish FDI. We also touched upon the dangers in these stereotypical representations and the contradiction between the globalization (or transnationalization) of the economy and the fact that the media continue to adhere to the traditional framework of international confrontation.

In their search to add drama to media texts, business media professionals not only create news stories on the basis of winners and losers, they also use a narrative framework based on historical analogies. This study confirms that media professionals frequently explain the present in light of the past. Media professionals are likely to tap into collective socio-cultural memory to make meaningful comparisons in order to process and simplify the complexity of contemporary news events. This research shows how, in the context of Spanish FDI, the English-language headline writers seemed only too eager to dive into the historical stereotypical narrative through which the Spaniards are depicted as forceful aggressors. In our corpus, this discursive metaphorical framework is materialized in the use of a conquest, Armada and, if only once, USS Maine scenario. Interestingly, the media professionals themselves seem to consider this framing to be predictable.

It is also no coincidence that precisely these three metaphor scenarios are exploited in our corpus. Our analysis suggests that, in the English-speaking world, the anti-Spanish discursive traditions continue to serve as a powerful framing device for news stories in which Spain is the powerful agent. The colonial exploitation of the indigenous population of the New World has been recounted over the years, and has made it into collective memory. The same holds for the Armada story as it still resonates as the symbol of all conflicts Spain and England/Great Britain have had over the centuries.

The USS Maine story is also about a Spanish attack on the territorial integrity of another nation. What these three stories have in common is that these violent Spanish actions resulted in a backlash against Spain, affecting its reputation at international and intercultural levels. Indeed, the journalistic use of these dramatic historical narrative frames has important consequences for the intercultural understanding of Spain in the English-speaking world, and ultimately for international relations as well. By using these narrative frames in their news stories, the media professionals not only help to carry these historical memories over from one generation to the other, they also help to transfer cultural prejudices and preconceptions.

However, this research also suggests that these narrative frames have more journalistic potential than one would perhaps first expect. Media professionals not only use these frames to present a stereotypical interpretation of the Spanish investors as Spanish conquistadors, but also use the same historical analogies to present Spain's economic internationalization in a positive way. Depending on which aspects best fit the broader scenario the writer of the news story wishes to set up, the Spanish investors can be either framed as forceful aggressors or as audacious pioneers.

Notes

1 It is crucial, of course, that the reader possesses the necessary socio-cultural background knowledge to establish the link between the investors from the present and the Spanish conquistadors from the past. However, even if the reader does not immediately establish the socio-cultural link, the headline is also likely to be explained in the body of the article. This is, for example, the case for the headlines 'Forget the Maine. Spain is back!' (*New York Times*, 15 February 1998) and 'Spain's ship comes in at last' (*The Times*, 8 June 2006), both of which are discussed in this chapter.

2 The journalist refers to an article published by *El Tiempo* on 1 May 1995 ('Expotecnia, la segunda conquista') about the inauguration of an important Spanish trade fair in Bogotá, Colombia, organized by the Spanish Institute of Foreign Trade (ICEX).

References

Ailon-Souday, G. and Kunda, G. (2003), 'The Local Selves of Global Workers: The Social Construction of National Identity in the Face of Organizational Globalization', *Organization Studies*, 24(7): 1073–96.

DeGuzmán, M. (2005), *Spain's Long Shadow: The Black Legend, Off-Whiteness, and Anglo-American Empire*. Minneapolis: University of Minnesota Press.

Deignan, A. (2003), 'Metaphorical Expressions and Culture: An Indirect Link', *Metaphor and Symbol*, 18(4): 255–71.

Desai, M. A. (2009), 'The Decentering of the Global Firm', *The World Economy*, 32(9): 1271–90.

Edy, J. A. (1999), 'Journalistic Uses of Collective Memory', *Journal of Communication*, 49(2): 71–85.

Eubanks, P. (2000), *A War of Words in the Discourse of Trade: The Rhetorical Constitution of Metaphor*, Carbondale: Southern Illinois University Press.

Feyaerts, K., and Brône, G. (2005), 'Expressivity and Metonymic Inferencing: Stylistic Variation in Nonliterary Language Use', *Style*, 39(1): 12–26.

Fishman, M. (1980), *Manufacturing the News*, Austin: University of Texas Press.

Greco, S. (2009), 'Metaphorical Headlines in Business, Finance and Economic Magazines', *Linguistica e Filologia*, 28: 193–211.

Hellgren, B., Löwstedt, J., Puttonen, L., Tienari, J., Vaara, E. and Werr, A. (2002), 'How Issues Become (Re)constructed in the Media: Discursive Practices in the AstraZeneca Merger', *British Journal of Management*, 13: 123–40.

Hellsten, I. (2009), 'Metaphors as Time Capsules: Their Uses in the Biosciences and the Media', in B. Nerlich, R. Elliott and B. Larson (eds), *Communicating Biological Sciences: Ethical and Metaphorical Dimensions*, Surrey: Ashgate, pp. 185–200.

Houchin-Winfield, B., Friedman, B. and Trisnadi, V. (2002), 'History as the Metaphor through Which the Current World Is Viewed: British and American Newspapers' Uses of History Following the 11 September 2001 Terrorist Attacks', *Journalism Studies*, 3(2): 289–300.

Johnson, M. (1992), 'Philosophical Implications of Cognitive Semantics', *Cognitive Linguistics*, 3: 345–66.

Juderías, J. (1914), *La Leyenda Negra y la Verdad Histórica: Contribución al Estudio del Concepto de España en Europa, de las Causas de Este Concepto y de la Tolerancia Religiosa y Política en los Países Civilizados*, Madrid: Tip. de la Revista de Archivos.

Koller, V. (2004), *Metaphor and Gender in Business Media Discourse: A Critical Cognitive Study*, Basingstoke: Palgrave Macmillan.

—(2005), 'Critical Discourse Analysis and Social Cognition: Evidence from Business Media Discourse', *Discourse and Society*, 16(2): 199–224.

Koteyko, N., Brown, B. and Crawford, P. (2008), 'The Dead Parrot and the Dying Swan: The Role of Metaphor Scenarios in UK Press Coverage of Avian Flu in the UK in 2005–2006', *Metaphor and Symbol*, 23: 242–61.

Kövecses, Z. (2005), *Metaphor in Culture: Universality and Variation*, Cambridge: Cambridge University Press.

Kuronen, M.-L., Tienari, J. and Vaara, E. (2005), 'The Merger Storm Recognizes No Borders: An Analysis of Media Rhetoric on a Business Manoeuvre', *Organization*, 12(2): 247–73.

Lakoff, G. (1987), *Women, Fire, and Dangerous Things: What Categories Reveal about the Mind*, Chicago: University of Chicago Press.

Lakoff, G. and Johnson, M. (1980), *Metaphors We Live By*, Chicago: University of Chicago Press.

Le, E. (2006), 'Collective Memory and Representations of National Identity in Editorials – Obstacles to a Renegotiation of Intercultural Relations', *Journalism Studies*, 7(5): 708–28.

López de Abiada, J. M. (2007), 'Spaniards', in M. Beller and J. Leerssen (eds), *Imagology: The Cultural Construction and Literary Representation of National Characters. A Critical Survey*, Amsterdam: Rodopi, pp. 242–7.

Musolff, A. (2006), 'Metaphor Scenarios in Public Discourse', *Metaphor and Symbol*, 21(1): 23–38.

Naisbitt, J. (1994), *Global Paradox*, New York: Avon Books.

Nerlich, B. (2005), '"A River Runs Through it"': How the Discourse Metaphor *Crossing the Rubicon* Structured the Debate about Human Embryonic Stem Cells in Germany and (not) the UK', *metaphorik.de*, 8: 71–104.

Nerlich, B., Hamilton, C. A. and Rowe, V. (2002), 'Conceptualising Foot and Mouth Disease: The Socio-cultural Role of Metaphors, Frames and Narratives', *metaphorik.de*, 2: 90–108.

Nerlich, B. and Koteyko, N. (2010), 'Carbon Gold Rush and Carbon Cowboys: A New Chapter in Green Mythology?', *Environmental Communication*, 4(1): 37–53.

Noya, J. (2004), 'La Imagen de España y Sus Inversiones en América Latina', *Universia Business Review*, 3: 46–61.

OED Online, *Oxford English Dictionary*, Oxford: Oxford University Press. <http://oxforddictionaries.com/<

Riad, S. and Vaara, E. (2011), 'Varieties of National Metonomy in Media Accounts of International Mergers and Acquisitions', *Journal of Management Studies*, 48(4): 737–71.

Schafraad, P., Wester, F. and Scheepers, P. (2006), 'Using "New" Data Sources for "Old" Newspaper Research: Developing Guidelines for Data Collection', *Communications*, 31: 455–67.

Schmidt, D. E. (2005), *The Folly of War: American Foreign Policy, 1898–2005*, New York: Algora Publishing.

Stern, S. J. (1992), 'Paradigms of Conquest: History, Historiography, and Politics', *Journal of Latin American Studies*, 24: 1–34.

Tienari, J., Vaara, E. and Björkman, I. (2003), 'Global Capitalism Meets National Spirit: Discourses in Media Texts on a Cross-Border Acquisition', *Journal of Management Inquiry*, 12(4): 377–93.

Vaara, E. and Tienari, J. (2002), 'Justification, Legitimization and Naturalization of Mergers and Acquisitions: A Critical Discourse Analysis of Media Texts', *Organization*, 9(2): 275–301.

Valdeón García, R. A. (2007), 'The Armada Is Coming: Editorialese Strategies in Economic Comment Columns', *Revista Electrónica de Lingüística Aplicada*, 6(1): 69–81.

White, M. (1998), 'A Cognitive Linguistic View of the Use of Metaphor in Headlines, Leads and News Stories', in A. Downing Rothwell, A. J. Moya Guijarro and J. I. Albentosa Hernández (eds), *Patterns in Discourse and Text*, Ciudad Real: Artes Gráficas, pp. 31–62.

White, M. and Herrera, H. (2003), 'Metaphor and Ideology in the Press Coverage of Telecom Corporate Consolidations', in R. Dirven, R. Frank and M. Pütz (eds), *Cognitive Models in Language and Thought: Ideology, Metaphors and Meanings*, Berlin: Mouton de Gruyter, pp. 277–323.

—(2009), 'How Business Press Headlines Get Their Message Across: A Different Perspective on Metaphor', in A. Musolff and J. Zinken (eds), *Metaphor and Discourse*, Basingstoke: Palgrave Macmillan, pp. 135–52.

Zelizer, B. (2008), 'Journalism's Memory Work', in A. Erll and A. Nünning (eds), *Media and Cultural Memory*, Berlin: Walter de Gruyter, pp. 379–88.

Zinken, J. (2003), 'Ideological Imagination: Intertextual and Correlational Metaphors in Political Discourse', *Discourse and Society*, 14(4): 507–23.

Zinken, J., Hellsten, I. and Nerlich, B. (2008), 'Discourse Metaphors', in R. Frank, R. Dirven, T. Ziemke and E. Bernárdez (eds), *Body, Language, and Mind – Volume 2: Sociocultural Situatedness*, Berlin: Mouton de Gruyter, pp. 363–86.

10

One Step Forward, Two Steps Back: Conceptualizing Serbia's EU Accession in Serbian and EU Discourse[1]

Nadežda Silaški and Tatjana Đurović[2]

Introduction

Being a highly complex political structure markedly different from the concept of state as defined by international law, the European Union (EU) still seems to be literally and figuratively unfathomable not only to people who live within its boundaries but even more so to those outside its overall framework, thus still being experienced as *un objet politique non-identifié*.[3] The way that the perplexing European space is conceived and how a number of countries geographically belonging to Europe but politically and economically outside the EU boundaries eagerly pursue a place in the new space are evidenced in discourse. This discourse, in both cognitive and linguistic terms, serves as a vehicle for conveying the concepts which should be understood by the general public.

Many studies which research EU discourse both inside and outside the EU (e.g. Musolff, 2000, 2004, 2006; Šarić, 2005; Šarić et al., 2010; Silaški et al., 2009; Zbierska-Sawala, 2004) convincingly show that highly abstract processes of joining and integration with the EU are effectuated by the linkages between language, cognition and reality, while metaphors, understood in Lakoffian terms (Lakoff and Johnson, 1980), become the most pervasive cognitive and linguistic devices for shaping and communicating conceptualizations of the given reality. In other words, a host of metaphors documented in the aforementioned studies are created and deployed with the aim of making the issue of the European political and economic union less abstract and more comprehensible. The conceptualization of Serbia's EU accession is no exception in this regard.

On 28 February 2012, officially effective as of 1 March 2012, after more than a decade of tough negotiations and ebbs and flows in mutual relations, Serbia was granted a full candidate status in the European Union. Although Serbia officially applied for the European Union membership on 22 December 2009, its commitment to join 'the

European family of nations' has been the political staple ever since 2000, that is, since the fall of Slobodan Milošević's regime. Joining the European Union was the hottest issue emerging in all previous presidential and parliamentary election agendas except the last one, held in May 2012, probably due both to the fact that Serbia's future in the EU is somewhat clearer upon getting the candidate status for EU membership and to a rise in Euroscepticism markedly discernible among Serbian citizens. This has been proved by surveys whose results clearly indicate that the support for EU accession has been declining noticeably in the last two years.[4]

Theoretical framework and data collection

Metaphors are regarded here as powerful persuasive tools used for generating specific value judgements thus constructing via discourse a certain point of view, and as a discursive means which aids in understanding certain social processes, more specifically the aspect of Serbia's entering the European Union and its underlying notions. The JOURNEY metaphor scenario, one of 'the most important discursive representations of the EU' (Drulák, 2006, p. 499), is analyzed within the framework of Critical Metaphor Analysis (CMA) (Charteris-Black, 2004). It will hopefully help us to conduct 'the ideological analysis of implicit textual content': 'texts are not as neutral as they at first appear' because 'the social processes that lead to unconscious choices being made are concealed or made opaque in the linguistic encoding' (p. 30).

Contemporary metaphor research from the late 1990s onwards has however completely shifted focus from viewing metaphor as a primarily cognitive phenomenon, placing great emphasis on 'the importance of language use in understanding metaphor' (Cameron and Deignan, 2006, p. 672). In other words, metaphor has now emerged as equally a cognitive and a linguistic phenomenon. In this new 'emergentist perspective' metaphor is viewed as a blend of linguistic, conceptual and socio-cultural aspects (p. 674). Charteris-Black (2004, p. 24) emphasizes the 'interconnecting aspects of metaphor', arguing for a definition of metaphor that incorporates its semantic, cognitive and pragmatic dimensions, where the pragmatic one arises from 'the underlying purpose of [metaphor] influencing opinions and judgements by persuasion' (p. 21), since metaphors are often used 'persuasively to convey evaluations and therefore constitute part of the ideology of texts' (p. 28).

On the other hand, the category of *scenario*, as propounded by Musolff (2006), draws on Charles Fillmore's (1975) notion of a conceptual 'scene' as well as on Lakoff's (1987) definition of 'scenario' as a subtype of idealized cognitive models. By integrating various approaches which relate to 'scenario', Musolff (2006, p. 28) views it 'as a set of assumptions made by competent members of a discourse community about "typical" aspects of a source-situation, for example, its participants and their roles, the "dramatic" storylines and outcomes, and conventional evaluations of whether they count as successful or unsuccessful, normal or abnormal, permissible or illegitimate, etc.' Scenarios seem to be very frequent and 'constitute an essential feature of metaphor use in public discourse registers' (p. 28) and they 'help to shape the course of public debates and conceptualizations of political target topics by framing the attitudinal and evaluative preferences in the respective discourse communities' (p. 28).[5]

The main aim of the chapter is to explore the 'loadedness' of the JOURNEY metaphor scenario, especially as realized in *step* and *traffic light* metaphors, which we consider 'discourse metaphors'. Discourse metaphors, according to Musolff (2010, p. 158), 'not only transfer individual items and abstract (topo-)logical relations between source and target domains, but also transport evaluative and narrative elements that draw a seemingly self-explanatory conclusion from a mini-story or "scenario"'. By deepening our analysis of the JOURNEY metaphor with a detailed account of the *step* and *traffic light* linguistic instantiations, we try to probe into the evaluative content of these two metaphors in order to establish the ideological meaning that they carry in real discourse, focusing on one of the main contemporary issues relevant not only to ordinary Serbian citizens, but also to the politicians in power.

Our data collection for the analysis comprises two structurally different parts: the first is taken from Serbian dailies and political weeklies in the period 2006–12 and includes texts with the examples of *step* and *traffic light* metaphors which relate to Serbian politicians talking about the EU accession; the second part encompasses the EU officials' statements on Serbia's EU accession, compiled from press releases and official documents mostly downloaded from the official website of the European Union (europa.eu).[6] Hence the two data sets refer to national and institutional discourse respectively, and the 'intercultural' differences highlighted later in the text are not those between the two national cultures but rather between a national discourse on the one hand and an institutional discourse or 'culture' on the other. Each data set totals about 100,000 words.

In order to verify the validity of our intuitive judgement as regards the metaphoricity of the lexical units linguistically realizing the JOURNEY metaphor scenario (since 'intuitions are not necessarily explicit and systematic'; Semino, 2008, p. 14), we applied the procedure for metaphor identification (MIP) proposed by the Pragglejaz Group (2007). It is claimed to be a reliable method as it eliminates any subjective criteria for metaphor identification. Having established the presence of metaphoricity modelled on the MIP, we then extracted the parts of text containing those expressions which both of us judged to be metaphorical. Some of these will be used to illustrate our points in the text which follows. Our goal is *not* to establish absolute or relative frequencies of metaphors or metaphor density in the data collection. Our main focus is on the qualitative analysis of the examples of the JOURNEY metaphor scenario in question to examine its intercultural character and evaluative content in Serbian and EU discourse.

JOURNEY metaphor scenario in Serbia's EU accession discourse

One of the most prevailing and recurrent metaphor scenarios underlying the aspect of joining the EU is the JOURNEY scenario, which is actually 'shorthand for a much more complex conceptual scenario that ultimately goes back to the metaphor PURPOSES ARE DESTINATIONS (Lakoff and Johnson, 1999) and the related SOURCE-

PATH-GOAL schema (Johnson 1987)' (Koller and Semino, 2009, pp. 19–20), giving rise to a more precise PURPOSEFUL ACTIVITY IS MOVING ON A PATH TOWARDS A DESTINATION metaphor (Lakoff, 1993). A highly rhetorical impact of the JOURNEY scenario, which has been profusely exploited in political discourse, stems from the fact that the SOURCE-PATH-GOAL schema is one of the most common structures, emerging from our constant bodily functioning, so it is pervasive in experience and thus well-understood and simply structured (Johnson, 1987). The JOURNEY scenario realized via its MOTION and PATH subdomains has a direct link to our embodied experiences and that is why the embodied goal-oriented motion is found to be very productive in political discourse dealing with the issue of the EU accession (e.g. Drulák, 2004; Musolff, 2004; Šarić et al., 2010), Serbian public discourse being no exception (see Đurović and Silaški, 2012; Silaški et al., 2009). For that matter, we concur with Zbierska-Sawala (2004, p. 408) who writes that by their nature the JOURNEY metaphors 'have a strong tendency to promote positive axiology', since 'a journey, once undertaken, creates strong expectations of reaching the goal, despite the challenges awaiting the traveller'.

The JOURNEY scenario in our data collection reflects all the complexity of Serbia's accession to the European Union, which is in compliance with Kövecses's (2006, p. 211) claim that '[c]omplex events are also commonly viewed involving an initial state (SOURCE), intermediate stages (PATHS), and a final state (GOAL)'. In addition, the JOURNEY metaphor scenario is frequent in political discourse 'especially in relation to plans, policies, and the histories of nation states' (Semino, 2008, p. 117), while the concrete goals are conventionally conceptualized as destinations to be reached 'so that movement forward tends to correspond to positive change, development and success' (p. 81). Thus Serbia's accession to the European Union, conceptualized by means of the JOURNEY metaphor scenario, is based on a more concrete PURPOSEFUL SOCIAL ACTIVITY IS TRAVELLING ALONG A PATH TOWARDS A DESTINATION metaphor (Charteris-Black, 2004, p. 74). Incorporating instances of discourses from two discourse communities, national – Serbia, and institutional – the EU, and two languages, Serbian and English, may allow for certain mappings or correspondences which place an emphasis on different inferences, as our analysis of *step* and *traffic light* metaphors will show later in the text, manifesting certain cultural differences despite a universal foundation of the SOURCE-PATH-GOAL image schema.

As already said, we focus on two linguistic metaphors – that of *step* and *traffic light* – in order to examine how the same issue, Serbia's accession to the EU, may lead to different uses of the same metaphor scenario in two data collections, one which relates to Serbian politicians talking about the EU accession, and the other which encompasses the EU officials' statements on Serbia's EU accession. The use of metaphors, as Musolff (2003, p. 13) asserts, 'often implies a specific perspective and bias which relates to particular political experiences, interests and traditions of usage.' Thus, although we deal with semantic equivalents in Serbian and English, a deeper analysis seems to reveal that *step* and *traffic light* expressions presuppose rather different political perspectives, expectations and interests of Serbian and European officials, respectively.

Step by step

The expression *step* is one of the conventional expressions of the JOURNEY metaphor scenario, based on the ACTIONS ARE SELF-PROPELLED MOVEMENTS metaphor. 'This idea of moving in a particular direction is used metaphorically to talk about an action which will help someone to achieve a particular goal, especially when that action is one of a number of actions that they will have to take' (Deignan, 1995, p. 194). The kinds of steps which should be taken to reach a destination correspond to the mapping MANNER OF ACTION IS MANNER OF MOTION, hence 'great strides', 'big step', 'a step closer' and so on, as the examples here show. The analysis of both Serbian and EU data samples highlights two ways of understanding this metaphorical expression. In the first case, *step* indicates the usual, conventional and neutrally evaluative expression of the JOURNEY metaphor scenario expressing the change of location in the physical sense and motion and progress on the road or path, as illustrated in the following examples:

(1) Mislim da mi **krupnim koracima** idemo ka EU, ali kriza u EU može da utiče na naš možda kasniji ulazak. (*B92*, 4 December 2009)
(I think that we are making **great strides** towards the EU, but the crisis within the EU may influence our possible late accession.)

(2) Direktorka Kancelarije za evropske integracije Milica Delević rekla je da je hapšenje haškog optuženika Ratka Mladića **veliki korak** u procesu evropskih integracija. (*S media*, 27 May 2011)
(Director of the European Integration Office Milica Delević said that the arrest of the Hague indictee Ratko Mladić is a **big step** in the process of European integration.)

(3) Srbija **korak** bliže Evropskoj uniji. (*Blic*, 24 June 2009)
(Serbia **a step closer** to the European Union.)

(4) The satisfactory implementation of the SAA will be Serbia's gateway to the next stage towards the EU. I am convinced that the country can make **great strides**, as we have said in our Progress Report, but Serbia should now meet its international obligation to fully cooperate with the ICTY, leading to the arrest of the remaining indictees. (Olli Rehn, EU Commissioner for Enlargement, The Commission's 2007 enlargement reports, Presentation at European Parliament, Brussels, 21 November 2007)

More importantly, however, *step* is perceived in both the Serbian and English data sets as a part of the mapping of the EVENT STRUCTURE metaphor – MANNER OF ACTION OR ITS MEANS IS A PATH TOWARDS A DESTINATION. As already said, *step* is, generally speaking, one of the conventional metaphors, and as such it is 'automatic, effortless, and generally established as a mode of thought among the members of a linguistic community' (Lakoff and Turner, 1989, p. 55). However, our data indicate that the *step* metaphor also has a covert persuasive function in its appeal to both Serbian and EU officials who thus want to communicate different messages to the general public.

Step *in the Serbian data*

The following analysis is intended to show how the discourse manifestations of the *step* metaphor in the Serbian data help to shape not only the perception Serbian people have of Serbia's EU accession, but also 'conceptualizations of political target topics by framing the attitudinal and evaluative preferences in the respective discourse communities' (Musolff, 2006, p. 28).

(5) Potpisujući Sporazum o stabilizaciji i pridruživanju 29. aprila 2008, Srbija je načinila jedan od najvažnijih **koraka na putu** ka članstvu u Evropskoj uniji. Još mnogo **koraka** predstoji. (*Politika*, 7 December 2009)
(By signing the Stabilization and Association Agreement on 29 April 2008, Serbia made one of the most important **steps** toward European Union membership. There are many more **steps** to come.)

(6) **Put** do članstva u Evropskoj uniji je dug, složen i skup, ali na svakom **koraku** tog **puta** prati nas EU obezbeđujući finansijsku, tehničku, stručnu i savetodavnu pomoć. (*Evropski forum*, 28 September 2006)
(The **road** to EU membership is long, complex and expensive, but at every **step** of that **road** we are accompanied by the EU that provides financial, technical, expert and advisory help.)

(7) Podnošenjem kandidature za punopravno članstvo u Evropskoj uniji decembra prošle godine Srbija je prešla lakšu polovinu **puta** u procesu evropskih integracija, a kada u parlamentima 27 zemalja članica EU počne ratifikacija Sporazuma o stabilizaciji i pridruživanju, otvoriće se vrata i za **nove, kompleksnije korake** – prihvatanje kandidature i početak pregovora o članstvu. (*Danas*, 14 June 2010)
(Having submitted the application for full-fledged membership of the European Union in December last year, Serbia got past the easier half of the **road** to European integration and, when the ratification of the Stabilization and Association Agreement starts in the parliaments of the 27 EU member states, the door will open to **new and more complex steps**: approval of its candidacy and commencement of membership negotiations.)

(8) Evropska unija najverovatnije će odobriti početak primene prelaznog sporazuma sa Srbijom, ali će za **svaki sledeći korak na putu** ka punopravnom članstvu u Uniji lociranje i hapšenje preostalih haških optuženika ostati uslov, saznaje „Blic" u diplomatskim izvorima u Briselu. (*Blic*, 23 July 2008)
(In all likelihood, the European Union will approve the commencement of the application of a transitional agreement with Serbia, but **each subsequent step along the road** to full-fledged membership of the EU will be conditioned on tracking down and arresting the remaining Hague Tribunal indictees, the *Blic* daily has learnt from diplomatic sources in Brussels.)

(9) Predsednik Srbije Boris Tadić izjavio je danas da je stavljanje Srbije na belu šengensku listu **prvi korak** ka njenoj punoj integraciji u EU. „Ovo je **praktičan i jasan korak na putu** evropskih integracija." (*Politika*, 30 November 2011)

(Serbian President Boris Tadić has said today that placing Serbia on the Schengen White List is a **first step** towards its full integration with the EU. 'This is a **practical and clear step on the road** to European integration.')

(10) **Korak napred, korak nazad**: Srbija je u novu 2012. ušla ohrabrena činjenicom da je u prethodnoj godini napravila krupan **korak napred** u reformama kako bi se približila EU, ali i sa punom svešću da na tom **putu** ima ozbiljne prepreke. (*Tanjug*, 3 January 2012)
(**One step forward, one step back**: Serbia has entered the year 2012 encouraged by the fact that last year it made a **big step forward** in its reforms in order to get closer to the EU, but also fully aware that there are serious obstacles on this **road**.)

The examples from the Serbian data indicate that the metaphorical expression *step* is a powerful rhetorical device for initiating an action. Every positively evaluated activity on the part of the Serbian government, for example, signing the Stabilization and Association Agreement, the CEFTA Agreement, placing Serbia on the Schengen White List, arresting war crimes fugitives and so on, is perceived by Serbian officials as one step closer to Serbia's reaching the final goal, entering the EU, in both real and abstract senses. A host of adjectives which qualify the *step* metaphor purposely contribute to a highly positive evaluation, which Serbian officials strive to impart on the nature of the activities undertaken. Thus they talk of 'the most important steps', 'new, complex steps', 'practical and clear step' and so on with the aim of conveying self-complacency and making the Serbian electorate aware of the progress made so far towards the final goal. The rhetorical impact of the character of *steps* hinges on convincing the electorate of the justifiability of the cause and hardship endured on the course, which should tone down the fact that the process has not been completed yet and that there are still sacrifices to be made. Taking steps in political discourse is not a voluntary activity likened to taking steps in real life, but a heavily controlled activity since, as seen in example (6), '**at every step** of that road we are accompanied by the EU that provides financial, technical, expert and advisory help', that is, there is a reward after every important step taken.

Although Serbian officials try to induce a positive perception of advancement towards the EU with the Serbian electorate, presenting steps as necessary and worthwhile activities on Serbia's path to the EU, they in fact tend to justify and mitigate their unwillingness, inability or incompetence to fulfil the conditions set by the EU, fuzzily viewed as steps. Hence Serbia's movement to the EU is not always a forward one, but is occasionally intercepted by moving backwards, and viewed as 'one step back' (example [10]), implying that UNDOING PROGRESS IS BACKWARD MOVEMENT (see Lakoff, 1993). The expression 'one step back' signals not only the incapability of Serbian authorities to comply with all the conditions set by the EU, but it also serves as a rationalization of why Serbia has not made the expected and visible advancement to the EU, thus handing over the responsibility for Serbia's impediment to progress solely to the EU. Among the forthcoming steps that Serbia still needs to take are fighting organized crime and corruption, judicial and other reforms, completion of Serbia's cooperation with the Hague Tribunal and continuation of negotiations between

Serbia and Kosovar Albanians. Nevertheless, it appears that the number of steps, that is, the concessions Serbia needs to make, are not limited. In other words, what this metaphorical expression hides is *how many* steps Serbia has to take and *how long* a road it needs to travel, as the part 'there are many more **steps** to come' of example (5) indicates.

Step *in EU discourse*

The patterns of collocations that qualify the *step* examples in the EU data sample bear only a superficial similarity to the Serbian data, by trading on the positive associations attached to the selected adjectives.

(11) After the SAA, **the next logical step** for Serbia would be to achieve the status of an EU candidate country. (Olli Rehn, EU Commissioner for Enlargement, Enlargement – the EU keeps its doors open for South Eastern Europe, European Economic and Social Committee, Brussels, 17 January 2007)

(12) It will help to clarify to Serbia that it has a clear perspective to join the Union, if it **takes the right steps in this direction**, and meets the conditions that are expected of a future Member State. (Olli Rehn, European Commissioner for Enlargement, Open debate on enlargement, European Parliament, Foreign Affairs Committee, Brussels, 7 May 2007)

(13) The Council welcomes the arrest of Radovan Karadzic, who is indicted by the ICTY for genocide, crimes against humanity and war crimes. This development illustrates the commitment of the new government in Belgrade to contribute to peace and stability in the Balkans regions. It is **a significant step** on Serbia's path towards the EU. (Press release of the Council of the European Union, 22 July 2008)

(14) As members are aware, the European Council agreed to grant the status of candidate country to Serbia last week. (. . .) Candidate status is only **the first step** on the road to EU membership. (Eamon Gilmore, Tánaiste and Minister for Foreign Affairs and Trade, The Government of Ireland Joint Committee on Foreign Affairs and Trade Debate, 7 March 2012)

(15) Štefan Füle stated that the submittal of the answers was a historic day for Serbia and **a key step** a potential EU candidate takes in order to potentially become a candidate for the EU membership. (Štefan Füle, Commissioner for Enlargement, commenting on the fact that Serbian Prime Minister Mirko Cvetković has delivered to him the answers to the European Commission's Questionnaire, 31 January 2011, www.europa.rs)

Thus the EU discourse qualifies steps Serbia has taken or needs to take as 'key', 'significant', 'right' and so on. Yet, although these adjectives ostensibly serve to give credit for what Serbia has previously done on her route to the EU, on a deeper level they may be understood as the ground for setting up new steps, that is, terms, put forward as being for the benefit of Serbian citizens. Characterizing every condition that Serbia needs to fulfil on her path to the European Union as one step closer to this objective, and granting Serbia the date for the opening of accession negotiations as pending on the steps Serbian authorities should take, is a discursive practice for exerting pressure by constantly devising new steps. In mental terms, the list of conditions perceived as steps transposes into a road or path whose length is infinite and changes incessantly, while the space of the European Union that Serbia needs to approach becomes converted into a number of smaller paths it has to travel on its main route. Strangely enough, example (14), dated 7 March 2012, reads '[c]andidate status is only **the first step** on the road to EU membership', thus not only obliterating any progress made so far via diverse 'steps' already undertaken (e.g. fulfilling conditions for Serbia being placed on the Schengen White List, cooperation with the Hague Tribunal, etc.), but also making the whole process of becoming one of the EU member states rather precarious, the road to EU appearing to be not only long but endless too.

By equating the country's candidate status with taking only the first step after so many years, the European officials tend to signal that Serbia is only at the beginning of its transformation from a non-European state into a European one – it has yet to obey and conform to European criteria and conditions, metaphorically perceived as *steps*. Thus although the institution of new steps is presented by the European officials as moving forward, it is usually viewed by the Serbian general public as throwing Serbia off balance and hampering its progress. More precisely, a positive evaluation of Serbia's move towards reaching the European Union so far, that is, the number of steps taken, at an abstract level should correspond to a travel schedule – the speed of the traveller (Serbia) to a pre-arranged destination at a pre-arranged time, but actually it masks how many steps Serbia has yet to take, the length of the road it has yet to travel, the speed of the steps yet to be taken and so on, that is, how many conditions still need to be met. Hence the use of *step* as evidenced by the EU data is an apt discursive tool for veiling the EU's reluctance to grant Serbia access to the EU, by way of setting new steps corresponding to new concessions to be made.

Therefore, while Serbian officials strive to mitigate the conditional part of *step*, by putting at the forefront the progress achieved so far in moving Serbia closer to the EU, the EU officials use *step* as a trigger for setting new steps, which they view as indispensable joining criteria for endorsing the accession of Serbia to the EU, further prolonging her 'journey'. Thus, despite the positive connotations of *step* that metaphor creators in both discourse communities probably argue for as well as the shared semantic content, *step* renders a cross-cultural misunderstanding which may help develop disillusionment of the Serbian general public and a negative sentiment of Serbian citizens towards the EU. Many surveys conducted so far have shown that support of Serbian citizens to EU accession markedly declines with the institution of new steps, particularly those referring to the sensitive Kosovo issue, which creates a fertile ground for gradually growing Euroscepticism, especially among youth groups.[7]

The green light on Serbia's road to the EU

The *traffic light* metaphor is yet another powerful rhetorical device whose role in political discourse is to expedite the action by giving a clear signal as to whether to proceed in the desired direction or to stop. Together with *step*, the *traffic light* expression may be regarded as '"spotlights" which focus the attention on specific aspects of the problem under discussion' (Musolff, 2003, p. 14).

Traffic light *in the Serbian data*

As some of our examples from the Serbian data show, getting the green light is a prerequisite to taking the next step on Serbia's road to the EU:

(16) **Zeleni semafor** na evropskom putu – **žuto svetlo**, odnosno privremeno čekanje do **zelenog**, za Srbiju je šansa da se otkloni poslednja prepreka za potpisivanje SAA. (. . .) **Žuto svetlo na semaforu** za Beograd zato će, sasvim izvesno, trajati prilično kratko pre nego što se **upali zeleno**. (*Blic*, 28 May 2008)
(The **green light** on the European road – **the amber light**, i.e. the temporary wait for it to change to **green**, is the chance for Serbia to eliminate the last obstacle to signing the SAA. (. . .) **The amber light** for Belgrade will therefore certainly **change to green** in a rather short time.)

(17) Ukoliko posao oko kandidature Srbija bude traljavo radila, onda je to **crveno svetlo** i na izbore moramo otići kako bismo dobili sposobniju i efikasniju vladu u sprovođenju unutrašnjih reformi koji su preduslov daljeg napredovanja Srbije ka EU. (*Blic*, 10 January 2010)
(If Serbia does the shoddy work with its candidacy bid, then it is the **red light** and we will have to have an election to get a government that will be more capable of and efficient in implementing internal reforms, which is a precondition for Serbia's further progress towards the EU.)

(18) Živorad Kovačević, predsednik Evropskog pokreta u Srbiji: Oli Ren je već pokušao da ublaži negativnu ocenu, koju je o saradnji Srbije s Haškim tribunalom dala Karla del Ponte. Mislim da odlaganje parafiranja sporazuma sa EU nije **crveno svetlo za Srbiju, već pre žuto ili zelenkasto**. (*Danas*, 18 October 2007)
(Živorad Kovačević, President of the European Movement in Serbia: Olli Rehn has already tried to play down Carla del Ponte's negative assessment of Serbia's cooperation with The Hague Tribunal. I don't think the postponement of the initialling of the agreement with the EU is a **red light to Serbia, but rather an amber or greenish one**.)

(19) U predlogu rezolucije o procesu evropskih integracija Srbije, koju je sačinio Jelko Kacin, izvestilac Evropskog parlamenta, odaje se priznanje Srbiji za napredak u reformama i pozdravlja odluka Saveta ministara EU koji je **dao zeleno svetlo** da se Beogradu odobri **novi korak** ka članstvu u Uniji. (*Blic*, 29 October 2010)
(The proposed resolution on the process of Serbia's European integration, prepared by Jelko Kacin, European Parliament Rapporteur, commends Serbia for its progress in reforms and welcomes the decision of the EU Council of Ministers to **give the green light** to Belgrade and allow it to take a **new step** towards EU membership.)

(20) „**Zeleno svetlo** za srpski voz prema Briselu biće upaljeno čim pogasimo neka naša **crvena svetla**", istakao je Drašković u izjavi za javnost, navodeći da ohrabruje odluka Saveta ministara EU da se Srbiji otvore vrata za sticanje statusa kandidata za pridužіvanje EU. (*S media*, 25 October 2010)
('**A green light** for Serbia's train to Brussels will be turned on as soon as we turn off some of our **red lights**,' Drašković stressed in his statement for the public, adding that the EU Council of Ministers' decision to open the door to Serbia's getting an EU accession candidate status was encouraging.)

(21) Srbija će verovatno sledećeg meseca podneti kandidaturu za članstvo u EU, ali će prvo sačekati **zeleno svetlo** iz Brisela pre nego što povuče taj **korak**, rekao je Boris Tadić, predsednik Srbije. (*Blic*, 9 November 2009)
(Serbia will probably submit its application for EU candidate status next month, but it will first wait for **a green light** from Brussels before it makes **the move**, said Serbian President Boris Tadić.)

Similarly to the *step* metaphor, these examples indicate that the forward movement is not the traveller's (Serbia's) voluntary activity, but an extremely controlled plan, conceptualized by means of the *traffic light* expression, with the green light conventionally signifying 'permission to proceed', and the amber light referring to the period between 'prohibition to proceed' (the red light) and 'permission to proceed' (the green light). The predominance of the 'green light' expressions in Serbian discourse has a role of creating in Serbian citizens a sense of better days ahead since 'getting the green light' enables taking new steps on Serbia's road to the EU and gaining in speed of movement. Thus, Serbian officials trade on this expression as a positive evaluation of the progress made, yet again obscuring a persuasive motive for using it – *green light* is portrayed in Serbian data sample as a way of allaying doubts of the electorate about the right course of actions undertaken and the direction chosen, but hiding the powerlessness of the Serbian government to proceed any further with integration until permitted to do so by an external agency, in this case the EU.

It is interesting to note the use of the *red light* expression in Serbian data, which has a dual role. On the one hand, it conceptualizes the conventional meaning as the prohibition to proceed until, in political discourse reality, some conditions are met, such as the improvement of the government's attempts to get the EU candidate status or promoting the cooperation with the Hague Tribunal. It is the Serbian officials who perceive unfulfilled conditions set by the EU as changing the lights on the European traffic light to red, which in turn impedes Serbia's journey, making it last longer and be uncertain. On the other hand, the marked absence of this metaphor in English data, as attested by the examples that follow, strengthens the intracultural aspect of this metaphor in Serbian – it functions as a creative extension of the conventional *green light* metaphor and as a part of the comprehensive JOURNEY scenario. Being viewed as the prohibition to proceed, the *red light*, similar to the previous 'one step back' expression, also connotes both spatial and abstract distance away from a better future with which the EU has so often been equated. According to Musolff (2006, p. 35), it is at the level of scenario 'that attitudinal biases and political preferences of discourse communities become discernible'.

Traffic light ***in EU discourse***

The EU data also use an extension of the JOURNEY metaphor scenario by way of the *traffic light* vocabulary to shape Serbia's progression on her road to EU membership.

(22) The Italian official (Giulio Terzi, Italy's Foreign Minister) could not say if the European Council would give **the green light**, but underscored Italy's position that Serbia deserved a positive opinion. ('Serbia deserves green light for accession talks', *Tanjug*, 5 December 2012)

(23) Serbia will then qualify for EU pre-accession money and might get **the green light** from EU leaders in December to open accession talks. ('EU diplomats: Serbia to get candidate status', *EU Observer*, 28 February 2012)

(24) The commissioner (EU Enlargement Commissioner Štefan Füle) said that it was important that Serbia had received **a green light** from the highest level for its cooperation with The Hague, fulfillment of the Copenhagen criteria and for an extremely important role in the reconciliation process in the Western Balkans. ('EU Wants Action, Not Words from Serbia', 12 December 2011, www.balkaninsight.com)

Although the EU officials tend to portray giving a green light to Serbia as encouragement and reward for the progress achieved so far, the motivation that lies behind the *traffic light* instantiation in the EU data seems to be different from the one recognized in Serbian data collection – every granting of the *green light* in case of European officials is a proof that their previous condition conceptually formulated as a *step* has been not only fulfilled but also justified. This, in turn, may set the ground for new conditions for the Serbian authorities to abide by whether they approve of them or not. As already said, the EU officials do not resort to the *red light* expression to mark unsatisfactory progress regarding Serbia's EU accession. This may be accounted for as intentional avoidance of any literal or abstract associations that the *red light* – as an impediment the EU wishes to set up on Serbia's movement – may impart, thus tending to evoke the positive image of the EU with Serbian citizens as the driving force behind Serbia's progress to the EU (by giving her only the *green light*).

On the other hand, it seems that Serbian officials are the ones who, by failing to meet the terms set by the EU labelled as *steps*, impose this metaphorical extension in the form of *red light*, although as the examples from the Serbian data show, the *red light* expression is triggered whenever the EU sets new steps to follow or at least when it is presented to the general public in Serbia in this particular manner. The citation that follows is the best illustration of how the European officials, via the *traffic light* metaphor, structure the issue of enlargement and accession. It also corroborates our argument that the EU officials do not tend to metaphorically portray their conditions and criteria via the *red traffic light* expression:

(25) We also need traffic lights. In this case, metaphorically speaking, we need two, rather than three colours. We should have **green and amber lights** but no **red light**. This means that no country should automatically be excluded

> from European Union membership. Showing any country **the red light** along the road to the European Community is inappropriate, but European traffic would also sink into chaos if the only **light** on the road was **green**. (Ryszard Czarnecki, Member of the European Parliament, an excerpt from his speech at the debate entitled 'Enlargement strategy and main challenges 2006–2007 – The institutional aspects of the European Union's capacity to integrate the new Member States', 13 December 2006)

Thus the *traffic light* metaphor, together with the previous *step* metaphor, is a subtle discursive means which seems to disguise the real intentions of metaphor creators. It reveals that the European officials opt for a combination of 'green' and 'amber' lights, which, in addition to mitigating the powerful 'banning' effect of the 'red light', allows them to totally control the whole process of integration and set the pace for the EU accession. The *traffic light*, accompanied by the *step* metaphor, underlies the heavily regulated character of the journey scenario interspersed with many 'waits' and sparse 'goes', in the case of Serbia, which in turn often generates the negative attitudes in Serbian citizens towards the process of EU integration as one granted grudgingly rather than willingly.

Conclusion

In this chapter an attempt has been made to describe the use of two metaphors, those of *step* and *traffic light*, within the JOURNEY metaphor scenario used for the conceptualization of Serbia's accession to the European Union in Serbian and EU discourse. The intercultural comparison of the two data sets pertaining to EU accession discourse used by politicians in Serbia and in the EU shows that while these two groups use identical *step* and *traffic light* metaphors, at the same time they use them to fit their respective communicative and political purposes and interests. Our analysis reveals that by the use of the *step* and *traffic light* metaphors it is possible to construct a discourse which, in the case of the Serbian authorities, serves to convey self-complacency with the progress made so far, with the intention of inducing a positive perception of such progress with the Serbian electorate and at the same time tending to justify the incompetence of Serbian leaders and their inability to fulfil the conditions set by the EU. In contrast, the *step* and *traffic light* metaphors also allow the EU officials to linguistically and conceptually express the evaluation of the efforts Serbia is making towards EU integration.

Despite positive connotations rendered by the *steps* undertaken and the alternation between the *red* and *green light*, the two metaphors serve as an apt metaphorical tool for masking the EU's reluctance to grant Serbia access to the EU by way of setting new steps, that is, conditions, that Serbia still has to meet. The difference in the use of the *step* and *traffic light* metaphors between the national (Serbian) and institutional (EU) discourse frequently results in misunderstanding by Serbian citizens, which in turn fuels Euroscepticism, increases negative sentiment towards the EU and occasionally backfires on the original intentions of the metaphor users.

If, according to Musolff (2003, p. 14), '[l]inguistic analysis cannot take sides in the form of endorsing one specific formulation or interpretation as "correct" or "truthful" but analyse and explain the political experiences and perspectives that are characteristic for their use in different discourse communities and thus help the respective communities to understand each other better', this chapter then belongs to similar endeavours which, by exposing the hidden, loaded connotations of conventional and inherently positively valued JOURNEY metaphor scenario, tend to offer a deeper insight into the discursive practices of the two communities and to help minimize the causes of misunderstanding, particularly in the general public. Our analysis has hopefully once again demonstrated how seemingly innocent metaphors may have an effective role in authentic discourse. We strongly believe that the use of the *step* and *traffic light* metaphors may at least be partially responsible for the general public in Serbia being so overwhelmed with the feeling that accession to today's European Union is now as implausible as it was a decade or so ago.

Notes

1 The chapter is the result of research conducted within project no. 178002 *Languages and cultures across time and space* funded by the Ministry of Education, Science and Technological Development of the Republic of Serbia.
2 The authors would like to thank two anonymous reviewers for their valuable and insightful comments which helped to improve the quality of this chapter substantially.
3 The expression is credited to Jacques Delors, one of the former presidents of the European Commission (see Chaban et al., 2009).
4 See, e.g., *Press Online*, 22 December 2011 <http://www.pressonline.rs/sr/vesti/vestI_dana/story/194005/Evroskeptici+sve+brojniji+u+Srbiji+-+Ve%C4%87ina+ne%C4%87e+u+EU.html>. In addition, according to a poll conducted in June 2012 and modelled on Eurobarometer standards, only 49 per cent of Serbian citizens support Serbia's EU accession, which is a dramatic fall in support of European integration compared to 2008 when it was as much as 75 per cent. <http://www.euractiv.rs/srbija-i-eu/4576-opada-podrka-graana-ulasku-u-eu>
5 For a somewhat different account of 'scenarios' related to metaphors, see Semino (2008, p. 219–22).
6 The sources of the examples are indicated after each individual example.
7 See <http://www.slobodnaevropa.org/content/raste-evroskepticizam-u-srbiji-mladi-se-najvise-protive-eu/24742776.html>. See also the Eurobarometer results of the Serbian public opinion poll about the images the EU conjures up, available at <http://ec.europa.eu/public_opinion/cf/showchart_column.cfm?keyID=2202&nationID=35,&startdate=2012.05&enddate=2012.05>. It is important to point out that Euroscepticism discernible among Serbian citizens is not so much due to their disappointment with the EU as a political or economic institution faced with a serious crisis, as it is due to the EU's firm conditionality policy in the accession process. See also <http://www.b92.net/info/vesti/index.php?yyyy=2011&mm=08&dd=30&nav_category=1262&nav_id=538413> for the results of another opinion poll which emphasizes this particular aspect of Serbian Euroscepticism.

References

Cameron, L. and Deignan, A. (2006), 'The Emergence of Metaphor in Discourse', *Applied Linguistics*, 27(4): 671–90.

Chaban, N., Schneider, C. E. and Malthus, R. (2009), 'Visibility, Framing and Importance: Images of the EU in Japan and South Korea', *The Copenhagen Journal of Asian Studies*, 27(1): 88–125.

Charteris-Black, J. (2004), *Corpus Approaches to Critical Metaphor Analysis*, Basingstoke and New York: Palgrave Macmillan.

Deignan, A. (1995), *Collins Cobuild English Guides 7: Metaphor*, London: Harper Collins.

Drulák, P. (2004), 'Metaphors Europe Lives By: Language and Institutional Change of the European Union', *EUI Working Paper SPS, 2004/15*, Florence: European University Institute.

—(2006), 'Motion, Container and Equilibrium: Metaphors in the Discourse about European Integration', *European Journal of International Relations*, 12(4): 499–531.

Đurović, T. and Silaški, N. (2012), 'How Heavy Do I Journey on the Way: Framing the Issue of the EU Visa Liberalisation Process in Contemporary Serbia', in C. Hart (ed.), *Selected Papers from UK-CLA Meetings*, pp. 64–77. <http://uk-cla.org.uk/files/proceedings/Durovic%20and%20Silaski.pdf> (accessed 22 January 2013)

Fillmore, C. J. (1975), 'An Alternative to Checklist Theories of Meaning', *Proceedings of the Berkeley Linguistics Society*, 1: 123–31.

Johnson, M. (1987), *The Body in the Mind: The Bodily Basis of Meaning, Imagination, and Reason*, Chicago: University of Chicago Press.

Koller, V. and Semino, E. (2009), 'Metaphor, Politics and Gender: A Case Study from Germany', in K. Ahrens (ed.), *Politics, Gender and Conceptual Metaphors*, Basingstoke and New York: Palgrave Macmillan, pp. 9–36.

Kövecses, Z. (2006), *Language, Mind, and Culture: A Practical Introduction*, Oxford: Oxford University Press.

Lakoff, G. (1993), 'The Contemporary Theory of Metaphor', in A. Ortony (ed.), *Metaphor and Thought*, Cambridge: Cambridge University Press, pp. 202–51.

—(1987), *Women, Fire, and Dangerous Things: What Categories Reveal About the Mind*, Chicago: University of Chicago Press.

Lakoff, G. and Johnson, M. (1980), *Metaphors We Live By*, Chicago: University of Chicago Press.

—(1999), *Philosophy in the Flesh: The Embodied Mind and Its Challenge to Western Thought*, New York: Basic Books.

Lakoff, G. and Turner, M. (1989), *More Than Cool Reason: A Field Guide to Poetic Metaphor*, Chicago: University of Chicago Press.

Musolff, A. (2000), 'Political Imagery of Europe: A *House* without *Exit Doors*?', *Journal of Multilingual and Multicultural Development*, 21(3): 216–29.

—(2003), 'Cross-Language Metaphors: Obstacles or Pathways of International Communication?'. <http://www.dur.ac.uk/resources/mlac/german/resources/crosslang.pdf> (accessed 16 February 2009)

—(2004), *Metaphor and Political Discourse: Analogical Reasoning in Debates about Europe*, Basingstoke: Palgrave Macmillan.

—(2006), 'Metaphor Scenarios in Public Discourse', *Metaphor and Symbol*, 21(1): 23–38.

—(2010), 'Metaphor in Discourse History', in M. E. Winters, H. Tissari and K. Allan (eds), *Historical Cognitive Linguistics*, New York: De Gruyter Mouton, pp. 70–90.

Pragglejaz Group (2007), 'MIP: A Method for Identifying Metaphorically Used Words in Discourse', *Metaphor and Symbol*, 22: 1–39.
Semino, E. (2008), *Metaphor in Discourse*, Cambridge: Cambridge University Press.
Šarić, Lj. (2005), 'Metaphorical Models in EU Discourse in the Croatian Media', *Jezikoslovlje*, 6(2): 145–70.
Šarić, Lj., Musolff, A., Manz, S. and Hudabiunigg, I. (eds) (2010), *Contesting Europe's Eastern Rim: Cultural Identities in Public Discourse*, Bristol, Buffalo and Toronto: Multilingual Matters.
Silaški, N., Đurović, T. and Radić-Bojanić, B. (2009), *Javni Diskurs Srbije – Kognitivističko-kritička Studija*, Beograd: CID Ekonomskog fakulteta.
Zbierska-Sawala, A. (2004), 'The Conceptualisation of the European Union in Polish Public Discourse, 2002–2003', *Journal of Multilingual and Multicultural Development*, 25(5&6): 408–23.

11

Metaphor and Self/Other Representations: A Study on British and Romanian Headlines on Migration

Mariana Neagu and Gabriela Iuliana Colipcă-Ciobanu

Introduction

The vital role of metaphor in forming opinions has been explained by its potential to arouse emotions (Charteris-Black, 2004; Goatly, 1997). As speakers choose metaphors that are consonant with their own attitudes, emotions and evaluations, examining metaphors can reveal something of their perspectives on the issues reported in newspapers as well as on their own identity. Metaphor as a cognitive tool seems to be especially important in relation to migration because of 'the range of conflicting representations in public discourse' (Charteris-Black, 2006, p. 565). For example, migration can be represented as desirable or undesirable, depending on whether it is viewed from the perspective of a sending or a receiving country or from a liberal or a conservative perspective. Identifying the role of metaphors in public discourse is important because it can lead to identifying the source and nature of social myths and stereotypes of and prejudices against migrants.

The topic of migration and its representation in the British press has been discussed by Baker et al. (2008), Fomina and Frelak (2008) and Dervinyte (2009). Baker et al.'s (2008) study investigated images of refugees, asylum seekers, immigrants and migrants in the UK press between 1996 and 2006 from the perspective of critical discourse analysis. Fomina and Frelak's (2008) work focused on the UK press coverage of migration from Poland to Britain, while Dervinyte's study (2009) approached the topic of migration in the British and the Lithuanian press between 2004 and 2008 from the perspective of conceptual metaphor theory. Although Dervinyte deals with conceptual EMIGRATION and IMMIGRATION metaphors in the language of the press, her cross-linguistic analysis of English and Lithuanian does not account for the differences found between the two languages.

Metaphorical language use in news as a register has received attention (e.g. Hart, 2011; Krennmayr, 2011; Santa Ana, 1999) but the subgenre of headlines has not been explored. As a subgenre of news, headlines are likely to emphasize subjective, dominant representation patterns that play an important role in naturalizing and normalizing power hierarchies and inequalities in the context of broader social phenomena, including intercultural interaction in the process of migration. Among the linguistic tools of communication used in headlines, metaphor is particularly important because of its interpersonal dimension and its evaluative function.

The main aim of this chapter is to explore how migration is approached in British and Romanian newspapers, with special emphasis on metaphoric headlines that encode, explicitly or implicitly, self/other representations, making them available to the public in the migrant-receiving and migrant-sending societies. The study thus addresses the following research questions:

1. What metaphors associated with Romanian migrants occur in British and Romanian newspaper headlines?
2. What differences and/or similarities are there between metaphors in each media corpus?
3. How can we account for the choice of metaphors in each media?

The theoretical framework of the present study has been provided by Critical Metaphor Analysis (CMA). This is an approach to metaphor analysis that 'aims to reveal the covert and possibly unconscious intensions of language users' (Charteris-Black, 2004, p. 34). Its methodology follows three stages: (1) metaphor identification; (2) metaphor interpretation; and (3) metaphor explanation.

Data and methodology

Data

The use of metaphor in the subgenre of headlines to characterize the semantic domain of migration was investigated in articles related to immigration in the United Kingdom, taken from the online versions of two British broadsheets (*The Times* and the *Guardian*, together with their Sunday editions, i.e. the *Sunday Times* and the *Observer*, respectively) and two Romanian newspapers (*Adevărul* and *Cotidianul*), issued between 2006 and 2011. To identify examples of metaphors, 500 headlines (208 British and 292 Romanian headlines) were examined. The search terms were 'Romanian (im)migrant' for the British papers, and 'Romanian immigrant' and 'Britain' for the Romanian ones. In addition, in order to sustain the identification of certain conceptual metaphors, other linguistic forms motivated by the same idea, that is, migration, were searched in articles published in the same newspapers, within the same time frame of 2006–11, but referring to other groups of migrants or to migration in general. In order to discuss the ideological motivation of metaphors, we compared the headlines in our British and Romanian corpora and, where possible, extended the scope of comparison by considering headlines of articles published in the same newspapers in 2012.[1]

The British newspapers selected for the study represent distinct political options, from liberal and social democratic to conservative. They are broadsheets or quality newspapers aimed at a middle-class audience, usually providing a complex analysis of the topics they tackle. The *Guardian* tends to appeal to Labour and Liberal Democrat voters; *The Times* does not adhere to one political outlook, but is generally regarded as appealing to moderate or conservative readers. *The Times* is owned by Rupert Murdoch, who is said to greatly influence the political outlook of his media publications.

The Romanian newspapers chosen for the study are the electronic versions of two of the most widespread and influential Romanian quality papers, *Adevărul* and *Cotidianul*. In spite of controversies and of editorial and administrative changes, *Adevărul* has remained one of most appreciated high-quality newspapers in Romania, appealing especially to middle-aged and older readers through a prominent and constant concern with mainly socio-cultural issues. *Cotidianul* was initially founded in 1927, and re-founded, after the fall of Communism, by the right-wing politician Ion Raţiu, publishing its first issue on 10 May 1991. During approximately two decades of constant publication, *Cotidianul* has gained a large readership, mostly younger people, due, on the one hand, to its witty and slightly aggressive approach to the events presented, and, on the other, to the regular collaboration with representatives of the Romanian cultural elite (especially for opinion articles). It temporarily ceased publication in December 2009, but was back on the Romanian written press market at the beginning of 2010 when it was taken over by Academia Caţavencu and Regent House (see Colipcă et al., 2010, pp. 17–18).

Method

Metaphor identification consists in collecting examples of linguistic metaphors used to talk about a topic. Charteris-Black's (2004, p. 35) approach to metaphor identification involves two stages: the first requires 'a close reading of a sample of texts with the aim of identifying candidate metaphors'. The second stage consists in examining corpus texts in order to determine whether each use of a key word (i.e. a word commonly used with a metaphoric sense) is metaphoric or literal. For this study, we used the Metaphor Identification Procedure (MIP; Pragglejaz Group, 2007), a practical, systematic and reliable method for identifying metaphorically used words in discourse. MIP compares contextual meanings of lexical units to their basic meaning: words are used metaphorically if these meanings belong to different domains but can be understood by some form of comparison. MIP describes the basic meaning as tending to be more concrete, related to bodily action, more precise, human-oriented and historically older. For example, in a headline like (1), the contextual meaning of *wave* is 'a large number of people moving or arriving somewhere at the same time', while its basic meaning is 'line of water that rises up on the surface of a sea, lake, or river' (*Macmillan Dictionary and Thesaurus*).

(1) Reid pushes the ban on next **wave of EU workers**[2] (*Guardian*, 12 August 2006)

The basic and contextual meanings are clearly distinct from each other, though they are related by similarity: a 'wave of EU workers' is compared to a concrete entity, that is, a sea wave, with all that that entails. In order to identify the contextual and the basic meaning of the lexical unit to be analysed and then to determine whether the two meanings can be contrasted and also understood in comparison to each other, we used the online versions of *Macmillan Dictionary and Thesaurus*, *Longman Dictionary of Contemporary English* and also the *Oxford English Dictionary*.

The second stage of metaphor analysis – metaphor interpretation – involved the identification of conceptual metaphors, that is, generalizing from examples of linguistic metaphors to conceptual metaphors. In order to make a claim for a conceptual metaphor, there is a need to provide further linguistic evidence (other linguistic forms) motivated by the same idea (Charteris-Black, 2004). In order to do this, we searched for the same metaphor-related word in other headlines on migration, not necessarily referring to Romanians or Eastern Europeans in the case of the British corpus, or to Britain as a migrant-receiving society in the case of the Romanian corpus. For example, headline (2) brings into discussion one of the negative socio-economic consequences of immigration, that is, the spread of disease, which, together with the ideas of financial burden and unemployment, can be noticed especially in the *Times* headlines:

(2) **New wave of immigration** blamed for doubling of hepatitis B cases (*The Times*, 21 November 2007)

Metaphor explanation implies the identification of the discourse functions of metaphor that permits us to establish their ideological and rhetorical motivation. According to Charteris-Black (2004, p. 39), evidence for the ideological and rhetorical motivation comes from 'comparing the findings for a particular mini-corpus with those for the same metaphor in a larger corpus . . . or by comparing different sections of the same corpus'. To do this, we compared some collocations found in our corpus (covering the years 2006–11) with those for the same metaphor in a larger corpus (including the year 2012). For instance, the categories of IMMIGRANT and CRIMINAL may sometimes overlap because of semantic contagion, facilitated by the construal of immigrants, in general, and (illegal) immigrants who commit crimes as members of the same category. This representation is reinforced by the collocation '(im)migrant crime wave' as in the headlines that follow:

(3) Riding the **immigrant crime wave** (*Guardian*, 16 April 2008)
(4) **Migrant crime wave** a myth – police study (*Guardian*, 16 April 2008)

Metaphor analysis

In what follows, we present and discuss the groups of migration metaphor-related words that we find significant for Self/Other representations in two distinct environments: the receiving country, that is, the United Kingdom, and the sending country, that is, Romania.

Moving water metaphors

In British headlines, by far the most popular metaphor seems to be that of IMMIGRATION AS MOVING WATER. Along with the headlines already cited, which use this metaphor to refer to Romanian immigrants in Britain, the following examples should be considered:

(5) **Worker influx** prompts EU migration debate (*The Times*, 22 August 2006)
(6) Permit scheme to cut **flow of East Europeans**: Ministers want specific skills test for Bulgarian and Romanian workers (*Guardian*, 31 August 2006)
(7) Britain shuts the door on new **wave of migrants** (*Observer*, 22 October 2006)
(8) East European migration **on the rise** (*The Times*, 27 February 2007)
(9) **Flood of Eastern Europeans** slows to a **trickle** (*The Times*, 22 August 2008)
(10) **Rising tide of immigrants** puts strain on our budget, say police (*The Times*, 17 April 2008)

The linguistic realizations of this metaphor in the British headlines favour nouns pertaining to the semantic domain of running water: '*influx*', '*flow*', '*flood*', '*tide*', '*wave*'. As Table 11.1 shows, the metaphor was used more frequently in 2006.

The presence of the IMMIGRATION AS MOVING WATER metaphor in headlines from both the *Times* and *Guardian* should not be interpreted as strictly indicative of these newspapers' attitude to Romanian immigration to the United Kingdom, but rather against the larger background of (already stereotypical) representations of immigration that rely upon similar linguistic realizations.

Previous research (Baker et al., 2008; Dervinyte, 2009) has already shown that quantifying migrants in terms of moving water metaphors is a common strategy in

Table 11.1 IMMIGRATION AS MOVING WATER metaphor in British headlines

Linguistic realizations	2006	2007	2008	2009	2010	2011
The Times: - worker *influx*; - *flow* of low-skilled immigrants; - migration *on the rise*; - *flood* of Eastern Europeans; - *rising tide* of immigrants; - *influx* of 1m migrants.	2	1	2	1	–	–
Guardian: - *wave* of EU workers; - *flow* of East Europeans; - *influx*; - *new wave* of migrants; - *flood* of Balkan migrants; - (im)migrant crime *wave*.	4	1	2	–	–	–
Total no. of metaphoric headlines	6	2	4	1	–	–
	13					

immigration discourse in the British press. Such representations trigger a number of ideological inferences in which immigration is viewed as possessing some of the characteristics of moving water. Since 'water' is a mass noun, the moving entities, that is, immigrants, are construed as a single moving mass, thus hiding 'individual identities, histories, motives and intentions' (Hart, 2011, p. 184). Comparable metaphoric expressions may be identified in Romanian headlines from *Adevărul* and *Cotidianul*:

(11) Deziluzie în presa de scandal engleză: primul **val de imigranţi** numără patru români (*Cotidianul*, 2 January 2007)
(English tabloids disappointed: first **wave of immigrants** made up of four Romanians)
(12) Un nou **val de cerşetori din Est**, la Londra (*Adevărul*, 24 February 2007)
(New **wave of East European beggars** in London)
(13) Britanicii se tem de **un val de imigranţi** români (*Adevărul*, 16 May 2009)
(Britons fear a **wave** of Romanian **immigrants**)
(14) Marea Britanie va introduce un regim sever de taxe pe fondul temerilor unui nou **aflux de români** (*Cotidianul*, 21 January 2010)
(Britain to raise taxes for fear of new **influx of Romanian immigrants**)
(15) Propunere Comisia Europeană. Reintroducerea vizelor la frontiere, în cazul unui **aflux de imigranţi foarte mare** (*Cotidianul*, 4 May 2011)
(European Commission Proposal: visa reintroduction in case of **immigrant flood**)

As Table 11.2 shows, moving water metaphors are less numerous in the headlines of the Romanian corpus. This may be largely accounted for by the Romanian journalists' common practice of quoting their sources, even if sometimes tongue-in-cheek (especially in *Cotidianul*), to criticize the British clinging to negative representations of migration, as in (11), (13) and (14), for instance. In some of these examples, water-related metaphoric expressions occur in contexts with words for

Table 11.2 IMMIGRATION AS MOVING WATER metaphor in Romanian headlines

Linguistic realizations	2006	2007	2008	2009	2010	2011
Adevărul: - *val* de imigranţi români/*wave* of Romanian immigrants; - *val* de cerşetori din Est/*wave* of East European beggars.	–	1	–	1	–	–
Cotidianul: - *val* de imigranţi/*wave* of immigrants; - *aflux* de români/*influx* of Romanian immigrants; - *aflux* de imigranţi foarte mare/ immigrant *flood*.	–	1	–	–	1	1
Total no. of metaphoric headlines	–	2	–	1	1	1
				5		

fear: '*a se teme*' (to fear) and '*temere*' (fear). This points to the Romanian journalists' awareness of the fact that even though the status of Romanian immigrants changed after Romania joined the EU, the British hosts' perspective on these newcomers seeking jobs has not improved. Romanian migration to the United Kingdom is conceived as the continuous inflow of a large number of people that can destroy the pre-established order on the labour market (since once restrictions that prevented Romanians from seeking employment abroad were lifted, they would come to take the British citizens' jobs) or in the public space (as Romanians are associated with criminality, e.g. in [12], with the proliferation of illegal networks of beggars). The enduring nature of such prejudice against the Romanian migrants is confirmed by headlines of articles published in 2012:

(16) Marea Britanie se pregătește pentru un **aflux de imigranți** (*Cotidianul*, 26 May 2012)
(Britain prepares for **influx of immigrants**)
(17) The Sun: Imigranții din România **scufundă** Marea Britanie (*Cotidianul*, 11 November 2012)
(The *Sun*: Romanian immigrants **to swamp** Britain)

In fact, British reactions to Romanian immigration, revealing a keen sense of differentiation verging on intolerance, specific to what Hofstede (1991) calls 'high uncertainty avoidance', appear circumscribable to general Western European attitudes to this phenomenon, emerging especially in the favourite destinations of Romanian immigrants, Italy and Spain. These are equally attested in a number of Romanian headlines that assimilate the IMMIGRATION AS MOVING WATER metaphor, like the following examples from *Adevărul*, which rely on the receiving-societies' sources to point to the anxiety triggered by major societal changes in the aftermath of Romania's accession to the EU:

(18) The Economist: 'Politicile guvernelor italiene au încurajat **afluxul de imigranți români**' (*Adevărul*, 10 November 2007)
(The *Economist*: 'Italian governments' policies have favoured the **influx of Romanian immigrants**')
(19) Emigranții în presă. **Aflux de români** (Madrid) (*Adevărul*, 5 December 2007)
(Emigrants in the news. **Influx of Romanians** [Madrid])

The fact that the IMMIGRATION AS MOVING WATER metaphor remains essentially attached to the host society's representation of the Romanian migrant as the Other becomes obvious from the disparity in numbers between the British and the Romanian headlines containing water metaphors, as can be seen in Table 11.3.

The United Kingdom's geographical position and the sense of insularity that seems defining of Britishness is likely to determine the Britons' way of conceptualizing abstract entities, like immigration, in terms of something familiar to them, like water. Besides, linguistic realizations such as 'flood' and 'rising tide' convey the idea of natural force and danger which, if allowed to continue, will cause some harm to the British

Table 11.3 IMMIGRATION AS MOVING WATER metaphor

	2006	2007	2008	2009	2010	2011	Total no. of metaphoric headlines
British headlines	6	2	4	1	–	–	13
Romanian headlines	–	2	–	1	1	1	5
Total no. of metaphoric headlines	6	4	4	2	1	1	18

island 'container'. We briefly consider the CONTAINER metaphor in the next section, which examines the UK AS A HOUSE metaphor.

House metaphors

The UK AS A HOUSE metaphor, a specific instance of the UK AS A CONTAINER metaphor, is mainly evidenced in British headlines on migration by lexical patterns containing the key-word 'door': '*open door(s)*', '*door opens*', '*backdoor*', '*key to Britain's door*', '*shut/close the (open) door*' and so on.

(20) Britain **shuts the door** on new wave of migrants (*Observer*, 22 October 2006)
(21) Scotland **opens its doors** to the east (*Guardian*, 1 November 2006)
(22) Romanians get **key to Britain's door** (*Sunday Times*, 31 December 2006)

Other linguistic realizations of this metaphor are also foregrounded in several British headlines, as can be seen from the examples below:

(23) Yes, you're right, Mr. Reid, but how are you going **to keep** the illegals **out**? (*The Times*, 10 August 2006)
(24) **Exits and entrances** that lift population by 500 every day (*The Times*, 3 November 2006)

As these examples show, like moving water metaphors, house metaphors are more frequent in the 2006 British headlines (Table 11.4).

As has been pointed out (Charteris-Black, 2006; Chilton, 2004; Hart, 2011), the IMMIGRATION AS MOVING WATER metaphor and the COUNTRY AS CONTAINER metaphor appear in conjunction, thus conveying the idea of danger and the need for a restrictive immigration policy in the migrant-receiving society. According to Charteris-Black (2006, p. 576), 'Containment and control are . . . two very closely related and mutually supportive concepts that integrate historical experience in right-wing political discourse' that may account, for instance, for the larger number of headlines that combine, explicitly or implicitly, these concepts in *The Times*. In addition, Charteris-Black argues that 'the existence of a clearly defined container also implies a conscious controlling entity that fills or empties the container – just as a government controls the flow of people into and out of the country' (p. 576). Similarly, when dealing with the use of 'deliberate metaphors' in the student immigration debate, Musolff (2011,

Table 11.4 UK AS A HOUSE metaphor in British headlines

Linguistic realizations	2006	2007	2008	2009	2010	2011
The Times: - *keep* the illegals *out*; - *closes door*; - *exits and entrances*; - *key* to Britain's *door*; - Britain is *taking in*; - *open the door*.	4	1	1	–	–	–
Guardian: - *shuts the door*; - *opens its doors*.	2	1	–	–	–	–
Total no. of metaphoric headlines	6	2	1	–	–	–
	9					

p. 14) observes that it might appear to represent 'a prime example . . . that exhibits deep seated xenophobic attitudes towards strangers who are seen as violating the boundaries of the container of collective identity and therefore must be brought under control, and whose unfettered access must be stopped'. Thus, examples (23) and (24) refer to loss of control and carry negative evaluations of the Romanian migration issue. The only HOUSE metaphor headlines with an explicitly positive stance towards immigration, even if not necessarily related to the Romanian newcomers, have been found in more recent issues of *Guardian*:

(25) Immigration policy 'will keep talented scientists **out of** UK' (*Guardian*, 25 November 2010)

In contrast, there is hardly any reference to the receiving country (Britain) as a house from the perspective of the sending country (Romania), as Table 11.5 shows, although some exceptions are found:

(26) Trei dintre statele vechi membre UE şi-**au deschis** piaţa muncii în 2009 pentru cetăţenii români (*Cotidianul*, 3 January 2009)
(Three old EU member states **open** labour markets for Romanian citizens in 2009)

Table 11.5 HOUSE/CONTAINER metaphors in Romanian headlines

Linguistic realizations	2006	2007	2008	2009	2010	2011
Adevărul	–	–	–	–	–	–
Cotidianul: - *au deschis/open*; - *vor umple/ to fill*.	–	–	–	1	1	–
Total no. of metaphoric headlines	–	–	–	1	1	–
	2					

Table 11.6 HOUSE/CONTAINER metaphors

	2006	2007	2008	2009	2010	2011	Total no. of metaphoric headlines
British headlines	6	2	1	–	–	–	9
Romanian headlines	–	–	–	1	1	–	2
Total no. of metaphoric headlines	6	2	1	1	1	–	11

Even when referring to other receiving countries, like Italy or Germany, the Romanian headlines do not favour the HOUSE/CONTAINER metaphor, although some examples of the kind can be found in the corpus:

(27) Germania **deschide porţile** muncitorilor imigranţi. Nu şi românilor! (*Cotidianul*, 9 May 2011)
(Germany **opens doors** to migrant workers, but not to Romanian ones!)

Though few, such headlines are meant to draw attention to the discriminatory attitudes of the in-groups that may be further nuanced by differentiating several degrees of otherness; certain out-groups may have come to appear, in time, more congenial, and therefore acceptable, while others (like the Romanians) seem to have remained stuck in the stereotypical frame of undesirability that keeps them out of the in-group's HOUSE/CONTAINER. Table 11.6 reveals the contrast between the number of instances of the HOUSE/CONTAINER metaphors in the selected British and Romanian corpora.

We believe that the presumably positive connotations of 'house' (i.e. a safe place, where usually only one family lives) account for the presence of HOUSE metaphors in the self-representation generated by British headlines on migration.

Conflict metaphors

Another group of metaphor-related words (which may imply an attitude towards migration) belongs to the semantic source domain of war/invasion which we will generically call CONFLICT: '*assault*', '*fortress*', '*invasion*', '*invade*', '*attack*', '*battle*'. Like water metaphors, conflict metaphors are more specific variants of the higher level metaphor IMMIGRATION AS FORCE (Charteris-Black, 2004; Hart, 2011) which justifies the perception of migrants as a threat, as something which the receiving country has to be defended against. A very interesting British headline from among those that see migration as invasion combines a metaphor of attack ('new assault') with a metaphor of defence ('fortress Europe'), the latter voicing a conservative, anti-immigrant stance.

(28) Migrants risk all in **new assault** on **fortress Europe** (*The Times*, 3 June 2007)

More explicitly connecting with the metaphoric representation of immigration, in general, as war, another headline from *The Times* refers to immigration as 'battle', thus emphasizing the differences between and intolerance of the two groups involved in this form of intercultural encounter, that is, the hosts and the migrants:

(29) Are you a winner or a loser in the **immigration battle**? (*The Times*, 8 June 2010)

As regards the headlines that refer specifically to Romanian migrants, two categories may be clearly distinguished. On the one hand, there are headlines (though not numerous) that, in line with the stereotypical, xenophobic representation of immigration as conflict-engendering, conceptualize the Romanian other as the 'enemy' that 'invades' Britain.

(30) Migration figures explode claims of **East European invasion** (*Guardian*, 22 May 2007)

On the other hand, through literal rather than metaphoric language, several British headlines depict immigrants as targets of racism in a conflict-ridden society that remains divided by the rigid 'us' versus 'them' dichotomy.

(31) Fears recession will ignite **racist attacks** in Scotland (*The Times*, 30 November 2008)
(32) Romanians hit by **racist attacks** in Northern Ireland 'want to go home' (*The Times*, 18 June 2009)
(33) Man charged as Romanians leave country after Belfast **race attacks** (*Guardian*, 23 June 2009)

A summary of the CONFLICT metaphors and their linguistic realizations in the selected corpus from *The Times* and *Guardian* may be found in Table 11.7.

The largest number of headlines about Romanian immigrants in Britain belongs to the second category, illustrated in examples (32) and (33), and refers to a difficult moment for the Romanian community in Belfast, when, in 2009, the local authorities encountered problems trying to control increasing xenophobic violence directed against the Romanian immigrants. The same series of violent clashes between the 'racist

Table 11.7 CONFLICT metaphors in British headlines

Linguistic realizations	2006	2007	2008	2009	2010	2011
The Times: - racist/race *attacks*; - *to defend*; - *is attacked.*	–	–	1	4	–	–
Guardian: - East European ***invasion***.	–	1	–	1	–	–
Total no. of metaphoric headlines	–	1	1	5	–	–
	7					

attackers' (as both *The Times* and *Guardian* call them) and the Romanian immigrants is duly recorded in 2009 Romanian headlines from both *Adevărul* and *Cotidianul.*

(34) Românii din Belfast, ţinta unui nou **atac** (*Adevărul* and *Cotidianul*, 18 June 2009)
(Romanians in Belfast, target of a new **attack**)

Most instantiations of this metaphor in the Romanian headlines use the same lexical patterns, that is, '*invazie*' (invasion) and '*a invada*' (to invade), reflecting the Romanian journalists' common practice of quoting or closely mimicking the British sources (Table 11.8).

(35) Graham Watson: 'Occidentalilor li s-a indus teama de o **invazie** a românilor' (*Cotidianul*, 3 January 2007)
(Graham Watson: 'Romanian **invasion**, induced fear in Westerners')
(36) Românii şi bulgarii **invadează** Marea Britanie (*Adevărul*, 10 May 2007)
(Romanians and Bulgarians **invade** Britain)
(37) **Invazia** muncitorilor estici în ţările UE, o spaimă indusă (*Adevărul*, 12 March 2008)
(East European workers **invasion** in EU countries, an induced fear)

Some of these metaphoric headlines, such as (35) and (37), emphasize, by the association of invasion metaphors with the phrase 'induced fear', that the British hosts' anxiety about the Romanian foreign Other is artificially fuelled by influential political leaders or groups that manage to transform their biased, high-uncertainty avoidance-oriented attitudes and policies into 'weapons' in the 'immigration battle'. The power of manipulating readers and maintaining social tensions that part of the British press (especially the tabloids) exerts – especially at times of major transformations in the

Table 11.8 CONFLICT metaphors in Romanian headlines

Linguistic realizations	2006	2007	2008	2009	2010	2011
Adevărul: - . . . *invadează/invade*; - *invazia* muncitorilor estici/East European workers invasion; - *ţinta unui nou atac/target of a new attack.*	–	1	1	1	–	–
Cotidianul: - *o invazie a românilor*/Romanian *invasion*; - *ţinta unui nou atac/target of a new attack*; - *va fi invadată* de moldoveni./Moldovans *to invade.*	–	1	–	1	1	–
Total no. of metaphoric headlines	–	2	1	2	1	–
				6		

status of migrant workers (like 2007 or 2013) – is clearly hinted at in the following headline from *Adevărul*:

(38) The Sun: În 2014, va fi o **invazie** de muncitori români şi bulgari în Marea Britanie (*Adevărul*, 11 November 2012)
(The *Sun*: **Invasion** of Romanian and Bulgarian workers in UK in 2014)

At least in the socially oriented *Adevărul*, the use of the MIGRATION AS CONFLICT metaphor in headlines that refer to the United Kingdom as a destination for Romanian migrants seems quite 'natural' against the larger background of the huge number of headlines that rely on the same metaphor to represent various trends of Romanian migration to the West, especially at crucial moments like 2007, when Romania became a member of the EU. The range of lexical patterns is more diverse: '*a cotropi*' or '*a invada*' (to invade); '*atac*' (attack); '*a ataca*' (to attack); '*bombă*' (bomb); '*a declara război*' (to declare war on); '*a lua cu asalt*' (to assault), but the same distinction between headlines that metaphorically conceptualize Romanian migrants to different destinations (Italy, Spain, Ireland, Greece, etc.) as (criminal) 'invaders', on the one hand, and headlines that, literally, refer to Romanian migrants as the target of intercultural violence, on the other, can be perceived in the following examples.

(39) Italia, **cotropită** de 105.000 de români şi bulgari (*Adevărul*, 4 January 2007)
(Italy **invaded** by 105,000 Romanians and Bulgarians)

(40) Românii **au luat cu asalt** piaţa muncii din Irlanda (*Adevărul*, 6 March 2007)
(Romanians **assault** labour market in Ireland)

(41) Treizeci de persoane **au atacat** o tabără de ţigani de lângă Roma (*Adevărul*, 20 September 2007)
(Thirty people **attack** gipsy camp near Rome)

(42) Românii din Italia, ameninţaţi cu **atacuri** şi **bombe** (*Adevărul*, 7 October 2007)
(Romanians in Italy, threatened with **attacks** and **bombs**)

(43) Rromii români din Italia, '**bomba cu ceas**' a Europei (*Adevărul*, 9 October 2007)
(Romanian Roma in Italy, Europe's '**time bomb**')

(44) Cerşetorii români au părăsit Roma şi **au invadat** Atena (*Adevărul*, 24 December 2007)
(Romanian beggars abandon Rome and **invade** Athens)

(45) **Atacuri cu tentă rasistă** la adresa românilor (*Adevărul*, 13 February 2008)
(**Racist attacks** on Romanians)

To sum up, the acute sense of difference between hosts and migrants becomes, in many cases, an obstacle that prevents intercultural communication and that causes the phenomenon of migration to be perceived and metaphorically conceptualized as conflict. Both the British and the Romanian headlines of the selected corpus prove the journalists' awareness of the fact that the sharp division between 'us' and 'them' may be the source of various manifestations of intercultural violence. Table 11.9 shows the prevalence of this metaphor in the British and Romanian headlines.

Table 11.9 CONFLICT metaphors

	2006	2007	2008	2009	2010	2011	Total no. of metaphoric headlines
British headlines	–	1	1	5	–	–	7
Romanian headlines	–	2	1	2	1	–	6
Total no. of metaphoric headlines	–	3	2	7	1	–	13

Slave-trade metaphors

The thirst for sensationalism that characterizes the present-day press makes journalists take interest in issues related to various forms of migration-triggered intercultural violence. That may account for the presence, in certain metaphoric headlines, of linguistic realizations of the conceptual metaphor MIGRATION AS SLAVE-TRADE ('*exploit*', '*exploitation*', '*slave*') (Table 11.10). They fall into two major categories indicative of the specific semantic features of the source domain that they intend to highlight. To be more specific, certain headlines seem to lay more emphasis on the slave-like condition of Romanian migrant workers, subject to coercion and exploitation, totally dependent on the employers for whom they work and whom they must obey. Others focus on human trafficking, in its different manifestations (mainly for sex, but also for begging), as the most extreme form of intercultural violence that most explicitly implies 'the procuring, transporting, and selling' (*Oxford English Dictionary*) of the victims by traffickers who treat them like goods to be exchanged. Two of the British headlines from *The Times* and *Guardian* that foreground representations of immigration in terms of SLAVE-TRADE, (46) and (47), point to the Romanian migrants' vulnerability to abuse and exploitation, while a third one (48) refers to sex trafficking in terms that recall the early twentieth-century conceptualization of traffic for prostitution as 'white slavery'.

(46) Hotel cleaners in London paid a pittance as immigrants are **exploited** (*The Times*, 31 July 2009)
(47) Migrant workers are **ripe for exploitation** (*Guardian*, 18 April 2011)
(48) Trafficked, raped, deported: story of a **sex slave** (*Sunday Times*, 3 April 2011)

Table 11.10 SLAVE-TRADE metaphors in British headlines

Linguistic realizations	2006	2007	2008	2009	2010	2011
The Times: - *exploited*; - *sex slave*.	–	–	–	1	–	1
The Guardian: - *ripe for exploitation*.	–	–	–	–	–	1
Total no. of metaphoric headlines	–	–	–	1	–	2
	3					

As regards the Romanian headlines from *Adevărul* and *Cotidianul*, though the aforementioned categories are indeed identifiable, the best represented is that of headlines which bring to Romanian readers' attention cases of human trafficking with the United Kingdom as a destination. Thus, whereas only one headline in *Cotidianul* (49) records (quoting *The Times*) Romanian migrant workers being reduced to 'slaves' in London hotels, many more, all from *Adevărul*, centre on trafficking in women for prostitution and trafficking in children for begging but also sexual exploitation (Table 11.11).

(49) Hotelurile de lux din Londra **exploatează** imigranți, printre care și români, scrie *The Times* (*Cotidianul*, 1 August 2009)
(*The Times*: London luxury hotels **exploit** immigrants, Romanians included)

(50) '**Licitații de sclavi**' în Marea Britanie (*Adevărul*, 6 June 2006)
('**Slave auctions**' in Britain)

(51) Slobozia: Puradeii din Țăndărei, **la mare căutare** printre traficanți (*Adevărul*, 28 June 2010)
(Slobozia: Gipsy kids from Țăndărei **in great demand** among traffickers)

(52) A făcut 30.000 de euro**, vânzând copii** români în Marea Britanie (*Adevărul*, 11 August 2010)
(30,000 euro for Romanian **children sale** in Britain)

(53) Cât '**costă**' un copil român pe **piața traficului uman** din Marea Britanie? (*Adevărul*, 17 January 2011)
(**Price** of Romanian child on **human trafficking market** in Britain)

(54) Copii români, '**marfă**' profitabilă de **export** (*Adevărul*, 18 January 2011)
(Romanian children, profitable **export** '**goods**')

Table 11.11 SLAVE-TRADE metaphors in Romanian headlines

Linguistic realizations	2006	2007	2008	2009	2010	2011
Adevărul:	1	1	1	–	2	3
- *licitații de sclavi /slave auctions* . . .;						
- Copii . . . *exploatați* . . . /children . . . *exploited* . . .;						
- Copii . . . *exportați* . . ./children . . . *exported* . . .;						
- *la mare căutare printre traficanți/in great demand among traffickers*;						
- *vânzând* copii . . ./children *sale* . . .;						
- . . . *costă* . . . *piața traficului uman/price* . . . *human trafficking market*;						
- *marfă de export/export goods*;						
- . . . *au exportat* tinere . . ./. . . *exporting* young girls . . .						
Cotidianul:	–	–	–	1	–	–
- . . . *exploatează imigranți* . . ./. . .*exploit immigrants* . . .						
Total no. of metaphoric headlines	1	1	1	1	2	3
				9		

The different approach of the two Romanian dailies to the exploitation and violence that may be fostered by migration becomes obvious upon thorough examination of the enlarged Romanian corpus. On the one hand, *Cotidianul* shows more interest in labour migration as the frame within which low-skilled workers (especially from the domestic, agricultural and construction sectors) are abusively treated by Western employers. In relatively recent headlines (2010 and 2012) from this newspaper, the most explicit linguistic realization of the IMMIGRATION AS SLAVE-TRADE metaphor, that is, '*sclavi*' (slaves), is favoured in an attempt to emphasize the precarious living and working conditions, psychological pressure and severe manipulation that (il)legal migrant workers (Romanians included) are forced to put up with.

(55) **Sclavi** pentru familiile unor diplomaţi străini de la Londra (*Cotidianul*, 30 August 2010)
(**Slaves** for families of foreign diplomats in London)

In contrast, in *Adevărul*, a much more explicitly sensationalist perspective on the negative social consequences of massive Romanian migration to the West has resulted in a wider range of articles dealing with different manifestations of exploitation that Romanian migrants have been subject to. Especially in the years following Romania's becoming an EU member state (2007–8), when the slow passage from mainly illegal to predominantly legal labour migration (with Italy and Spain as their favourite destinations) still caused many Romanian migrant workers to become easily 'enslaved' victims of either migrant smugglers or abusive employers in the receiving countries, *Adevărul* journalists often resorted to the IMMIGRATION AS SLAVE-TRADE metaphor: '*a exploata*' (to exploit); '*sclavi*' (slaves) to report on such cases.

(56) Muncitorii români dispăruţi în Spania erau **sclavii** unor romi (*Adevărul*, 19 September 2007)
(Romanian workers missing in Spain as Roma **slaves**)

(57) Muncitorii români, **sclavi** la Roma (*Adevărul*, 9 November 2007)
(Romanian workers, **slaves** in Rome)

However, a much more constant and perennial concern was shown in *Adevărul* for human trafficking. It is difficult to say, though, whether the large number of reports on human trafficking was simply motivated by the penchant for sensationalism or by the desire to raise awareness among Romanian readers of the dangers of migration. Irrespective of the Western country (Italy, Spain, the United Kingdom) where criminal networks of sex traffickers transported and sold their victims, the IMMIGRATION AS SLAVE-TRADE metaphor finds its place in *Adevărul* headlines that draw on lexical constructions which emphasize either the victims' condition as sex-slaves: '*sclavie sexuală*' (sex slavery); '*prostituţie cu forţa*' (forced prostitution); '*a exploata*' (to exploit) or their objectification and treatment as if they were goods: '*a exporta*' (to export); '*a vinde*' (to sell). The following two examples illustrate these patterns:

(58) O româncă a salvat câteva sute de femei din **sclavia sexuală** (*Adevărul*, 29 January 2007)
(Romanian woman saves hundred others from **sex slavery**)

(59) Filierele **sclaviei sexuale exportă** mii de românce (*Adevărul*, 10 February 2008)
(Sex **slavery networks export** thousands of Romanian women)

The subsuming of the HUMAN BEINGS AS GOODS cross-domain mapping to the larger metaphoric frame of MIGRATION AS SLAVE-TRADE that characterizes these examples may be detected in the increasingly numerous headlines on child trafficking, mainly for begging. Most likely drawing on information provided by both the Romanian and the British police, the articles that reflect on the trafficking of Romanian children in Britain are given headlines that display the same shift from the conceptual source domain of trade, realized linguistically by '*licitație*' (auction), '*export*' (export), '*la mare căutare*' (in great demand), '*a vinde*' (to sell), '*a costa*' (to cost), '*piață*' (market), '*marfă*' (goods), to the conceptual target domain of migration.

All in all, it is worth noticing that the IMMIGRATION AS SLAVE-TRADE metaphor is more frequently present in the Romanian headlines, as Table 11.12 shows. Given the semantic features that it preserves from the source domains of SLAVERY and SLAVE-TRADE, this metaphor highlights the vulnerability of migrant victims and, hence, may function, for the readers, as a warning about the multiple causes, forms and effects of migration-related intercultural violence.

Hunt metaphors

Last but not least, as a peculiarity of Romanian journalistic discourse reporting on migration, several headlines contain metaphor-related words from the semantic source domain of hunting (Table 11.13).

(60) Anglia **vânează** românii (*Cotidianul*, 3 September 2006)
(Britain **hunts** Romanians)

(61) Londra lansează '**vânătoarea**' ilegalilor din Marea Britanie (*Adevărul*, 8 March 2007)
(London sets off illegal migrant '**hunt**' in Britain)

(62) Universități '**vânate**' de tinerii români (*Adevărul*, 26 July 2010)
(Universities '**hunted**' by Romanian youth)

Table 11.12 SLAVE-TRADE metaphors

	2006	2007	2008	2009	2010	2011	Total no. of metaphoric headlines
British headlines	–	–	–	1	–	2	3
Romanian headlines	1	1	1	1	2	3	9
Total no. of metaphoric headlines	1	1	1	2	2	5	12

Table 11.13 HUNT metaphors in Romanian headlines

Linguistic realizations	2006	2007	2008	2009	2010	2011
Adevărul: - *vânătoarea* . . ./. . . *hunt* . . .; - . . .*vânate* . . ./. . . *hunted* . . .; - *vânează* . . . /. . . *hunted* . . .	–	1	–	–	2	–
Cotidianul: - . . . *vânează* . . ./. . . *hunts* . . .	1	–	–	–	–	–
Total no. of metaphoric headlines	1	1	–	–	2	–
				4		

Interestingly, the same metaphor is used to portray different aspects of Romanian migration. On the one hand, around the time of Romania's accession to the EU in 2006–7, both Romanian dailies use the HUNT metaphor to report and/or to ironically comment on the tense relations between the British majority and the mostly illegal Romanian migrants, for example, (60) and (61). In this case, clearly preserving the semantic features of 'hunt', that is, 'to chase animals and birds in order to kill or catch them' (*Longman Dictionary*), Romanian journalists construe the British authorities as agents (the 'hunters') whose actions/policies contribute to reinforcing the conflation of migration with illegality and that are meant to prevent the migrant others (the 'hunted') from finding a place in the British 'house'.

On the other hand, a few Romanian headlines give an unexpectedly positive connotation to the HUNT metaphor. Instead of traditionally representing Romanian migrants as victims that have to put up with discrimination, pressure and harassment in the receiving society, example (62) reveals young Romanian migrants travelling to the United Kingdom for study as active agents, diligently pursuing the goal of completing their education in prestigious foreign universities, among which British ones occupy a privileged position.

Conclusions

To sum up, the analysis of the selected corpus resulted in the identification of five main metaphor groups which, according to their overall frequency, are the following: (1) MOVING WATER metaphors; (2) CONFLICT metaphors; (3) SLAVE-TRADE metaphors; (4) HOUSE metaphors; and (5) HUNT metaphors.

In the British headlines, out of the five source domains identified, the MOVING WATER metaphors have the highest occurrence, followed by the HOUSE metaphors. What is interesting to note is that, with both types, more than half of the British headlines containing them are from 2006. We have argued that the high number of MOVING WATER metaphors in both *The Times* and *Guardian* should not be interpreted as being strictly indicative of these newspapers' stance towards Romanians' immigration to the

United Kingdom. It should be viewed within the larger framework of stereotypical representations of immigration in general.

While MOVING WATER metaphors are suggestive of representations of the Other and are generally viewed as carrying negative connotations, HOUSE metaphors, which rank second as frequency in the British headlines, have provided the opportunity to discuss representations of the Self and its association with positive connotations.

For CONFLICT metaphors we have found approximately the same number of linguistic realizations in the British and Romanian headlines. Analysing the British headlines, we have identified two categories: one which conceptualizes the Romanian Other as the 'enemy' or the 'invader' of the British 'house' and another which construes immigrants as targets of extreme xenophobic reactions motivated by the hosts' rigidly clinging to the 'us' versus 'them' distinction. The higher number of headlines from the second category is accounted for by the 2009 clash between members of the Romanian community in Belfast and racist attackers.

The approach to migration in the Romanian headlines resembles that in the British headlines probably because some metaphors themselves *migrate* from the British to the Romanian press. Many of the Romanian articles with metaphoric headlines draw on British sources and thus aim at mediating the access of Romanian readership to the image of and attitudes to the Romanian diaspora in British public discourse. That is why most of the foregrounded metaphoric patterns actually function as traces of intertextuality in Romanian journalistic discourse and merely reproduce stereotypical conceptualizations of migration (e.g. MOVING WATER metaphors and CONFLICT metaphors) that characterize the journalistic discourse in the receiving society.

Whether to fuel a more general interest in sensationalist, crime-related topics or to raise awareness of different manifestations of migration-related violence – human trafficking in particular – certain Romanian headlines foreground different linguistic realizations of the metaphor MIGRATION AS SLAVE-TRADE, occasionally narrowing its scope to CHILDREN/WOMEN AS GOODS. In Romanian headlines, slave-trade metaphors seem to have the highest frequency out of the five main metaphor groups identified.

The presence of the metaphor MIGRATION AS HUNT is particularly interesting in the Romanian headlines as the changes in the economic, social and political contexts influencing migration flows determine the occurrence of different linguistic realizations. Thus, prior to Romania's accession to the EU and immediately after it (in 2006 and 2007), when, at the end of their legal ninety-day stay, many Romanian migrants assumed the status of illegal migrants in their pursuit of the Western dream, the metaphoric expressions of MIGRATION AS HUNT tended to view Romanian migrants as in a vulnerable position, constantly threatened with deportation by the British authorities. However, after 2007, as labour migration came to be predominantly legal after the elimination of restrictions for Romanian migrant workers in several EU member states, the same metaphor came to be used in response to another major trend in migration (migration for study); hence Romanian students were presented as active agents in pursuit of a praiseworthy goal: professional achievement.

We acknowledge that most of the metaphors we have discussed are 'dying metaphors', simply clichés that have lost their real imaginative power and are used by journalists to spare the effort of inventing phrases for themselves. They resort to them out of habit of using sensational language and catchy phrases. Nevertheless, what one has to bear in mind is that such language still affects the perception of the migration phenomenon discussed in the press and certainly does not help to build a positive picture of it.

Notes

1 The unavailability of the archives of *Adevărul* and *Cotidianul* made it impossible to include headlines from 2005 as well in the enlarged corpus.

2 All emphases in the examples are ours.

References

Baker, P., Gabrielatos, C., Khosravinik, M., Krzyżanowski, M., McEnery, T. and Wodak, R. (2008), 'A Useful Methodological Synergy? Combining Critical Discourse Analysis and Corpus Linguistics to Examine Discourses of Refugees and Asylum Seekers in the UK Press', *Discourse and Society*, 19(3): 273–305.

Charteris-Black, J. (2004), *Corpus Approaches to Critical Metaphor Analysis*, Basingstoke: Palgrave Macmillan.

—(2006), 'Britain as a Container: Immigration Metaphors in the 2005 Election Campaign', *Discourse and Society*, 17(5): 563–81.

Chilton, P. (2004), *Analysing Political Discourse. Theory and Practice*, London: Routledge.

Colipcă, G. I., Ivan-Mohor, I., Praisler, M., Dima, G., Dumitraşcu, A. M. and Neagu, M. (2010), *National Case Study – National Identity and the Media (WP4): Romania*. <http://www.gemic.eu/wp-content/uploads/2010/07/WP4-Report-Romania-final.pdf.> (accessed 31 January 2013)

Dervinyte, I. (2009), 'Conceptual EMIGRATION and IMMIGRATION Metaphors in the Language of the Press: A Contrastive Analysis', *Kalbų Studijos. Studies about Languages*, 14: 49–55.

Fomina, J. and Frelak, J. (2008), *Next Stopski London. Public Perceptions of Labour Migration within the EU. The case of Polish Labour Migrants in the British Press*, Warszawa: Fundacja Instytut Spraw Publiczych.

Goatly, A. (1997), *The Language of Metaphors*, London: Routledge.

Hart, C. (2011), 'Moving beyond Metaphor in the Cognitive Linguistics Approach to CDA: Construal Operations in Immigration Discourse', in C. Hart (ed.), *Critical Discourse Studies in Context and Cognition*, Amsterdam and New York: John Benjamins, pp. 171–92.

Hofstede, G. (1991), *Cultures and Organizations: Intercultural Cooperation and its Importance for Survival. Software of the Mind*, London: Harper Collins Publishers.

Krennmayr, T. (2011), *Metaphor in Newspapers*, Utrecht: LOT.

Longman Dictionary of Contemporary English <http://www.ldoceonline.com/>.

Macmillan Dictionary and Thesaurus <http://www.macmillandictionary.com/>.

Musolff, A. (2011), 'Migration, Media and "Deliberate" Metaphors', *metaphorik.de*, 21: 7–19.

Oxford English Dictionary, Oxford: Oxford University Press. <http://oxforddictionaries.com/>

Pragglejaz Group (2007), 'MIP: A Method for Identifying Metaphorically Used Words in Discourse', *Metaphor and Symbol*, 22(1): 1–39.

Santa Ana, O. (1999), 'Like an Animal I Was Treated': Anti-immigrant Metaphor in US Public Discourse', *Discourse and Society*, 10(2): 191–224.

Subject Index

Name Index